Empirical Methods in International Trade

Empirical Methods in International Trade

Essays in Honor of Mordechai Kreinin

Edited by

Michael G. Plummer

Johns Hopkins University SAIS-Bologna

Edward Elgar
Cheltenham, UK • Northampton, MA, USA

Published by
Edward Elgar Publishing Limited
Glensanda House
Montpellier Parade
Cheltenham
Glos GL50 1UA
UK

Edward Elgar Publishing, Inc.
136 West Street
Suite 202
Northampton
Massachusetts 01060
USA

A catalogue record for this book
is available from the British Library

ISBN 1 84376 838 0

Typeset by Cambrian Typesetters, Frimley, Surrey
Printed and bound in Great Britain by MPG Books Ltd, Bodmin, Cornwall

Contents

Tables

Figures

Acknowledgements

This volume would not have existed without the generous efforts of many. First, we would like to thank the Washington, DC campus of the Johns Hopkins University School of Advanced International Studies (SAIS-DC) for its kind offer to allow us to use its conference facilities in holding our two-day conference. In particular, we would like to extend our appreciation to Dean Jessica Einhorn, Associate Dean John Harrington and Associate Dean Ted Baker. We also profited from the strong support of the Economics Department of SAIS-DC, especially from Professors Charles Pearson and Enzo Grilli and staff members Ms Patricia Calvano, Ms Rosa Bullock and Ms Robin Washington. At the SAIS-Bologna campus, we obtained invaluable help from the former Director of the Bologna Center, Dr Robert Evans, when the conference was being planned, and from the new Director, Ambassador Marisa Lino, during the manuscript preparation phase. Tremendous staff and editorial support were offered by Ms Barbara Wiza, Ms Brooke Neuman and Ms Yonit Golub.

Second, we received financial and logistical help, as well as much encouragement, from Michigan State University. While the list is long, special thanks go to President Peter McPherson, Dean Charles Greenleaf, Dean Marietta Baba and Chair of the Economics Department, Professor Rowena Pecchenino. On the academic side, all of Professor Kreinin's colleagues – past and present – were generous with their assistance, but Professors Carl Davidson and Steven Matusz were particularly kind with their time and input at all phases of the project.

Finally, we would like to thank all the conference participants for making Professor Kreinin's Festschrift not only a memorable academic event but also a wonderful personal tribute to this exceptional international economist. Moreover, many of Professor Kreinin's colleagues who could not make the conference sent in warm messages of congratulations, often with interesting anecdotes. These were greatly appreciated and added much to the conference ambiance.

Contributors

EDITOR

Michael G. Plummer is Professor of International Economics at Johns Hopkins University SAIS-Bologna. He received his Ph.D. in Economics from Michigan State University, and has been, *inter alia*, Research Fellow at the East–West Center in Honolulu; Research Professor at Kobe University; and Assistant and Associate Professor of Economics at Brandeis University. He has been a Fulbright Chair in Economics and Pew Fellow of International Affairs, Harvard University. His interests are mainly in the area of international economic integration and Asian economic development. He has published extensively on issues related to these areas. Many of his articles and books have been co-authored with Professor Kreinin, who was his major professor at Michigan State.

CHAPTER CONTRIBUTORS

Sven W. Arndt is the Charles M. Stone Professor of Money, Credit and Trade, and Director of the Lowe Institute of Political Economy at Claremont McKenna College. He received his Ph.D. in economics from the University of California, Berkeley in 1964. He has served on the faculties of the University of California, Los Angeles and the University of California, Santa Cruz, and has been visiting professor at Stanford University, Johns Hopkins University, SAIS-Bologna, the Institute for Advanced Studies, Vienna and the Universities of Mannheim and Konstanz in Germany. He has served as Director, Office of International Monetary Research, US Department of the Treasury, as Visiting Scholar, Board of Governors of the Federal Reserve System, and as trade project director at the American Enterprise Institute in Washington, DC. He has served as president of the North American Economics and Finance Association and is Managing Editor of the *North American Journal of Economics and Finance*. He has authored and edited several books and written articles in a variety of professional journals. His current research interests include trade and trade policy, cross-border production networks, exchange rate stability and macro modeling of open economies.

Chad P. Bown is an assistant professor in the Department of Economics and International Business School at Brandeis University in Waltham, Massachusetts. Professor Bown holds a Ph.D. in Economics from the University of Wisconsin at Madison. His recent publications include articles on GATT/WTO dispute settlement and the use and proliferation of antidumping measures.

James Cassing is Professor of Economics at the University of Pittsburgh and holds a B.A. in economics from the University of Kansas, and an M.A. and Ph.D. from the University of Iowa (1975). His special areas of interest include international economics and he has held visiting positions at the Australian National University, Johns Hopkins University SAIS-Bologna, and Bar-Ilan University in Tel Aviv. He has also served as Senior Trade Analysis Advisor to the Government of Indonesia, residing in Jakarta, and worked on trade and development projects in Southeast Asia, Egypt, Kenya and Zimbabwe.

Carl Davidson joined the faculty at Michigan State University in 1982 after completing his Ph.D. in economics at the University of Wisconsin with a specialty in microeconomics. He has published extensively on a wide variety of topics in academic journals. Recently, he has devoted most of his attention to the implications of international trade for labor market outcomes. He and his colleague Steven Matusz have established a broad research agenda aimed at understanding how changes in trade or trade policy affect the job prospects of workers and their wages. They are also interested in the way in which the link between trade, job prospects and the distribution of income is affected by the underlying structure of the labor market. Since 2001, Professor Davidson has been External Research Fellow with the Leverhulme Centre for Research on Globalization and Economic Policy at the University of Nottingham, UK.

Fernando De Paolis has been an assistant professor at the Monterey Institute of International Studies since receiving his Ph.D. in Urban Planning from UCLA in 2000. His research covers a number of issue areas in the Americas and beyond: preferential trade agreements (particularly NAFTA), regional development, income distribution, urbanization and development, and the links among these topics.

Jorge G. Gonzalez obtained his Ph.D. in Economics from Michigan State University. Since 1989 he has been at Trinity University, where he currently holds the titles of Professor and Chairman of the Department of Economics. His research focuses on foreign investment, the economics of undocumented immigration, international trade between the United States and Latin America, the political economy of trade liberalization and of immigration restrictions, and the Mexican economy.

Steven Husted, Professor of Economics and Associate Dean for Graduate Studies & Research, joined the University of Pittsburgh faculty in 1980 and became Dean in 1999. Professor Husted has published widely in the areas of international trade, international finance and monetary economics, and is co-author with Michael Melvin of a popular textbook in international economics. He has had wide-ranging international experience, including visiting appointments to the Australian National University and the University of Strathclyde in Glasgow, Scotland.

Joon-Kyung Kim is a Senior Fellow at the Korea Development Institute (KDI), Seoul. He gained his doctorate from the University of California at San Diego and served as Assistant Professor at Virginia Polytechnic Institute and State University before joining KDI. His recent research focuses on economic restructuring and related institutional reforms in the financial and corporate sectors in Korea. He has published various articles on Korean financial markets locally and overseas.

Chung H. Lee is Professor of Economics at the University of Hawaii at Manoa, where he has served as Chair of the Department of Economics and Director of Center for Korean Studies. He has also served as senior fellow and project leader at the East–West Center, Honolulu, Hawaii. He has held teaching/research positions at the University of Essex, University of Manchester, Miami University (Ohio), Kobe University, OECD Development Centre, the Kiel Institute of World Economics, the European Institute of Japanese Studies at the Stockholm School of Economics, and Johns Hopkins University SAIS-Bologna. He received a Ph.D. in Economics from the University of California at Berkeley in 1966. He has published numerous papers and edited volumes on Asian economies, their financial systems and foreign direct investment.

Peter J. Lloyd is Emeritus Professor at the University of Melbourne, after teaching and researching there for 20 years. His main interests are international policy and theory and microeconomic theory. He has worked as a consultant for many Australian and New Zealand Government departments and organizations and for a number of international organizations, including the GATT, WTO, OECD and World Bank.

Steven J. Matusz has been a member of the faculty at Michigan State University since completing his Ph.D. at the University of Pennsylvania in 1983. His doctoral thesis represented one of the earliest attempts in the literature to formally embed endogenously determined unemployment within general equilibrium models of international trade. His interest in this topic was sparked by the disconnect that he observed between popular views of the effect of trade on employment and the existing body of trade theory, which assumed that labor was always fully employed. He has published extensively in this area.

Since 2001, Matusz has been an External Research Fellow with the Lever-hulme Centre for Research on Globalization and Economic Policy at the University of Nottingham, UK.

Robert K. McCleery is an associate professor at the Monterey Institute of International Studies. He received his Ph.D. in Economics from Stanford University, and has worked for the East–West Center in Honolulu, Kobe University (Japan), and Claremont McKenna College. His research areas are immigration, FDI and preferential trade agreements in Asia and the Americas.

Rachel McCulloch is the Rosen Family Professor of International Finance at Brandeis University. Professor McCulloch received her Ph.D. from the University of Chicago and taught at Chicago, Harvard and Wisconsin before joining the Brandeis faculty in 1987. Her research focuses on international economic policy.

Marcus Noland is a Senior Fellow at the Institute for International Economics and an Associate of the International Food Policy Research Institute. He was a senior economist at the Council of Economic Advisers in the Executive Office of the President of the United States, and has held research or teaching positions at the Johns Hopkins University, the University of Southern California, Tokyo University, Saitama University, the University of Ghana, the Korea Development Institute and the East–West Center. He has been the recipient of fellowships sponsored by the Japan Society for the Promotion of Science, the Council on Foreign Relations, the Council for the International Exchange of Scholars and the Pohang Iron and Steel Corporation (POSCO). His book, *Avoiding the Apocalypse: the Future of the Two Koreas*, won the prestigious Ohira Memorial Prize.

Gretchen Anne Phillips is currently a student in the Master in Public Administration in International Development program at the John F. Kennedy School of Government. Her research focuses on private sector development initiatives in South America and Asia. Prior to Harvard, Gretchen worked for Goldman Sachs & Company in the International Finance/Capital Markets Group. She received her B.A. from Duke University in 2000.

Richard Pomfret has been Professor of Economics at the University of Adelaide in Australia since 1992. He was previously at the Johns Hopkins University (1979–91), Concordia University in Montreal (1976–79) and the Institut für Weltwirtschaft at the University of Kiel (1974–76). He has published 16 books and numerous articles in the areas of international trade and economic development.

Dominick Salvatore is Distinguished Professor and Director of the Ph.D. Program in Economics at Fordham University in New York. He is the author of many articles and books on international economics. He is a Fellow of the New York Academy of Sciences and Research Fellow of the Institute for European Affairs of the Vienna University of Business and Economics, as well as a consultant to the United Nations, World Bank, International Monetary Fund and the Economic Policy Institute in Washington, DC. He has taught and lectured at many universities in the United States and abroad.

Robert C. Shelburne is a senior international economist in the Division of Foreign Economic Research of the US Department of Labor. He received his Ph.D. in Economics from the University of North Carolina at Chapel Hill and has taught at Ohio University and North Carolina State University. Dr Shelburne's areas of research are the effects of international trade on employment and wages; the macroeconomics of trade policy; the theory and estimation of intra-industry trade; trade and labor standards; Caribbean and Latin American trade patterns; and the geographical concentration of manufacturing. Dr Shelburne has published numerous articles in a number of journals throughout the world, and has authored over a dozen Congressional reports concerning the operation of US trade preference programs.

Edward Tower is a professor of economics at Duke University. After earning his Ph.D. from Harvard, he taught at Tufts, the University of Auckland, Simon Fraser University and Nanjing University, and held visiting fellowships at the Australian National University. He has also consulted with USAID, the World Bank and the Harvard Institute for International Development.

Foreword

Peter McPherson

When I returned to Michigan State University (MSU) as President in 1993, I was determined to continue and enhance the long-standing tradition of international involvement that had characterized the University largely as the result of initiatives instituted by John Hannah in the 1950s. Of course faculty, led by people like Max Kreinin, had similar aims and indeed had worked effectively to maintain MSU as a place where the international community and American academia came together. It is no wonder, then, that Professor Kreinin and I came to collaborate on a number of projects in recent years. One of these was the book, *Building a Partnership: The Canada–United States Free Trade Agreement* (MSU Press, 2000), which stemmed from a major conference that we organized on the subject at MSU. Thus it is a particular pleasure to have this opportunity to join his esteemed colleagues and students in recognizing Max Kreinin's extraordinary career and impact.

For more than 45 years, Professor Kreinin has exemplified the ideal of a faculty member at a research-based, land-grant university. He has been a dedicated teacher of students at all levels. Thousands of MSU students – from freshmen studying economics at the introductory level to the most advanced graduate students seeking the intricacies of trade policy – have benefited from his engaging, insightful and challenging classes. And even beyond MSU, Max has extended his teaching impact through his leading textbooks and service around the world as a visiting professor.

Professor Kreinin – as is reflected by the work reported in this volume – has also been an internationally recognized scholar whose research and written work has informed both the economics and finance professions as well as the world of economic policy. Most of this research has focused on the empirical foundations of international trade and finance policy. I understand that his publications are so numerous and significant that he has been one of the most cited authors in economics. The combination of Max's research productivity and teaching excellence serves as a reminder that these two aspects of academic life can – and should – be complementary.

Importantly for a university with the history and objectives of MSU, Max has always been committed to sharing his expertise outside the narrow academic community. For example, he has served as the past president of the International Trade and Finance Association and has been a consultant to many institutions, including the United Nations, the US Department of State and the US Department of Commerce. Whether working with the US government, other nations, international organizations, other universities, or the media, he has recognized the importance of transmitting his knowledge, understanding and ideas to others. Thus Max's interests and professional involvement have advanced Michigan State's own international perspective and activity.

My congratulations and thanks to Michael Plummer for organizing and coordinating the conference and this volume and to all of the participants for their excellent contributions.

Peter McPherson, President
Michigan State University,
East Lansing

Foreword

Jagdish Bhagwati

Max Kreinin, as all his friends call him, is one of the most creative and influential international economists of his generation, which happens to be the same as mine. Who has not used his celebrated textbook? And who has not profited from the steady stream of professional contributions that have marked his prolific career?

Max's range has also been tremendous, though we know him best from his seminal articles on economic integration. I have learnt from him also when we disagreed, as on whether Japanese entrepreneurs displayed an unjustified bias towards buying from Japanese sources; he was always a tough opponent whom one opposed only to profit from the exchange.

Even as we honor him with this Festschrift, splendidly edited by his student Michael Plummer, we know that he will continue for several more years to write and illuminate our understanding of international trade and even finance. His voice and his pen are as strong as ever. In honoring him, we also honor a warm and generous teacher and friend.

Jagdish Bhagwati,
Columbia University

PART I

Introduction

1. Contributions of Professor Kreinin to international economics

Michael G. Plummer

1. INTRODUCTION

Professor Mordechai Kreinin, University Distinguished Professor of Economics at Michigan State University (MSU), has been one of the most prolific writers in international economics of his time. He has published a few dozen books, including nine editions of a best-selling textbook (*International Economics: A Policy Approach*); over 150 journal articles, many of which appear in the profession's top journals; and myriad other publications. He has clearly left an indelible imprint on the discipline of international economics, including international trade *and* finance. This volume, which brings together selected papers from a January 2003 conference at the Johns Hopkins University School of Advanced International Studies (SAIS) in celebration of his 73rd birthday, is entitled *Empirical Methods in International Trade*, mainly because his most extensive and influential contributions have been in this area.

In addition to his scholarly publications, Professor Kreinin has been an influential economist in many other ways. He has been the major professor of 37 doctoral students at MSU and a committee member of countless others, and has taught tens of thousands of undergraduate and graduate students, mostly at MSU but also while visiting other campuses in every continent bar Antarctica (where there are no campuses). His pedagogic approach and economic perspectives continue to dominate the classroom style and academic orientation of many of his former students. He has won a number of teaching awards.

Moreover, Professor Kreinin has been a key international economics adviser and/or consultant to various departments of the US and foreign governments, as well as to international organizations such as the IMF (International Monetary Fund) and UNCTAD (United Nations Conference on Trade and Development). He has also been active in professional associations, including the American Economic Association, Western Economic Association, Midwestern Economic Association and the International Trade and Finance Association, for which he served as a Board Member (1991–98) and as President (1993).

In short, Professor Kreinin has been a major figure in economics and in the lives of many of us economists. This volume celebrates his many contributions. This introductory chapter has two goals. The first is intended to summarize some of his more influential publications in empirical international trade, international trade theory, international finance and other areas (Section 2). Second, in Section 3 we give a brief survey of the papers included in this collection. Section 4 offers some concluding remarks.

2.   PROFESSOR KREININ'S ACADEMIC CONTRIBUTIONS

While Professor Kreinin's research has covered a wide range of the international economics literature over the past 40 years, his work has spanned many other aspects of economics as well, from consumer economics to analysis of the Israeli economy. In fact, he is one of the few international economists of his generation to have published influential work in the areas of both international trade and international finance, as well as outside international economics. To do justice to his *opus* would take an entire volume in itself (in fact, he has been asked twice to publish collections of his articles on specific topics[1]). Hence, in this section, we limit ourselves to a brief review of some of the major issues he has tackled during his career and which have had an important influence on the profession.

2.1   Empirical International Trade

Professor Kreinin's approach to empirical analysis is always practical: he is interested in real-world problems and has developed solid methods to address them. Most of these tools, some created as far back as the late 1950s, continue to be used in international economics. He is widely cited for new as well as old work in this area.

Certainly one of his most important academic contributions relates to international economic integration. In 1961, he published in the *American Economic Review* an influential econometric technique that could be used to generate parameters necessary for the *ex-ante* estimation of trade creation and trade diversion (Kreinin, 1961), which became an integral part of the 'price-elasticities approach' to *ex-ante* modeling.[2] Together with other emerging approaches to estimating the effects of economic integration in the literature, he used this technique in a variety of contexts, including the possibility of an Atlantic free-trade area and its effects on the United States (Kreinin, 1966) and the static effects of the Kennedy Round (Belassa and Kreinin, 1967). A variant of this approach was also used to estimate the effects of the First

Enlargement of the EEC on GSP (generalized system of preferences) concessions for developing countries (Kreinin, 1975). In the early 1970s, he developed a similar econometric technique to estimate these parameters at a
disaggregated level (Kreinin, 1973a). As trade policy tends to be dominated by
political-economy considerations at the sectoral level, this contribution added
an important dimension to empirical modeling. The insights gained from these
approaches were important building blocks to the development of more
sophisticated *ex-ante* economic paradigms used today, such as computational
general equilibrium (CGE) models.

Moreover, Professor Kreinin undertook pioneering work in *ex-post* empirical analysis. *A priori*, the political market for such work is less obvious than
in the case of *ex-ante* estimation: policymakers are more interested in what
will happen if a certain policy is adopted, rather than what actually did happen.
Such modeling is inherently difficult, as it requires the creation of a reliable
counterfactual (or *antimonde*). That is, data as to what actually happened are
readily available; what would have happened in the absence of the policy
innovation needs to be estimated. Still, *ex-post* estimation is of great importance if one is to learn from the effects of policy change, particularly in the
context of second-best initiatives such as regional economic integration
accords. In a series of articles in the late 1960s and the 1970s (e.g., Kreinin,
1969b, 1972, 1973b, 1976, 1979), Professor Kreinin developed an *ex-post*
approach in which a control country's trade performance, independent of the
integration process and properly adjusted for differences in income growth
and changes in real exchange rates, could be used to proxy the *antimonde*. His
work was first used to estimate the effects of the creation of the EEC and
EFTA (European Free Trade Area), at aggregate and disaggregate levels. The
approach spurred a great deal of excitement in the literature and continues to
be used today (of course, the contemporary problem is that with so many
countries negotiating free-trade areas of their own, finding a control country is
extremely difficult these days, though not impossible with proper adjustments). Professor Kreinin continued to use the model throughout the years, for
example, in estimating the effects of the EU Single Market Program and
NAFTA (North American Free Trade Agreement) on developing countries
(Kreinin and Plummer, 2002).

The theory of economic integration would suggest that, *a priori*, net trade
creation will be a negative function of the similarity of exports between partners and non-partner countries, and a positive function of the facility with
which partner exports can compete with domestic production. Hence the
degree of export similarity might be an important indicator of the *ex-ante*
effects of integration. It can also address other export-competitiveness questions, such as the extent to which China is actually a competitive export
'threat' to Southeast Asia. Together with Michael Finger, Professor Kreinin

developed a simple index to capture such export similarity (Finger and Kreinin, 1979). Given the ease with which such an index can be calculated, and transparency in interpretation, it has become one of the most popular indices used in empirical international trade, along with Balassa's revealed comparative advantage (RCA) index and the Grubel–Lloyd index. Peter Lloyd in his contribution to this volume (Chapter 2) surveys some of the economic literature's important contributions that have employed the Finger–Kreinin index.

Professor Kreinin and I also developed two types of empirical approaches related to the concept of export similarily in the context of regional integration. The first (Kreinin and Plummer, 1992) involved the creation of an export 'matching' technique to estimate the likely (*ex-ante*) effects of NAFTA on developing Asia, and the second (Kreinin and Plummer, 1994) related to the 'natural economic bloc' debate, in which we posit a 'natural bloc' to be one which preserved the structure of a country's comparative advantage.

Finally, in two widely publicized articles on 'supplier preferences' (Kreinin, 1988, 1996), he shed light on the exclusive purchasing behavior of Japanese companies that contributed to the closed nature of Japan's market.

2.2   International Trade Theory

As in the case of empirical international trade, Professor Kreinin has been influential in the more general mainstream of international trade theory and various topical areas, including international economic integration. Regarding the former, he resolved an important debate surrounding the ostensible stylized fact that tariff elasticities appeared to be consistently higher than what would be theoretically derived (Kreinin, 1967a, 1967b). He noted that the paradox could be solved by differentiating between estimated liberalization-induced effects on finished goods on the one hand and intermediate/primary goods on the other. Hence the reconciliation related to the need to control for effective – rather than mere nominal – rates of protection. He continued to work on various aspects of the effective rate of protection, publishing, for example, an important piece with James Ramsey and Jan Kmenta in which they incorporate an effective-rate dimension to a standard neoclassical trade model (Kreinin, Ramsey and Kmenta, 1971).

Professor Kreinin also contributed to the great debate surrounding the 'Leontief paradox' (e.g., Kreinin, 1965b). This debate exemplifies the type of economic inquiry on which he thrives, that is, empirical testing of standard theoretical models and careful attention to the explanation of the results. He demonstrates that, although Leontief was right in assuming that US labor was more productive than foreign labor, the superiority is not large enough to explain the paradox completely.

As the 1980s progressed, non-tariff barriers became increasingly popular even as tariff barriers had fallen considerably under the GATT and continued to fall due to the Tokyo and Uruguay Rounds. These non-tariff barriers (e.g., anti-dumping duties, countervailing duties, voluntary export restraints and the like) seemed to be emerging to take the place of tariff barriers in protecting domestic markets under an international regime that could do little to stop them. It is widely agreed that these non-tariff barriers tend to be more pernicious than tariff barriers in obstructing international trade. Yet, hitherto most of the trade literature had focused on tariff barriers; economic analysis of non-tariff barriers proved to be an important challenge to the discipline. Often with his colleagues at MSU and others, Professor Kreinin endeavored to formalize our theoretical understanding of the economic effects of non-tariff barriers in standard neoclassical models, including: the effects of voluntary export restraints on the welfare of imposing, recipient and specific third parties (Dinopoulos and Kreinin, 1988 and 1989; Kreinin, 1991); the welfare effects of quota-allocation schemes (Dinopoulos and Kreinin, 1992); comparative analysis of import quotas and voluntary export restraints (Dinopoulos and Kreinin, 1989); the economic implications of bilateral quota wars (Syropoulos, Dinopoulos and Kreinin, 1995); and the economic implications of voluntary import expansion programs (Dinopoulos and Kreinin, 1990). In addition to presenting novel theoretical insights, many of these theory-based articles also included an empirical dimension as a way of underscoring their relevance.

With respect to the area of economic integration, Professor Kreinin contributed significant insights to the theoretical understanding of the economics of preferential trading accords, again often as a means to support empirical analysis. For example, he presented a critical assessment of the theory of the dynamics of regional economic integration in a classic piece in the *Journal of Political Economy* (1964a). In this article, he coins for the first time the concepts of 'investment creation' and 'investment diversion,' and noted later that it was likely that these effects would be closely correlated with Vinerian trade creation and diversion (Kreinin and Plummer, 1992). He also was the first to develop a dynamic dimension to the 'equivalence of tariffs and quotas' framework, showing that the conclusions reached in the literature to date broke down when one considered tariffs and quotas in a dynamic context (Kreinin, 1970, 1975). He contributed to partial-equilibrium approaches to regional integration by dropping the small-country assumption that had previously been used in the literature (Kreinin, 1963a).

2.3 International Finance

In many ways, the close relationship between international trade and finance suggests that the emergence of these two areas as separate fields is unfortunate.

8 *Introduction*

Progress in one area is greatly hindered if it does not recognize this interdependence with the other. A salient contribution of Professor Kreinin to international economics is to underscore the reality of this trade–finance nexus in the real world. He began to address related issues as far back as the mid-1960s, when he published research on free trade and capital flows (e.g., Kreinin, 1965a), and later on the effect of exchange-rate changes on trade flows (1977b). More recently, he has focused on trade–direct foreign investment (DFI) links in an empirical context and continues to publish extensively in the area (e.g., Kreinin and Plummer, 1998a, 2003 and Kreinin et al., 1999). Results from this work reveal a clear and robust relationship between the two, and causality tests (as well as theory) underscore that the two are determined simultaneously. Econometric models of trade determination, therefore, need to include DFI – or, better yet, an instrumental variable for DFI – as an explanatory variable, otherwise risking an important misspecification problem.

Throughout the years, Professor Kreinin has also been fascinated by various issues related to exchange-rate determination, regime choice and its relationship to the real economy. In particular, he has focused on the determination and implications of balance of payments imbalances, mostly in the context of the United States. His work in this area began in the mid-1960s and continues to the present. He has testified frequently before the US Congress on this issue. Along with his colleague at MSU, Lawrence Officer, he published a classic integration of approaches to the balance of payments, 'The Monetary Approach to the Balance of Payments: A Survey,' in the *Princeton Special Studies in International Economics* (Kreinin and Officer, 1978). This work became an important reference for professional economists and a staple in the academic diet of many economics graduate students. Given that this area of international economics is of great interest to the general public, his publications in the popular press also tend to relate to international finance. Further, his work on optimum currency areas (e.g., Kreinin and Heller, 1975) has been receiving increased attention in the literature over the past ten years, as monetary union in the EU progressed and other regions contemplate monetary integration. Pomfret, Chapter 4 in this volume, emphasizes the importance of this earlier work.

Finally, in analyzing the US trade deficit, he predicted the 2003 appreciation of the euro (in speeches throughout Europe in 2002), at a time when many in the profession were predicting a stable dollar–euro exchange rate, or even a continued strengthening of the US dollar.

2.4   Contributions in Areas Other than International

Professor Kreinin has researched areas other than international economics which include: consumer economics (Kreinin, 1957a, 1957b, 1959a, 1959b) based on his work at the Survey Research Center; a test of Friedman's permanent income hypothesis (Kreinin, 1964d) and several papers on the Israeli economy (Kreinin, 1956, 1958a, 1958b, 1964b). Indeed, his first published paper, entitled 'Suppressed Inflation in Israel,' published in the *Journal of Political Economy* (Kreinin, 1956), found its way into the development literature of that time.

2.5   University Finances

Professor Kreinin's professional activities, apart from teaching and research, were many and varied, including consulting and lecturing around the world. Prominent among his activities was work on university finances. During the recession of the early 1980s, Michigan State University encountered a deep financial crisis and Professor Kreinin (in his capacity as member of the academic council and chairman of its steering committee) developed and helped introduce a buy-out plan for tenured faculty that resolved the crisis (Kreinin, 1982a, 1982b). This was the first time that buy-outs were used in academia. Following that experience he served as a consultant to about ten universities that encountered similar financial exigencies.

3.   SUMMARY OF VOLUME

The contributions to this volume cover a wide range of topics in the area of international trade, with a strong bias toward empirical modeling. In this section, we give a brief abstract of these chapters, which are organized under two broad themes: 'New approaches to empirical trade analysis,' which considers issues generally in the broad area of international trade, and 'Empirical approaches to economic integration,' which focuses more specifically on the economics of preferential trade arrangements.

In Chapter 2, Lloyd considers measurement issues related to similarity indices and matching techniques in international trade, an area in which, as noted above, Professor Kreinin has made some important contributions. Lloyd notes that there are two different strands in the trade literature on matching indices, each having different goals. One deals with matching proportions in two distributions; the other deals with matching the absolute value of different flows, usually exports and imports classified by industry or product group. This chapter discusses the use of similarity and matching indices in empirical research in international trade, focusing on the choice of measure and the properties of the chosen indices. It also discusses measures of dissimilarity.

Salvatore in Chapter 3 examines the relative international competitiveness of the United States *vis-à-vis* Europe, Japan and the rest of Asia in all manu-factured goods and in high-technology products, and how it has evolved over the past two decades. In doing so, he considers three different measures of competitiveness: revealed comparative advantage; an index of international competitiveness, such as that calculated yearly by the Institute for International Management (IMD); and changes in labor productivity. He presents, evaluates and compares the results of these three methods in the context of the United States and its major international competitors. In doing so, he is able not only to provide important insights into the changing struc-ture of US trade, but also to assess various measurement concerns in evaluat-ing international trade in general.

Chapter 4 by Pomfret argues that the European experience of monetary cooperation and integration in the 1990s presents a complicated economic process that was far from inevitable. Indeed, with the collapse of the Soviet Bloc, Europe in 2002 actually had more independent currencies than it did in 1991. Pomfret analyzes these processes in Western and Eastern Europe. He argues that while political considerations were important, economic forces were critical for both monetary union and disunion. Still, these factors do not fall under the traditional framework of optimum currency area (OCA) theory. Instead, the most salient issues concern who determines the conduct of mone-tary and fiscal policy, rather than the more technical issues emphasized in OCA theory of whether macro policy will be effective or not. Finally, in light of the European experience and in the context of OCA theory, Pomfret consid-ers monetary and financial cooperation in East Asia today. He notes that many proposals for closer monetary and financial cooperation have been negotiated and even launched in Asia since September 1997, that is, near the beginning of the Asian financial crisis. He also notes that the relevance of OCA theory does have implications for the prospects for monetary union in East Asia. Discussing the matter as a technical one of economic benefits versus economic costs misses the point of whether any of the independent countries, apart from the very small states, are willing to cede national autonomy over monetary and part of fiscal policy to a supranational institution.

The fact that international trade can have important effects on labor markets is recognized in the literature, but the exact nature of the link between trade and labor market outcomes is often the center of controversy. In Chapter 5, Davidson and Matusz summarize and integrate the major conclusions of three of their key contributions to this debate, both theoretical and empirical. They show, first, how differences in labor market structure, as characterized by job break-up rates and the efficiency of the matching process, could alter the pattern of comparative advantage and, hence, influence trade patterns. Second, they consider the manner in which changes in trade can affect the distribution of income, showing that this depends upon the underlying structure of the labor market. Finally, they use data on turnover rates, trade patterns and political lobbying activity to test these two predictions. The conclusion is that there is considerable empirical support for the predictions of the model.

Over the past twenty years there has been a remarkable amount of change in world trade conditions. The Uruguay Round has been largely implemented. Important new regional trade agreements have been created. Individual countries have experienced significant differences in growth rates, and biases induced by differential rates of factor accumulation across countries have been substantial. In addition, there have been substantive changes in the commodity composition of trade over this period. Given all of this, most theories of comparative advantage would lead us to expect considerable changes in trade patterns over these years. But this is not the case. Countries tend to have as their trading partners by rank and share of trade the same partners as they had decades ago. This pattern holds remarkably broadly across many countries, especially major industrialized countries that account for the bulk of world trade.

In Chapter 6, Cassing and Husted establish this absence of change in trade patterns and then hazard some theories to explain it. The chapter focuses on import shares for about one hundred countries between 1980 and 2000, constructing several statistical tests to determine whether trade partners have changed over the sample period. They find a remarkable amount of constancy in these relationships. In the second part of the chapter, the authors explore which, if any, trade theories are consistent with this behavior. They argue that an economic geography model is the only theory that seems to be consistent with the finding of relatively constant trading patterns even in a fairly dynamic world.

In spite of its growing importance, the international trade literature has neglected the study of the service sector. Chapter 7, by Shelburne and Gonzalez, begins to bridge that gap by studying the structure of trade in services. Specifically, it inquires into the prevalence of intra-industry trade in this sector. The results show that intra-industry trade is an important characteristic of this sector and is probably of a similar magnitude as the level of intra-industry trade in goods. The analysis presented indicates that GDP per capita and the relative size of the domestic service sector are significant determinants of the level of intra-industry trade across countries.

Chapter 8 by Arndt examines several aspects of cross-border production sharing. The implications for production and welfare of offshore component sourcing is examined in a general-equilibrium framework for several types of trade policy. While cross-border production sharing is welfare-enhancing in a standard free-trade arrangement, its welfare effect is ambiguous under most-favored-nation (MFN) trade protection. A partial-equilibrium framework is used to explore the trade-creating and trade-diverting elements of an economic area with production sharing and a standard preferential trade area. Cross-border production sharing affects the relationship between exports and imports and the exchange rate by making both less sensitive to the exchange rate as the importance of trade related to production sharing rises. Finally, Arndt shows that, as production sharing increases, it becomes important to distinguish between the value of trade and trade in value-added for proper trade-balance accounting purposes.

Part III opens with a contribution by Bown and McCulloch (Chapter 9) on the Uruguay Round Agreement on safeguards, which represents an effort to improve the GATT safeguards (SG) process and thereby encourage countries to choose this option over anti-dumping and 'gray-area' measures such as bilaterally negotiated export restraints. The chapter offers first a detailed analysis of the way safeguards initiated under the agreement have been implemented in practice. Bown and McCulloch examine the actual trade effects of 14 safeguard actions, covering 85 different 6-digit Harmonized System product categories, implemented by WTO signatories between 1995 and 2000. The main focus is the extent to which safeguard actions conform to the GATT/WTO MFN principle. They identify two types of discrimination that arise in the application of safeguards: explicit departures from MFN treatment through formal exclusion of some exporters, and implicit departures from MFN as reflected by systematic differences in impact across trading partners. The results indicate that the impact of SG action on a given exporter depends on the specific form of the safeguard policy. An SG implemented as a quota tends to preserve historical market shares more than an SG implemented as a tariff. When an SG is implemented as a quota, countries that have recently increased market share face reductions in market share relative to other suppliers. More generally, SG actions tend to favor established suppliers, whether large or small, over new suppliers and those whose market share has recently increased. The authors also find evidence that formal exemptions for developing countries and partners in a preferential trading arrangement allow these countries to gain market share at the expense of other suppliers.

Prior to the congressional vote, organized labor threatened to punish legislators who voted for NAFTA (the North American Free Trade Agreement). Building on work by Engel and Jackson, Phillips and Tower in Chapter 10 explore whether or not organized labor made good on its threat by reducing campaign contributions to House members who voted in favor of NAFTA. They postulate contribution functions for both Democrats and Republicans, with pre-NAFTA vote contributions on the horizontal axis and post-NAFTA vote contributions on the vertical axis. For members of both parties, Phillips and Tower find that a 'yes' vote on NAFTA resulted in a change in the contribution function, which is a combination of a downward proportional shift and a downward parallel shift.

Chapter 11 by Kim and Lee investigates Korea's direct investment in China and its implications for economic integration in Northeast Asia by examining its effect on bilateral trade between the two countries. The empirical part of the research is based on two recent surveys on Korea's overseas direct investment (ODI), one carried out by the Korea Institute for Industrial Economics and Trade and the other by the Korean Export–Import Bank. The chapter concludes that although the motives for investing in China are diverse, Korea's ODI in China as a whole had a positive effect on bilateral trade and thus on the economic integration of the two economies.

The literature demonstrates that trade agreements are about much more than just how trade flows respond to margins of preference. As was noted in Section 2 above, trade and factor flows are fundamentally linked, and studies of the impacts of preferential trade agreements should reflect such linkages. In Chapter 12 McCleery and De Paolis show that DFI in the NAFTA case seems not to be motivated by access to cheap labor, but rather access to the US market. Mexico's pattern of growth, in turn, is much more closely related to DFI inflows than tariff reductions. Hence traditional trade theory, with its focus on comparative advantage, trade barriers and scale economies, is insufficient to understand the complexities of NAFTA, if not modern trade agreements in general.

Chapter 13, by Noland, attempts to determine whether conditions amenable to successful selective interventions to capture cross-industry externalities are likely to be fulfilled in practice. Three criteria are proposed for good candidates for industrial promotion: (1) that they have strong inter-industry links to the rest of the economy; (2) that they lead the rest of the economy in a causal sense; and (3) that they be characterized by a high share of industry-specific innovations in output growth. According to these criteria, likely candidates for successful intervention are identified in the Korean data. Noland finds that, with one exception, none of the sectors promoted by the heavy and chemical industry (HCI) policy fulfills all three of the criteria.

4.   FINAL COMMENTS

Professor Kreinin is an extremely prolific, influential and innovative economist. Above, we reviewed a 'sampling' of his research, noting that he has accomplished much more than can be summarized in a brief survey like this.

It should be noted that his vast contributions to the area of international economics and his prominence in the profession constituted an important (sometimes, overriding) reason why MSU became such a popular doctoral program in economics. Some of his former students (including the volume's editor) have contributed to this volume; others participated at his Festschrift Conference at Johns Hopkins University SAIS in January 2003. The volume

14 *Introduction*

also consists of chapters written by colleagues at MSU, former and present, and other distinguished economists whom he met on various occasions and in various capacities around the globe. Many who could not make the conference sent along warm congratulatory messages, always with insightful and entertaining stories about Professor Kreinin as a colleague and friend.

Indeed, as was clearly demonstrated during the conference, Professor Kreinin has contributed more to the profession than mere publications. Through his many professional activities, dedication to his students and the economics department at MSU, and the friendship he has extended to all, he has presented an excellent model to *economists*. No doubt he will continue to deepen this model over the long term and beyond his retirement (should he choose to retire some day, that is).

NOTES

1. Kreinin (1974a) and Kreinin and Plummer (2000).
2. The price-elasticities approach estimates trade creation by multiplying the percentage change in a product's price due to regional integration by the elasticity of demand for that product and base-line partner imports (and also non-partner imports in the case of a customs union). Trade diversion is estimated by multiplying the elasticity of substitution of partner and non-partner production of a product by the marginal percentage change in preferential treatment of partner imports and base-line non-partner imports.

REFERENCES

Belassa, Bela and Mordechai E. Kreinin (1967), 'Trade Liberalization Under the Kennedy Round – The Static Effects,' *Review of Economics and Statistics*, **47** (2), 125–37.
Dinopoulos, Elias and Mordechai E. Kreinin (1988), 'Effect of the U.S.–Japan Auto VER on European Prices and U.S. Welfare,' *Review of Economics and Statistics*, **70** (3), 484–91.
——— (1989), 'Import Quotas and VERs: A Comparative Analysis in a Three-Country Framework', *Journal of International Economics*, **26** (1/2), 169–78.
——— (1991), 'The US VER on Machine Tools: Causes and Effects,' in R.E. Baldwin (ed.), *Empirical Studies of Commercial Policy*, Chicago: University of Chicago Press (NBER), pp. 113–34.
Finger, Michael and Mordechai E. Kreinin (1979), 'A Measure of Export Similarity and Its Uses', *Economic Journal*, **89** (356), 905–12.
Kreinin, Mordechai E. (1956), 'Suppressed Inflation in Israel 1949–1954,' *Journal of Political Economy*, **64** (2), 111–27.
——— (1957a), 'Factors Associated with the Use of Consumer Credit,' *Consumer Installment Credit*, National Bureau of Economic Research, Part II, Volume I.
——— (1957b), 'Analysis of Life Insurance Premiums,' *Review of Economics and Statistics*, **39** (1), 46–54.
——— (1958a), 'Israel's Survey of Consumer Finances,' *Journal of Finance*, **13** (4), 488–98.

————— (1958b), 'Israel's Export Problem and its Policy Implications,' *Southern Economic Journal*, **25** (2), 202–12.
————— (1959a), 'Analysis of Used Car Purchases,' *Review of Economics and Statistics*, **41** (4), 419–25.
————— (1959b), 'European Integration and American Trade,' *American Economic Review*, **49** (4), 615–27.
————— (1959c), 'On the Trade Diversion Effect of Trade Preference Areas,' *Journal of Political Economy*, **67**, August, 398.
————— (1959d), 'Factors Associated with Stock Ownership,' *Review of Economics and Statistics*, **41** (1), 12–23.
————— (1960), 'Flexible Exchange Rates in the Common Market – Suggested Implementation,' *Social Research*, **27** (1), 105–10.
————— (1961a), 'Effect of Tariff Changes on the Prices and volume of Imports,' *American Economic Review*, **51** (3), 310–24.
————— (1961b), 'Regional Interest in Foreign Trade,' *Review of Economics and Statistics*, **44** (1), February, pp. 91–94.
————— (1963a), 'Trade Creation and Diversion in a Customs Union – A Graphical Presentation,' *Kyklos*, **16** (4), 660–61.
————— (1963b), 'An Analysis of the Brookings Institution Study of the U.S. Balance of Payments,' *Compendium of Papers*, Joint Economic Committee, United States Congress.
————— (1963c), 'Introduction of Israel's Land Settlement Plan to Nigeria,' *Journal of Farm Economics*, **45** (3), 535–46.
————— (1963d), 'Windfall Income and Consumption,' *American Economic Review*, **53** (3), 442.
————— (1964a), 'On the Dynamic Effects of a Customs Union,' *Journal of Political Economy*, **72**, April, 193.
————— (1964b), *Israel and Africa: A Study in Technical Cooperation*, New York: Praeger.
————— (1965a), 'Freedom of Trade and Capital Movement,' *The Economic Journal*, **7** (1/2), 748–58.
————— (1965b), 'Comparative Labor Effectiveness and the Leontief Scarce Factor Paradox,' *American Economic Review*, **55** (1/2), 131–40.
————— (1966), 'Effect of an Atlantic Free Trade Area on the U.S. Economy,' *Southern Economic Journal*, **33** (1), 96–111.
————— (1967a), 'Price Elasticities in International Trade,' *The Review of Economics and Statistics*, **49** (4), 510–16.
————— (1967b), 'Price vs. Tariff Elasticities in International Trade: A Suggested Reconciliation,' *American Economic Review*, **57** (4), 891–4.
————— (1967c), 'Direct Foreign Investments and the American Interest,' *Economia Internazionale*, **XX** (3), August, pp. 501–11.
————— (1968), 'Israel and the EEC,' *Quarterly Journal of Economics*, **82** (2), 297–312.
————— (1969a), 'Price vs. Tariff Elasticities – A Reply,' *American Economic Review*, **59** (1), 200.
————— (1969b), 'Trade Creation and Diversion by the EEC and EFTA,' *Economia Internazionale*, **22** (2), 273–280.
————— (1970), 'On the Equivalence of Tariffs and Quotas,' *Kyklos*, **23** (1), 75–9.
————— (1971), *International Economics – A Policy Approach,* New York: Harcourt, Brace Jovanovich, reprinted 1975, 1983, 1987, 1991, 1995, 1998, 1999, 2002.

Kreinin, Mordechai E. (1972), 'Effects of the EEC on Imports of Manufactures,' *Economic Journal*, **82** (327), 897–920.

———— (1973a), 'Disaggregated Import Demand Functions,' *Southern Economic Journal*, **40** (1), 19–25.

———— (1973b), 'Effect of EEC Enlargement on Trade Flows,' *Southern Economic Journal*, **39** (4), 559–68.

———— (1973c), 'Economic Consequence of Reverse Preferences,' *Journal of Common Market Studies*, **xi** (3), 161–72.

———— (1974a), *Trade Relations of the EEC – An Empirical Investigation*, New York: Praeger, Special Studies.

———— (1974b), Book review: 'The European Community,' *Kyklos*, **27** (2), 407–9.

———— (1975), ' "Equivalence of Tariffs and Quotas," A Reply,' *Kyklos*, **28** (3), 647–8.

———— (1976), 'The Static Effects of EC Enlargement and Trade Diversion: A Reply to Comment,' *Southern Economic Journal*, **42** (4), 764.

———— (1977a), 'Living With Floating Exchange Rates,' *Journal of World Trade Law*, **11** (6), 514–36.

———— (1977b), 'Effect of Exchange Rate Changes on the Prices and Volume of Trade', *IMF Staff Papers*, **24** (2), 297–329.

———— (1979), 'Effect of European Integration on Trade Flows in Manufactures', *Proceedings of the Tilburg Conference on European Integration*, Holland, June.

———— (1982a), 'Preserving Tenure Commitments in Hard Times,' *ACADEME*, **68** (2), 37–42.

———— (1982b), 'For a University in Financial Trouble a Faculty "Buy-Out" Plan Can Save Money and Face,' *The Chronicle of Higher Education*, **23** (28) 56.

———— (1988), 'How Closed is Japan's Market? Additional Evidence,' *The World Economy*, **11** (4), 529–42.

———— (1990), 'VIEs: An Economic Analysis of Trade Expansion Policies,' *Economic Inquiry*, **28** (1), 99–108.

———— (1991), 'The U.S. VER on Machine Tools; Causes and Effects,' in R.E. Baldwin, editor, *Empirical Studies of Commercial Policy*, University of Chicago Press (NBER).

———— (1992), 'Alternative Quota and VER Allocation Schemes: A Welfare Comparison,' *Economica*, **59** (235), 337–49.

———— (1996), 'Israel's Trade Policy Reviews', *The World Economy*, **19** 119–32.

———— (1999), 'The Global Financial Crisis of 1997–98,' in *Asia-Pacific Economic Linkages*, Elsevier, pp. xix–xxxiii.

Kreinin, Mordechai and Leonard Cheng (1996), 'Suppliers Preferences and Dumping: An Analysis of Japanese Corporate Groups,' *Southern Economic Journal*, **63** (1), 51–9.

Kreinin, Mordechai E. and Elias Dinapoulos (1990), 'An Analysis of Import Expansion Policies,' *Economic Inquiry*, Huntington Beach: **28** (1), Jan, pp. 99–108.

———— (1992), 'Alternative Quota and VER Allocation Schemes: A Welfare Comparison, *Economica*, **59** (235), Aug. pp. 337–349.

Kreinin, Mordechai E. and Robert Heller (1975), 'Adjustment Cost, Optimum Currency Areas, and Optimum International Reserves,' in *International Trade and Finance*, Festschrift in Honor of Jan Tinbergen, Macmillan International, pp. 127–40.

Kreinin, Mordechai and Lawrence Officer (1975), 'Tariff Reductions Under the Tokyo Rounds – A Review of Their Effects on Trade Flows, Employment and Welfare,' *Weltwirtschaftliches Archiv*, **115** (3), 541–72.

———— (1978), 'The Monetary Approach to the Balance of Payments: A Survey,' *Princeton Special Studies in International Economics*, No. 43.

Kreinin, Mordechai E. and Michael G. Plummer (2002), *Economic Integration and Development: Has Regionalism Delivered for Developing Countries?*, Cheltenham, UK and Northampton, USA: Edward Elgar.

———— (1992), 'Effects of Economic Integration in Industrial Countries on ASEAN and the Asian NIEs,' *World Development*, **20** (9), 1345–66.

———— (1994) ' "Natural" Economic Blocs: An Alternative Formulation,' *International Trade Journal*, **VIII** (2), Summer, pp. 193–205.

———— (1998a), 'The Trade–DFI Nexus,' in F. Contractor, *Economic Transformation in Emerging Countries: The Role of Investments, Trade and Finance*, London: Elsevier.

———— (1998b), 'Effect of EC92 on the Export of Developing Countries,' *ASEAN Economic Bulletin*, **15** (2), 206–14.

———— (1999), 'Regional Integration in Asia,' in K. Fatemi, *The New World Order*, London: Elsevier, pp. 95–108.

———— (2000), *Economic Integration in Asia*, Cheltenham, UK and Northampton, USA: Edward Elgar.

———— (2003), 'Effect of Regional Integration on DFI,' presented at the American Economics Association Annual Meeting, Washington, DC (submitted for publication).

Kreinin, Mordechai and Dennis Warner (1983), 'Determinants of International Trade Flows,' *Review of Economics and Statistics*, **65** (1), 96–104.

Kreinin, Mordechai E., Thomas Lowinger and Anilko Lal (1998), 'Determinants of Inter-Asia Direct Investment Flows,' in J. Dunning (ed.), *Globalization, Trade and Direct Foreign Investments*, Oxford: Elsevier, pp. 194–203.

Kreinin, Mordechai E., Michael G. Plummer and Shigeyuki Abe (1999), 'Exports and DFI Links: A Three-Country Comparison,' in Mordechai E. Kreinin, Shigeyuki Abe and Michael G. Plummer (eds), *Asia-Pacific Economic Linkages*, London: Elsevier, pp. 47–64.

Kreinin, Mordechai E., J. Ramsey and J. Kmenta (1971), 'Factor Substitution and Effective Protection Reconsidered,' *American Economic Review*, **61** (5), 891–900.

Syropoulos, Costas, E. Dinopoulos and M. Kreinin (1995), 'Bilateral Quota Wars,' the *Canadian Journal of Economics*, **28** (4a), 939–44.

PART II

New Approaches to Empirical Trade Analysis

2. Measures of similarity and matching in international trade[*]

Peter J. Lloyd

1. INTRODUCTION

Finger and Kreinin (1979) devised an index of 'export similarity' to calculate the overlap between the distributions of exports by commodity group of two countries to the markets of a third country. As they noted, 'A number of propositions in international economics can be examined by the use of an index measuring the similarity of the exports of any two countries (or groups of countries) to a third market' (Finger and Kreinin, 1979, p. 905). They specifically mentioned the situations of non-reciprocal preferences granted by developed countries to developing countries (and therefore not to other developed countries which also exported to the preference-granting country under consideration), the multilateral extension on an MFN (most-favoured-nation) basis of reductions in tariff rates agreed among the developing countries to developing countries, and the relationship between export patterns of two countries and the convergence or divergence of economic structure of the economies of these countries over time.

Subsequently, the Finger–Kreinin (FK) index of export similarity has been used to compare the distribution of exports of two countries or country group by a number of other authors in a number of different contexts. Pomfret (1981) used the measure in a similar way to examine the impact of EEC enlargement on non-member countries' exports to the EEC. More recently the Australian Productivity Commission (2002) used it to examine the impact of introducing free entry into Australian markets for all least developed countries. Xu and Song (2000) used the FK index of export similarity to explore trade linkages between East Asian economies. Glick and Rose (1998) used it to examine the pattern of contagion in currency crises.

The Finger–Kreinin index of similarity can be used to compare any two distributions of trade flows or, in some contexts, stocks. For example, it might be used to compare the distribution of *imports* into two countries from a third country or group of countries (Ng, 2002). Alternatively, it might be used to compare the *geographic* distribution of the exports of two countries, or the geographic distribution of imports into two countries. It has been used by Kol and Mennes (1986) to compare the distributions of *exports* and of *imports* by commodity groups into one country. Further, in any of these domains, the two distributions compared may be observations of some distribution at two different times.

It turns out that measures of similarity or matching have been used in a number of contexts. There are in fact two different strands in the trade literature on matching indices that derive from different purposes. One of these deals with matching proportions in two distributions, the other with matching the absolute value of different flows, usually exports and imports classified by industry or product group. As an example of the latter, intra-industry trade is the matching of exports and imports within commodity categories. For ease of description, the first set is referred to as similarity indices and the second as matching indices.

This chapter discusses the use of similarity and matching indices in empirical research in international trade, focusing on the choice of measure and the properties of the chosen indices. It also discusses measures of dissimilarity.

2. MEASURES OF SIMILARITY IN PROPORTIONS

Indices of similarity can be developed to compare any two distributions. However, for the sake of concreteness, I shall begin with measures of similarity in patterns of export flows.

Suppose there are n commodity groups traded by an economy that are indexed by $i = 1, \ldots, n$. We can match the proportions or shares of exports in each category for countries a and b. Let X_{ia} and X_{ib} be the value of exports of category i from country a and country b respectively to some other country (or a group of countries), country c. Then $X_{ia}/\sum_i X_{ia}$ and $X_{ib}/\sum_i X_{ib}$ are the proportions of exports of countries a and b in category i. Finger and Kreinin (1979) proposed the index

$$S = \sum_i \min\left(\left[X_{ia}/\sum_i X_{ia}\right], \left[X_{ib}/\sum_i X_{ib}\right]\right) \qquad (2.1)$$

The summations are across all relevant categories of exports of goods from the country concerned. This could refer to all goods or a subset of goods; Finger and Kreinin in fact examined only exports of manufactures.

By construction, all components in the summation are positive fractions. Consequently, $S \in [0,1]$ which implies $S \geq 0$. The index takes on the maximum value of unity when the distributions are identical and the minimum value of zero when there is zero overlap in the distributions.

The FK index can be expressed as a weighted average. Define the match in category i relative to the average proportion of the exports and imports of the category in the total exports of country a and b respectively. That is,

$$S_i = \min\left(\left[\frac{X_{ia}}{\sum_i X_{ia}}, \frac{X_{ib}}{\sum_i X_{ib}}\right] / \frac{1}{2}\left[\frac{X_{ia}}{\sum_i X_{ia}} + \frac{X_{ib}}{\sum_i X_{ib}}\right]\right) \qquad (2.2)$$

Then,

$$S = \sum_i S_i \cdot \frac{1}{2}\left[\frac{X_{ia}}{\sum_i X_{ia}} + \frac{X_{ib}}{\sum_i X_{ib}}\right] \qquad (2.3)$$

The weights are the simple average share of category i in the total exports of the two countries.

The value of the index is not invariant with respect to the level of disaggregation used to define the export categories. Disaggregation of a given flow necessarily lowers the value of the index, or leaves it unchanged. For any category i, X_{ia} and X_{ib} are defined at some level of aggregation in the international trade statistics. At the next (lower) level of disaggregation, $X_{ik} = \sum_j X_{ik}^j$ for $k = a, b$ where j is the set of sub-categories within category i for the country concerned. It is convenient here to define the proportions as a new variable $x_{ik} = [X_{ik}/\sum_i X_{ik}]$ and similarly, at the next level of disaggregation, $x_{ik}^j = X_{ik}^j/\sum_i X_{ik}$. Then, for category i,

$$\min(x_{ia}, x_{ib}) = \sum_j \min(x_{ia}^j, x_{ib}^j) + \min(x_{ia}', x_{ib}') \qquad (2.4)$$

where $x_{ik}' = x_{ik} - \sum_j \min(x_{ia}^j, x_{ib}^j)$. That is, the matching at the higher initial level of aggregation for category i is equal to the matching within the lower sub-categories plus the matching within all of category i which is across sub-categories. When the calculations are done at the more disaggregated level, the second set of matches drops out.

Kellman and Schroder (1983) called this difference in the measure at different levels of aggregation 'aggregation bias'. This term is misleading as there is no bias, unless one can establish that, for the purpose in hand, one level of disaggregation is *a priori* to be preferred to other levels.

The FK index can be written in an alternative form:

$$S = 1 - \frac{1}{2} \sum_i \left| \frac{X_{ia}}{\sum_i X_{ia}} - \frac{X_{ib}}{\sum_i X_{ib}} \right| \qquad (2.5)$$

The identity of equations (2.1) and (2.5) follows immediately from the equality

$$2 \min \left[\frac{X_{ia}}{\sum_i X_{ia}}, \frac{X_{ib}}{\sum_i X_{ib}} \right] = \frac{X_{ia}}{\sum_i X_{ia}} + \frac{X_{ib}}{\sum_i X_{ib}} - \left| \frac{X_{ia}}{\sum_i X_{ia}} - \frac{X_{ib}}{\sum_i X_{ib}} \right| \forall i \qquad (2.6)$$

The form in equation (2.5) had been developed by Grubel and Lloyd (1975, Equation (2.14)) in the different context of matching exports and imports across categories (= 'industries'), although they rejected it as an inappropriate measure in that context.

In this form, one can regard

$$D = \frac{1}{2} \sum \left| \frac{X_{ia}}{\sum_i X_{ia}} - \frac{X_{ib}}{\sum_i X_{ib}} \right| \qquad (2.7)$$

as an index of *dissimilarity*. Substituting equation (2.7) into (2.5) and rearranging, we have $D + S = 1$. For every index of similarity between two distributions that lies in the unit interval, one can obtain an index of dissimilarity simply by subtracting the index of similarity from unity, or *vice versa*. Similarity and dissimilarity are exact complements, an index of one defining the corresponding index of the other. By construction, all of the components in the summation in D are positive fractions. Consequently, $D \geq 0$ and $D \in [0,1]$. Of the two forms, that defined as $D = S - 1$ where S_i is given by equation (2.1) is the simplest and easiest to calculate.

Michaely (1962a, pp. 87–9) developed the index of dissimilarity between the commodity distribution of exports and of imports for one country, though he did not incorporate the adjustment factor 1/2 and consequently his index lies awkwardly in the closed interval from 0 to 2. Michaely (1962b) used the index of dissimilarity in the different domain of the balance of trade of one country with each of its trading partners. In this application, he did adjust the index by the factor (1/2). Here it was called the index of multilateral balancing.

Other measures of similarity have been put forward. An obvious choice is the correlation coefficient but this varies within the limits of −1 and +1. A second measure used in statistics is $\sum_i (x_{ia} - x_{ib})^2/2$. Squaring the differences is another method of producing an index with positive components and lying in the unit interval. However, it puts more weight on the larger differences that may not be appropriate in trade contexts. Linneman (1966, pp. 140-43) uses the cosine of the angle between the two vectors of proportions in countries *a* and *b*. Like the FK index, this measure has the desirable property that it lies in the unit interval but it has no simple interpretation and requires more computation.

Sun and Ng (2000, Theorem 3) show that the index in equation (2.1) is the only index that satisfies certain elementary axioms for an index of similarity and is some function of the differences for each category $(x_{ia} - x_{ib})$. The axioms are the properties that the index lies in the unit interval, is continuous, symmetric and strongly separable and a property relating to sub-classifications. These axioms and the use of category differences are reasonable in the case of comparisons of trade proportions.

The question of how to compare two distributions arises in the economic analysis of problems in other areas of economics. The FK similarity index, or its complement the index of dissimilarity, can be applied to two distributions in any domain. It is not, therefore, surprising that one or the other has been discovered independently and used in a number of different economic contexts. The dissimilarity index, *D*, has been widely used in location theory since the 1940s, where it is known as the coefficient of localization (see Isard, 1960, pp. 251–3).[1] Schiavo-Campo (1978) has used the index of dissimilarity in equation (2.5) to measure structural change in the distribution of some economic variable, say industrial output or exports, between two dates. More generally, Sun and Ng (2000) propose this index as a measure to analyse structural differences between two economies. There are probably applications in other domains of which the author is unaware.

Even more generally, the FK index of similarity can be regarded as an example of a family of similarity or matching indices used to measure the similarity or match between two objects (T_i, U_i) which take the form $\sum_i^n f(T_i, U_i) \cdot w_i$. Here f is some index of similarity and the w_i are weights. These indices are widely used in psychology, spatial analysis and other areas of the social sciences (see Watson, 1997).

3. MEASURES OF MATCHING INTRA-INDUSTRY TRADE

The second set of measures is based on values rather than proportions. The focus in this section is on measures of intra-industry trade as this is the most important application. In the field of intra-industry trade analysis, a measure or index of matching is required because goods trade flows are two-way. One measure has become standard. This is the measure that is known as the Grubel–Lloyd measure after the originators (Grubel and Lloyd, 1971 and 1975, chapter 2).

Suppose there are n industries in the economy that are indexed by $i = 1, \ldots, n$ and that exports and imports of all goods can be allocated to industries. For a multiple-product industry, industry i, let X_i be the aggregate value of exports of industry i and M_i be the value of imports of industry i. As Grubel and Lloyd (1975, p. 20) put it, 'Intra-industry trade is defined as the value of exports of an "industry" which is exactly matched by the imports of the same industry'. That is,

$$I_i = (X_i + M_i) - |X_i - M_i| \tag{2.8}$$

The complement of intra-industry trade is called inter-industry trade

$$J_i = |X_i - M_i| \tag{2.9}$$

The value of intra-industry trade in equation (2.8) is then normalized by dividing by $(X_i + M_i)$ to give

$$B_i = \{(X_i + M_i) - |X_i - M_i|\}/(X_i + M_i) \tag{2.10}$$

This is simply the proportion of the total trade of the industry that is intra-industry trade as distinct from inter-industry trade.

The economy-wide measure of intra-industry trade can now be obtained by averaging each industry measure B_i across all n industries, using the relative shares of industry exports plus imports as weights:

$$B = \sum_i B_i \cdot [(X_i + M_i)/\sum_i (X_i + M_i)] \tag{2.11}$$

$$= \frac{\sum_i (X_i + M_i) - \sum_i |X_i - M_i|)}{\sum_i (X_i + M_i)} \tag{2.12}$$

There is an equivalent statement of the measure. I_i can also be written

$$I_i = 2 \min (X_i, M_i) \tag{2.13}$$

as Grubel and Lloyd (1975, p. 20n) noted. Hence,

$$B = \frac{\sum_i 2 \min (X_i, M_i)}{\sum_i (X_i + M_i)} \qquad (2.14)$$

This can also be rewritten as

$$B = \sum_i \left[\frac{2 \min (X_i, M_i)}{(X_i + M_i)} \right] \cdot \left[\frac{(X_i + M_i)}{\sum_i (X_i + M_i)} \right] \qquad (2.15)$$

The properties of the measure in equation (2.12) or (2.14) are well established. It is the weighted mean of the proportions of intra-industry trade in each industry. The elements and weights are all positive fractions. Consequently $B \geq 0$ and $B \in [0,1]$. The mean is equal to intra-industry trade summed across all industries as a proportion of the total trade.

As with the FK index, the value of the Grubel–Lloyd index of intra-industry trade is not invariant with respect to the level of disaggregation at which the flows of exports and imports are matched. Disaggregation of a given flow of exports and imports necessarily lowers the value of the index, or leaves it unchanged. (The proof follows that in Section 2). Indeed, this aspect of the measurement of intra-industry trade attracted a great deal of attention in the early days of empirical research on intra-industry trade. (See Grubel and Lloyd, 1971, 1975, chapter 4 and Gray, 1979. For a review of recent literature on this aspect, see Gullstrand, 2002).

The most basic feature of the measure is that it was derived by matching the value of exports and imports in each industry and then averaging these industry measures. Trade theory indicates that this is the appropriate definition in analysing patterns of international trade. Helpman (1981) was the first to show rigorously the role of the Grubel–Lloyd measure in a trade model. He begins with an analysis of net (= inter-industry) trade. The measure of inter-industry trade is $| X_i - M_i |$. Before the recognition of intra-industry trade, this measure was widely used in the empirical study of trade patterns and comparative advantage. Then intra-industry trade is simply the complement of inter-industry trade, as in equations (2.8) and (2.9) above. As he seeks propositions concerning the share of intra-industry trade, Helpman uses the Grubel–Lloyd measure in equation (2.12). In his model the manufacturing sector produces closely differentiated products. He derives propositions relating the share of intra-industry trade in the manufacturing sector to factor proportions.

There is now a variety of trade models that yields two-way trade within industries that are defined as product groups related in some way in either demand or supply. These include models with vertical and horizontal product differentiation, models with trade in intermediates and models with jointness in supply. In all of these models, the goods actually traded by some country are a mixture of traditional inter-industry and intra-industry trade. Because comparative advantage and other causes of trade determine value of exports and imports, the Grubel–Lloyd index is the appropriate measure of intra-industry trade in analysing the intra-industry component of international trade. This explains why the Grubel–Lloyd measure became the standard one in empirical studies of commodity trade.

Other measures have been used to measure the levels of intra-industry trade. For discussions of these measures, see Grubel and Lloyd (1975, chapter 2) and Kol and Mennes (1986).

In fact, the main alternative to the Grubel–Lloyd measure that has been advanced is the FK measure in the same domain. The FK measure is here

$$S = \sum_i \min \left(\left[X_i / \sum_i X_i \right], \left[M_i / \sum_i M_i \right] \right) \qquad (2.16)$$

In the trade domain, it is the proportions of exports and imports in industry i that are matched. This measure has the same form as the Grubel–Lloyd index in equation (2.14) but with the proportions of imports and exports replacing the values of exports and imports.

First, we can note that the Grubel–Lloyd and Finger–Kreinin measures are identical if there is an exact equality between total exports and total imports (compare equations (2.14) and (2.16)). This case holds with a probability of zero as all countries have a deficit or surplus in the balance of trade and most countries have either a chronic deficit or a chronic surplus. At other times the measures will differ.

The FK measure of intra-industry trade has also arisen in another way. Because trade is unbalanced, the Grubel–Lloyd index in equation (2.12) lies below the upper bound of 1. Grubel and Lloyd (1975, p. 22) recommended the 'adjusted' measure

$$C = \frac{\sum_i (X_i + M_i) - \sum_i \left| X_i - M_i \right|}{\sum_i (X_i + M_i) - \left| \sum_i X_i - \sum_i M_i \right|} \qquad (2.17)$$

Note that $C \in [0,1]$, as desired, but C cannot be expressed as a weighted mean.

The need for some form of adjustment in the presence of a trade imbalance has been generally accepted. A number of authors have, however, criticized the method of adjustment in equation (2.17) and offered alternative adjustments. This literature is surveyed by Greenaway and Milner (1981).

Aquino (1978, p. 280) objected that C applies to total trade only and does not have a counterpart at the individual commodity level to B_i. Instead, Aquino believed that there should be an adjustment or correction to the value of B_i in every industry. He proposed an adjustment to provide 'an estimate of what the values of exports and imports of each commodity would have been if total exports had been equal to total imports' (ibid.). By making the same equiproportionate adjustment in each industry,

$$X_i^e = X_i \cdot \frac{1}{2} \frac{\sum_i (X_i + M_i)}{\sum_i X_i} \text{ and } M_i^e = M_I \cdot \frac{1}{2} \frac{\sum_i (X_i + M_i)}{\sum_i M_i}$$

he obtains the measure

$$D = \frac{\sum_i (X_i^e + M_i^e) - \sum_i \left| X_i^e - M_i^e \right|}{\sum_i (X_i^e + M_i^e)} \qquad (2.18)$$

Kol and Mennes (1986) showed that this measure is equivalent to that in equation (2.16), the FK measure. The Aquino index is not, therefore, really an adjustment for the balance of trade. It is a measure of the extent to which import and export *shares* are matched at the industry level. The question of whether and how to adjust the measures of intra-industry trade for trade imbalances remains unresolved.

The Grubel–Lloyd measure can be used to measure two-way exchange of goods in categories other than the products of 'industries'. Originally, this measure was used by Hirschman (1945) to measure the extent to which the trade between nations was an exchange within or between two broad categories of goods, 'manufactures' and 'raw materials and foodstuffs'. The Grubel–Lloyd measure has also been used for the analysis of matching two-way flows between countries in trade other than in goods. Lee and Lloyd (2002) have used it to measure and analyse two-way trade between countries in services. It has been used to analyse two-way affiliate production (see Markusen and Maskus, 2002 and Ekholm, 2002). Similarly, Greenaway, Lloyd and Milner (2001) have used the measure to analyse two-way market penetration by means of trade in goods and affiliate production combined. There is another body of literature seeking to measure the extent to which *changes* in exports and imports over some time are matched within industries. This has given rise to a family of indices called marginal intra-industry trade indices. One of the measures favoured here is an adaptation of the Grubel–Lloyd index, with an adjustment in the denominator of the index because changes in exports and imports may be negative or positive. Brülhart (2002) reviews this literature.

Michaely (1962b) used the index

$$C = \frac{\sum_i \left| X_i - M_i \right|}{\sum_i (X_i + M_i) - \left| \sum_i X_i - \sum_i M_i \right|} \tag{2.19}$$

in the analysis of bilateral versus multilateral balancing of a country's trade with its trading partners. In this domain X_i and M_i are the exports and imports of the country with trading partner i. This measure is the complement of that in equation (2.17). It is a measure of the extent to which trade between pairs of countries is not balanced or matched. Interestingly, it includes the same adjustment for the trade imbalance as that used by Grubel and Lloyd (1975) in the context of intra-industry trade.

To my knowledge, these measures of matching or non-matching, unlike the FK measure, have not been used outside the domain of international trade.

4.   CHOICE OF MEASURE

There are close connections between the measures of similarity and the measures of matching. Both are based on the overlap between corresponding elements in the two distributions, which is appropriate in the international trade context. (The complementary measures of dissimilarity are based on the differences between the corresponding elements, which is also appropriate.) Both are category averages with category share weights. Both sets of measures are not invariant with respect to the chosen level of aggregation.

Yet they are different measures, apart from the improbable case of an exact equality of the category totals in the relevant domain. One is a measure of matches between the proportions and the other a measure of the matching of values. Take, for illustration, the measure of similarity/matching in intra-industry trade analysis. For category i, the components of the indices of similarity and matching are respectively (from equations (2.2) and (2.15))

$$S_i = \min \left\{ \left[\frac{X_{ia}}{\sum_i X_{ia}}, \frac{X_{ib}}{\sum_i X_{ib}} \right] / \frac{1}{2} \left[\frac{X_{ia}}{\sum_i X_{ia}} + \frac{X_{ib}}{\sum_i X_{ib}} \right] \right\}$$

and

$$B_i = \frac{2 \min (X_i, M_i)}{X_i + M_i}$$

The index of similarity and the index of matching are then obtained by weighting and summing these different components. The same choice applies to the measures of dissimilarity.

Perhaps the most important lesson from this survey of measures of similarity or matching concerns the choice of measure. The choice depends on the purpose of the empirical study. For the purpose of explaining specialization and comparative advantage in international trade, a matching of values is appropriate. For the purpose of measuring similarity between two distributions, however, one needs to match the proportions rather than the values.

In most cases, the choice is clearly a measure based on proportions or one based on values. One example where this choice was debated is the discussion above of ways to correct the measure of average intra-industry trade for the aggregate trade imbalance. Another closely related example is the choice of measure of multilateral balancing of a country's trade with other countries. The League of Nations (1933) used an index based on values whereas Michaely (1962b) preferred an index based on proportions. Michaely's choice was criticized by Ahmad (1964) and Grubel and Lloyd (1975, chapter 4, n. 7), both of whom argued that a measure based on values was more appropriate in this context.

This necessity to derive the measure from the relevant body of theory holds generally. There are a number of economic contexts in which comparisons are made between two distributions but the matching indices discussed here are *not* used.

For example, in discussions on income distribution, analysts frequently want to compare two distributions. These could be the distribution of income among income classes for some unit (households, families or individuals) between two countries, or a change in the distribution for some country over some time. In this context, it is usual to use a measure such as the Gini coefficient. Such measures capture the inequality of the distributions across income classes. They use information concerning the whole distribution. In this context, the concern is with the relationships between income classes. For this purpose, the order of the classes is important. The ordered income classes can be cumulated, as in a Lorenz curve, and used to calculate some statistic of inequality for each distribution or to calculate the shares of the highest or lowest income classes. By contrast, in the matching indices of international trade discussed above, the focus is not on the relationship between the shares in each category as this is of little interest to trade economists. It is on the comparison of each class across the two distributions.

There are contexts in international trade where the analyst is concerned with some aspect of inequality such as concentration or diversification in the distribution of a variable. For example, there is an extensive literature on the role of concentration in the distribution of exports by commodity as a determination of year-to-year fluctuations in export earnings or the terms of trade. For this purpose, various measures of concentration such as the Hirschman index of concentration[2] or the entropy index have been used. Once more, the form of the index should be derived from the relevant body of theory. In the context of industrial concentration, there is a literature justifying the choice of the Hirschman measure (see, for example, Tirole, 1989, chapter 5.5 and references therein) but there is no comparable literature justifying the use of this index in international economics.

Clearly, trade economists doing empirical work must pay close attention to the nature of the problem before making a choice of an index of similarity or matching.

NOTES

* This note uses some of the material in Lloyd (2002).
1. I owe this reference to Robert Dixon. In this application, the measure is calculated in yet another equivalent way: adding either the positive or the negative differences, taking the absolute value of the sum and dividing by the category total. This method of calculation takes advantage of the fact that the sum of the differences must be zero.
2. Hirschman used his index to measure geographic concentration of goods trade rather than commodity concentration. The Hirschman index has been widely used to measure industrial concentration, where it is sometimes known as the Herfindahl index, but Herfindahl adopted the index from Hirschman (see Hirschman, 1964).

REFERENCES

Ahmad, S. (1964), 'Multilateral Balancing in International Trade: Comment', *American Economic Review*, **54**, 754–7.
Aquino, A. (1978), 'Intra-Industry Trade and Inter-industry Trade Specialization as Concurrent Sources of International Trade in Manufactures', *Weltwirtschaftliches Archiv*, **114**, 275–96.
Australian Productivity Commission (2002), *Removing Tariffs on Goods Originating from Least Developed Countries*, Productivity Commission, Canberra, ACT, Australia.
Brülhart, M. (2002), 'Marginal Intra-industry Trade: Towards a Measure of Non-disruptive Trade Expansion' in P.J. Lloyd and H. Lee (eds), *Frontiers of Research in Intra-industry Trade*, Basingstoke: Palgrave.
Ekholm, K. (2002), 'Factor Endowments and Intra-industry Affiliate Production by Multinational Enterprises' in P.J. Lloyd and H. Lee (eds), *Frontiers of Research in Intra-industry Trade*, Basingstoke: Palgrave, pp. 109–130.
Finger, J.M. and M.E. Kreinin (1979), 'A Measure of "Export Similarity" and its Possible Uses', *Economic Journal*, **89**, 905–12.

Glick, R. and A.K. Rose (1998), 'Contagion and Trade: Why are Currency Crises Regional?', NBER Working Paper Series No. 6806.

Gray, H.P. (1979), 'Intra-industry Trade: The Effects of Different Levels of Data Aggregation', in H. Giersch (ed.), *On Intra-industry Trade*, Tübingen: Mohr, pp. 87–110.

Greenaway, D. and C. Milner (1981), 'Trade Imbalance Effects in the Measurement of Intra-industry Trade', *Weltwirtschaftliches Archiv*, **117**, 756–62.

Greenaway, D., P.J. Lloyd and C. Milner (2001), 'Intra-industry Foreign Direct Investment and Trade Flows: New Measures of Global Competition', in L.K. Cheng and H. Kierzkowski (eds), *Global Production and Trade in East Asia*, Norwell, MA: Kluwer Academic Publishers, pp. 111–28.

Grubel, H.G. and P.J. Lloyd (1971), 'The Empirical Measurement of Intra-Industry Trade', *Economic Record*, **47**, 494–517.

———— (1975), *Intra-Industry Trade: The Theory and Measurement of International Trade in Differentiated Products*, London: Macmillan.

Gullstrand, J. (2002), 'Does the Measurement of Intra-industry Trade Matter?', *Weltwirtschaftliches Archiv*, **138** (2), 317–39.

Helpman, E. (1981), 'International Trade in the Presence of Product Differentiation, Economies of Scale and Monopolistic Competition: A Chamberlinian–Heckscher–Ohlin Approach', *Journal of International Economics*, **11**, 305–40.

Hirschman, A.O. (1945), *National Power and the Structure of Foreign Trade*, Berkeley and Los Angeles: University of California Press.

———— (1964) 'The Paternity of an Index', *American Economic Review*, **54**, 761–2.

Isard, W. (1960), *Methods of Regional Analysis*, Cambridge, MA: MIT Press.

Kellman, M. and T. Schroder (1983), 'The Export Similarity Index: Some Structural Tests', *Economic Journal*, **93**, 193–8.

Kol, J. and L.B.M. Mennes (1986), 'Intra-Industry Specialization and some Observations on Concepts and Measurement', *Journal of International Economics,* **21**, 1173–81.

League of Nations (1933), *Review of World Trade*, Geneva: League of Nations.

Lee, H.-H. and P.J. Lloyd (2002), 'Intra-industry Trade in Services' in P.J. Lloyd and H. Lee (eds), *Frontiers of Research in Intra-industry Trade*, Basingstoke: Palgrave Macmillan, pp. 159–79.

Linneman, H.H. (1966), *An Econometric Study of International Trade Flows*, Amsterdam: North-Holland.

Lloyd, P.J. (2002), 'Controversies Concerning Intra-industry Trade' in P.J. Lloyd and H.-H. Lee (eds), *Frontiers of Research in Intra-industry Trade*, Basingstoke: Palgrave Macmillan, pp. 13–30.

Markusen, J.R. and K. Maskus (2002), 'A Unified Approach to Intra-industry Trade and Foreign Direct Investment', in P.J. Lloyd and H.-H. Lee (eds), *Frontiers of Research in Intra-industry Trade*, Basingstoke: Palgrave Macmillan.

Michaely, M. (1962a), *Concentration in International Trade*, Amsterdam: North-Holland.

———— (1962b), 'Multilateral Balancing in International Trade', *American Economic Review*, **52**, 685–702.

Ng, S. (2002), 'The Effects of Growth of Its Trading Partners on Malaysia,' in Alan D. Woodland (ed.), *Economic Theory and International Trade: Essays in Honour of Murray C. Kemp*, Cheltenham, UK and Northampton, USA: Edward Elgar, pp. 311–20.

Pomfret, R. (1981), 'The Impact of EEC Enlargement on Non-member Mediterranean Countries' Exports to the EEC', *Economic Journal*, **91**, 726–30.

Schiavo-Campo, S. (1978), 'The Simple Measurement of Structural Change: A Note', *Economic Record*, **54**, 99–106.
Sun, G.-Z. and Y.-K. Ng (2000), 'The Measurement of Structural Differences between Two Economies', *Economic Theory*, **16**, 313–22.
Tirole, J. (1989), *The Theory of Industrial Organization*, Cambridge, MA: MIT Press.
Watson, I. (1997), *Applying Case-Based Reasoning: Techniques for Enterprise Systems*, Amsterdam: Morgan Kaufman.
Xu, X. and L. Song (2000), 'Export Similarity and the Pattern of East Asian Development', in P.J. Lloyd and X. Zhang (eds), *Global Economy*, Cheltenham, UK and Northampton, USA: Edward Elgar, pp. 145–64.

3. Changes in the relative international competitiveness of the United States during the past two decades

Dominick Salvatore

1. INTRODUCTION

The chapter examines the relative international competitiveness of the United States *vis-à-vis* Europe, Japan and the rest of Asia in all manufactured goods and in high-technology products, and how this has changed over the past two decades. International competitiveness is a crucial aspect of all modern economies, but a great deal of disagreement exists on how to measure it (see Salvatore, 1992 and 1993; McKibbin and Salvatore, 1995). One way to measure international competitiveness is by implicit or revealed comparative advantage. Another method is by the index of international competitiveness, such as that calculated yearly by the Institute for International Management (IMD), and the third by the change in labor productivity. Each of these different measures of international competitiveness has some shortcomings. They are also not directly comparable and provide somewhat different results. This chapter presents, evaluates and compares the results of these three methods of measuring the international competitiveness of nations.

Section 2 of this chapter examines the meaning and importance of the concept of international competitiveness itself. Section 3 discusses measuring the international competitiveness of nations and regions by revealed comparative advantage, Section 4 by measuring international competitiveness directly, and Section 5 by improvements in labor productivity. Section 6 concludes.

2. THE IMPORTANCE OF INTERNATIONAL COMPETITIVENESS AND ECONOMIC RESTRUCTURING

In a 1994 article, Paul Krugman stated that international competitiveness is an irrelevant and dangerous concept because nations simply do not compete with each other the way corporations do, and that increases in productivity rather than international competitiveness are all that matter for increasing the standard of living of the nation. In trying to prove his point, Krugman points out that US trade represents only about 10–15 percent of US GDP (and so international trade cannot significantly affect the standard of living, at least in the United States), international trade is not a zero-sum game (so that all nations can gain from international trade), and that concern with international competitiveness can lead governments to the wrong policies (such as adopting trade restrictions and engaging in industrial policies).

Of course, it is true that if a nation experiences a higher productivity growth than its trade partners it will experience an improvement in its international competitiveness, and so the nation need not worry about the latter. But it is not true that since international trade is only 10 to 15 percent of US GDP it cannot significantly affect the US standard of living. For example, eliminating its huge trade deficit would have added $344 billion or 0.3 percent to the US GDP in 2001. This is about the size of the tax stimulus package that President Bush pushed through. More generally, if a nation's corporations innovate and increase productivity at a faster rate than foreign corporations, the nation will export products which are technologically more advanced and thus permit faster growth in the future. For example, the US superiority in software makes possible faster productivity growth in the United States both directly (because productivity growth is faster in the software industry than in many other industries) and indirectly (by increasing the productivity of many other sectors, such as automobiles, which make great use of computer software in design and production). Thus changes in international competitiveness are crucial to the nation's standard of living even though international trade repents only 10–15 percent of US GDP.

Pointing out, as Krugman does, that some high-tech sectors artificially protected by trade policies and/or encouraged by industrial policies have grown less rapidly than some low-tech sectors, such as cigarettes and beer production, misses the point. This only proves that wrong policies can be costly. Productivity growth and international competitiveness must be encouraged not by protectionist or industrial policies but by improving the factors that affect its degree of international competitiveness (such as liberalizing its economy and improving its industrial structure). In short, a country's future prosperity depends on its growth in productivity and international competitiveness, and these can certainly be influenced by government policies. Thus nations compete in the sense that they choose policies that promote productivity. As pointed out by Dunning (1995) and Porter (1990), international competitiveness does matter.

This can be seen by comparing the United States with Europe. Although Europe has been able to keep wages and standards of living relatively high and rising during the past two decades, the rate of unemployment is now about 50 percent higher than the US and the Japanese rates. Furthermore, the United States has created many more jobs during the past 30 years than Europe, except for a few years during the second half of the 1990s. The United States has also been much more successful than European countries in meeting the growing competition from NIEs (newly industrializing economies) and other emerging economies in Asia (see Rausch, 1995).

The restructuring and downsizing that rapid technological change and increasing international competition made necessary resulted in average wages and salaries not rising very much in real terms in the United States during the past decade, but millions of new jobs were created. In Europe, on the other hand, real wages and salaries grew faster than in the United States but fewer new jobs were created, and this left Europe less able to compete on the world market than the United States. Being unable to fire workers when not needed, firms have tended to increase output by increasing capital per worker rather than by hiring more labor, and this has made the return to capital lower and the wage of labor higher in Europe than in the United States.

Since the 1970s, the United States has moved faster than Japan, Germany, France and other nations in deregulating (i.e., in removing government regulations and controls of economic activities on) airlines, telecommunications, trucking, banking and many other sectors of the economy. For example, cut-throat competition makes American airlines about a third more productive than the larger regulated or government-run foreign airlines. General merchandise retailing is twice as efficient in the United States than in Japan, and so is American telecommunications in relation to German telecommunications. Most American firms today face much stiffer competition from domestic and foreign firms than their European and Japanese counterparts. Stiff competition makes most American firms lean and mean – and generally more efficient than foreign firms. Despite the announcement in Lisbon in March 2000 of a strategy to make the European Union the most competitive economy in the world by 2010, not much has been accomplished to date to realize that goal.

3. MEASURING INTERNATIONAL COMPETITIVENESS BY REVEALED COMPARATIVE ADVANTAGE

One way of measuring the relative international competitiveness of nations is by their implicit or revealed comparative advantage. In this section, we provide data on the relative comparative advantage of the United States *vis-à-vis* Europe, Japan and the rest of Asia in manufactured goods as a whole and in high-technology products from 1980 to 2001.

3.1   Changes in US Relative Competitiveness in Manufactured Goods

Table 3.1 shows the change in the international competitiveness in all manufactured goods as a whole of the United States with respect to Western Europe, Japan and the rest of Asia from 1980 to 2001. The rest of Asia refers here primarily to the dynamic Asian economies (DAEs), which include China, Hong Kong, Korea, Malaysia, Singapore, Taiwan and Thailand. The change in the international competitiveness in manufactured goods of the United States gives an indication of the degree of de-industrialization allegedly taking place in the United States. This is not necessarily bad if the US gains in international competitiveness in high-technology products, and services exceed its loss in international competitiveness in manufactured goods as a whole. After all, the United States is the most advanced *technological* and *service* economy in the world.

Table 3.1 gives data on the manufactured exports and imports, the net balance, and the net balance as a percentage of total manufactured exports of the United States with respect to Europe, Japan, and the rest of Asia in 1980, 1990 and from 1995 to 2001. The last column of the table gives the change in the (revealed) comparative advantage and thus provides a measure of the change in the international competitiveness of the United States in manufactured goods as a whole from 1980 to 2001.

The table shows that in 1980 the United States exported to Europe $41.58 billion of manufactured goods, imported $36.05 billion, for a net balance of $5.53 billion, which represented 3.79 percent of the total exports of all manufactured goods of the United States. The positive sign indicates that the United States had a comparative advantage in manufactured products with respect to Europe in 1980. The absolute value of the index provides a measure of the degree or strength of the comparative advantage or international competitiveness of the nation. In 1990, US manufactured exports to Europe jumped to $86.71 billion, but its imports increased even more, to $90.60 billion, for a net balance of –$3.89 billion, which represented –1.34 percent of US total exports of manufactured goods. Thus the revealed comparative advantage that the US had with respect to Europe in manufactured goods in 1980 turned into a small revealed comparative disadvantage by 1990, and this increased almost continuously until 2001, when it was –9.12.

Table 3.1 also shows that the United States had a very strong comparative disadvantage in manufactured goods with respect to Japan, with an index of –16.30 in 1980. This increased to a high of –21.39 by 1990 and then declined to –13.72 in 2001. With respect to other Asian nations, the United States started with a small comparative disadvantage (–1.36) in 1980, but this increased rapidly as a result of the rapid industrialization of the DAEs during the past two decades, and it became the largest comparative disadvantage with an index of –26.58 in 2001.

Table 3.1   US trade in manufactured goods (billions of dollars)

	Exports	Imports	Net balance	Comp. adv. (+) or disadv. (−)*
Europe				
1980	41.58	36.05	5.53	3.79
1990	86.71	90.60	−3.89	−1.34
1995	104.34	125.61	−21.27	−4.72
1996	110.05	134.34	−24.29	−5.01
1997	125.18	148.67	−23.49	−4.24
1998	134.87	167.85	−32.98	−5.91
1999	140.39	183.75	−43.36	−7.54
2000	153.36	203.79	−50.43	−7.77
2001	147.91	202.87	−54.96	−9.12
Japan				
1980	7.91	31.70	−23.79	−16.30
1990	28.38	90.53	−62.15	−21.39
1995	44.01	123.95	−79.94	−17.75
1996	44.35	114.57	−70.22	−14.49
1997	45.41	120.20	−74.79	−13.51
1998	40.64	120.56	−79.92	−14.32
1999	40.03	129.23	−89.20	−15.50
2000	46.65	144.73	−98.08	−15.11
2001	41.35	124.01	−82.66	−13.72
Asia–Japan				
1980	20.86	22.84	−1.98	−1.36
1990	51.69	95.49	−43.80	−15.08
1995	99.17	178.46	−79.29	−17.61
1996	105.97	87.57	−81.60	−16.84
1997	116.32	208.51	−92.19	−16.66
1998	100.51	222.90	−122.39	−21.93
1999	106.76	250.79	−144.03	−25.03
2000	127.12	297.71	−170.59	−26.29
2001	112.79	272.93	−160.14	−26.58

* Comparative advantage (+) or disadvantage (−) is measured by the net balance as a percentage of the total manufactured exports of the nation (here the United States).

Source: GATT/WTO.

3.2   Changes in US Relative Competitiveness in High-Technology Products

Much more important is how the international competitiveness position changed in high-technology goods over time. High-technology products refers to chemicals, machinery and transport equipment. Chemicals includes pharmaceuticals. Machinery refers to power-generating machinery, electrical machinery and apparatus, non-electrical machinery, office equipment and telecommunications equipment. Transport equipment includes automotive products and other transport equipment. Automotive products incorporate many new technologies and can increasingly be regarded as a high-technology product. Other transport equipment refers to aircraft and locomotives.

Table 3.2 shows that the United States had a comparative advantage index of 4.69 in high-technology products with respect to Europe in 1980. This comparative advantage declined to 2.96 in 1990 and turned into a comparative disadvantage of –0.68 in 1995, which then increased to –5.19 in 2001. Thus, despite the widely held belief to the contrary, according to this measure the United States seems to have lost competitiveness in high-technology products with respect to Europe even during the 1990s. The contrary belief that the United States had become more competitive *vis-à-vis* Europe during the decade of the 1990s was based on (1) the elimination of the 1980s dollar overvaluation, (2) the much greater computerization of the American than the European economies, (3) the much more extensive spread of computer-aided design and computer-aided manufacturing in the US economy based on its superiority in software, and (4) the much greater restructuring of the US economy than European economies during the 1980s and early 1990s. This belief has also been encouraged by the Lausanne-based Institute for Management Development (IMD), which ranked the United States as the most competitive economy in the world since 1994, taking the top spot away from Japan, which had occupied that position from 1984 until 1993 (to be discussed later).

The United States, already with a large comparative disadvantage in high-technology products (shown by the index of –11.73 in the last column of Table 3.2) in 1980 with respect to Japan, continued to lose competitiveness until 1990 (see Salvatore, 1995), but regained some of the lost ground since then, so that in 2001 it was only marginally lower than it was in 1980. With respect to other Asian countries, the United States went from a comparative advantage index of 6.33 in 1980 to the index of comparative disadvantage of –2.89 in 1995. The index then continued to fall until it reached –8.61 in 2000, to some extent as a result of the serious financial and economic crisis that engulfed most of Asia from 1997 to 2000. With the end of the crisis, the US competitive position improved a little, but the index of –7.72 was much lower than in 1996, before the East Asia crisis.

Table 3.2   US trade in high-technology products (billions of dollars)

	Exports	Imports	Net balance	Comp. adv. (+) or disadv. (–)*
Europe				
1980	29.59	22.74	6.85	4.69
1990	66.57	57.98	8.59	2.96
1995	80.21	83.28	–3.07	–0.68
1996	84.54	89.48	–4.94	–1.02
1997	96.78	100.50	–3.72	–0.67
1998	104.93	115.87	–10.94	–1.96
1999	110.44	128.99	–18.55	–3.22
2000	119.40	142.48	–23.08	–3.56
2001	113.94	145.20	–31.26	–5.19
Japan				
1980	5.88	23.00	–17.12	–11.73
1990	19.92	74.12	–54.20	–18.66
1995	30.16	105.52	–75.36	–16.74
1996	32.30	96.42	–64.12	–13.23
1997	33.49	100.11	–66.62	–12.04
1998	30.31	99.12	–68.81	–12.33
1999	29.91	108.41	–78.50	–13.64
2000	34.42	122.28	–87.86	–13.54
2001	29.98	103.27	–73.29	–12.17
Asia–Japan				
1980	16.73	7.49	9.24	6.33
1990	42.39	38.84	3.35	1.22
1995	81.36	94.10	–12.74	–2.89
1996	86.59	100.35	–13.76	–2.84
1997	95.15	110.71	–15.56	–2.81
1998	83.28	114.91	–31.63	–5.67
1999	88.91	132.19	–43.28	–7.52
2000	105.59	161.46	–55.87	–8.61
2001	93.60	140.08	–46.48	–7.72

*   Comparative advantage (+) or disadvantage (–) is measured by the net balance as a percentage of the total manufactured exports of the nation (here the United States).

Source: GATT/WTO.

Taken at face value and viewed as a whole, the data in Table 3.2 show that the US competitive position in high-technology products greatly deteriorated from 1980 and 1990 to 2001 *vis-à-vis* Europe and the rest of Asia. Only with respect to Japan did the US more or less hold its own from 1980 to 2001.

3.3   Changes in US Relative Competitiveness in Office and Telecommunications Equipment

Table 3.3 shows the changes in the international competitiveness in office equipment and telecommunications of the United States with respect to Europe, Japan and the rest of Asia from 1980 to 2001. Office equipment and telecommunications are, of course, part of high-technology products, but they are here singled out because they are often considered the most important high-tech sectors and as of strategic importance to the future international competitiveness and growth of the nation.

Table 3.3 shows that in 1980 the United States had a revealed comparative advantage index of 3.94 in office equipment and telecommunications with respect to Europe. By 1990, this comparative advantage had increased to 4.62, but it then declined to 2.69 in 2001. Table 3.3 also shows that the United States had a comparative disadvantage index with respect to Japan in office equipment and telecommunications of –2.70 in 1980. This disadvantage increased to –6.62 by 1990, but then it declined to –2.38 in 2001. The United States had a comparative disadvantage of –1.06 in office equipment and telecommunications with respect to the rest of Asia in 1980. This disadvantage increased sharply to –8.95 by 1995, and it was –9.01 in 2001. Thus the US comparative advantage with respect to Europe and comparative disadvantage with respect to Japan in office and telecommunication equipment declined from 1980 to 2001, and its comparative disadvantage increased sharply with respect to the rest of Asia. Nevertheless, the US international competitive position is somewhat better in this sector as compared with the high-tech and manufacturing sectors as a whole.

3.4   Revealed Comparative Advantage and Dollar Overvaluation

The use of revealed comparative advantage to measure the international competitive position of a nation is appropriate only when the nation's trade balance is in equilibrium or nearly so. If the nation's currency is grossly overvalued and results in huge trade deficits, this method of measuring changes in the international competitiveness of a nation over time loses its usefulness. A grossly misaligned exchange rate distorts the pattern of specialization and trade. Changes in the revealed comparative advantage or disadvantage of a nation may reflect such distortions more than changes in the underlying competitive position of the nation.

Table 3.3 US trade in office equipment and telecommunications
(billions of dollars)

	Exports	Imports	Net balance	Comp. adv. (+) or disadv. (−)*
Europe				
1980	7.12	1.37	5.75	3.94
1990	18.02	4.60	13.42	4.62
1995	25.29	10.81	14.48	3.22
1996	25.04	10.46	14.58	3.01
1997	27.83	11.02	16.81	3.04
1998	27.43	11.46	15.97	2.86
1999	28.90	12.39	16.51	2.87
2000	33.34	14.45	18.89	2.91
2001	28.57	12.37	16.20	2.69
Japan				
1980	1.01	4.96	−3.95	−2.70
1990	6.02	24.66	−18.64	−6.62
1995	10.50	39.06	−28.56	−6.34
1996	12.35	33.98	−21.63	−4.46
1997	12.28	33.97	−21.69	−3.92
1998	10.40	30.74	−20.34	−3.64
1999	10.47	33.13	−22.66	−3.94
2000	13.07	37.04	−23.97	−3.69
2001	10.69	25.05	−14.36	−2.38
Asia–Japan				
1980	3.60	5.14	−1.54	−1.06
1990	12.94	25.68	−12.74	−4.39
1995	31.13	71.44	−40.31	−8.95
1996	32.71	74.78	−42.07	−8.68
1997	37.13	81.63	−44.50	−8.04
1998	33.41	83.73	−50.32	−9.02
1999	40.06	95.77	−55.61	−9.67
2000	50.28	115.44	−65.16	−10.04
2001	39.67	93.97	−54.30	−9.01

* Comparative advantage (+) or disadvantage (−) is measured by the net balance as a percentage of the total manufactured exports of the nation (here the United States).

Source: GATT/WTO.

Nowhere is this more evident than during the overvaluation of the dollar in the first half of the 1980s. It was estimated that from 1981 to February 1985, the US dollar had become overvalued by about 40 percent on a trade-weighted basis with respect to the nation's main trade partners. This led to a doubling of the US trade deficit from $70 billion to $140 billion in 1985 and to the loss of more than 2 million jobs (Council of Economic Advisors, 1986, chapter 3; Crockett and Goldstein, 1987, pp. 1–6). It also led to increased demand for trade protection even by firms that were more efficient than their foreign competitors but could not compete with them at home and abroad because of the dollar overvaluation.

Table 3.4 shows that the US revealed comparative advantage index in manufacturing with respect to Western Europe of 3.79 in 1980 changed to the very large revealed comparative disadvantage index of –18.26 by 1985, which then declined to –6.37 in 1988 when all the dollar overvaluation had been eliminated and to –1.34 in 1990 if we allow for the pass-through lag trade response. The same is true with respect to Japan (no data were available for the rest of Asia). Although the US international competitive position improved as the dollar overvaluation was eliminated, the data show clear evidence of hysteresis, with the index not returning to the 1980 level. The same is true for trade in high-technology goods, but not for trade in office and telecommunication equipment, where other fundamental competitive forces seem to have overwhelmed the exchange-rate effect.

The same (but to a much smaller extent) seemed to have occurred during the latter part of the 1990s, when the dollar became gradually overvalued with respect to most other currencies. Assuming, for argument's sake, that a 10 percent dollar overvaluation with respect to the euro, the yen and other currencies is removed, that there is complete and immediate pass-through, and that

Table 3.4   Changes in US revealed comparative advantage and disadvantage with dollar overvaluation

Year	In manufacturing		In high-tech		In office & telecom equip	
	Europe	Japan	Europe	Japan	Europe	Japan
1980	3.79	–16.30	4.69	–11.73	3.94	–2.70
1985	–18.26	–39.95	–6.28	–27.16	4.06	–5.47
1988	–6.37	–22.03	–1.13	–18.76	3.58	–6.33
1990	–1.34	–21.39	2.96	–18.66	4.62	–6.62

Source: GATT.

the price elasticity of demand for US exports and imports is –1, the elimination of the 10 percent dollar overvaluation would reduce the 2001 US index of revealed comparative disadvantage in high-tech goods from –5.19 to –0.87 with respect to Europe, from –12.17 to –10.00 with respect to Japan, and from –7.72 to –3.84 with respect to the rest of Asia. This would eliminate most or all of the deterioration in the US comparative advantage since 1996 with respect to Europe and with respect to Asia minus Japan, and would make the US index with respect to Japan in 2001 lower than in 1980. Thus we see that grossly misaligned exchange rates invalidate the use of revealed comparative advantage or disadvantage to measure a change in the international competitive position of a nation.

4.   A DIRECT MEASURE OF INTERNATIONAL COMPETITIVENESS

Another method of estimating the international competitiveness of nations is to try to measure it directly, as done, for example, by the Institute of Management Development (IMD) in Lausanne, Switzerland. According to this measure, the United States ranked as the most competitive economy in the world in each year since 1994, when it replaced Japan, which had held that position for several years up to 1994. Since taking the number one spot in 1994, the United States increased its lead over the other G-7 nations. These results seem to contradict those obtained by the revealed comparative advantage method presented above.

The international competitiveness ranking of the G-7 nations for 2002 calculated by IMD is shown in Table 3.5. The table shows that by assigning a

Table 3.5   National competitiveness scores, 2002

Country	Score
United States	100.0
Canada	79.0
Germany	70.9
United Kingdom	68.9
France	61.6
Japan	54.3
Italy	51.9

Source: Elaboration on IMD (2002).

competitive index of 100 to the United States, Canada came in second with an international competitiveness index of 79.0 (this means that Canada was about 21 percent less efficient on an overall basis with respect to the United States), Germany was third with an index of 70.9, the United Kingdom was fourth with an index of 68.9, followed by France with 61.6, Japan with 54.3 and Italy with 51.9. It should be noted that although Canada ranked second among the G-7 countries, it was actually in eighth place when all 49 countries for which the competitive index was calculated were included. Ahead of Canada (with the competitive index in parentheses) were Finland (84.4), Luxembourg (84.3), Netherlands (82.8), Singapore (81.2), Denmark (80.4) and Switzerland (79.5). Germany was 15th among the 49 countries, the United Kingdom was 16th, France 22nd, Japan 30th and Italy 32nd. Note the sharp decline of Japan from being the most competitive economy in the world for several years up to 1994 but now having fallen to sixth place among the G-7 countries and 32nd among all 49 countries as a result of the serious economic and financial problems that the nation has been facing since the early 1990s.

Competitiveness was defined as the ability of a country to generate more wealth for its people than its competitors in world markets, and was calculated as the weighted average of 314 individual competitiveness criteria grouped into four large categories: (1) economic performance (macroeconomic evaluation of the domestic economy); (2) government performance (extent to which government policies are conducive to competitiveness); (3) business efficiency (extent to which enterprises perform in an innovative and profitable way); (4) infrastructure (extent to which basic, technological scientific and human resources meet the needs of business). As Table 3.6 indicates, the United States ranked number 1 on all four of these broad criteria in 2002.

Table 3.6   Ranking on competitiveness factors, G-7 countries, 2002

Country	Score*	Economic performance	Government performance	Business efficiency	Infrastructure
US	100.0	1	1	1	1
Canada	79.0	5	2	2	2
Germany	70.9	2	4	4	3
U.K.	68.9	3	3	3	6
France	61.6	4	6	5	5
Japan	54.3	7	5	7	4
Italy	51.9	6	7	6	7

*   Overall competitiveness score (from Table 3.5).

Source: Elaboration on IMD (2002).

However, measuring international competitiveness directly is a very ambitious and difficult undertaking. The very concept of providing an overall competitive index for a nation faces some serious shortcomings. One is the grouping and the measuring of international competitiveness of developed and developing countries, and of large and small countries, together. It is well known that developed and developing countries, on the one hand, and large and small countries, on the other, have very different industrial structures and face different competitiveness problems. Therefore, using the same method to measure the international competitiveness for all types of countries may not be appropriate: the results may not be very informative and may be difficult to interpret. Nothing prevents us, however, from comparing only the large, the small, and the developed and the developing countries among themselves, separately (as we have done above) rather then comparing them all together.

Another serious shortcoming with the above competitiveness measure is that the correlation between real per capita income and the standard of living of the various nations may not be very high. For example, the United Kingdom has a higher competitiveness index than Japan even though its real per capita income is more than a quarter lower than Japan's. Similarly, the United Kingdom has a competitiveness index much higher than Italy even though its real per capita income is practically the same as Italy's. The questions that naturally arise are: (1) if the United Kingdom is more competitive than Japan, how can its per capita income and standard of living be so much lower? (2) Similarly, if Italy is so much less competitive than the United Kingdom, how can it have a similar real per capita income? Specifically, where do Italy's high per capita income and standard of living come from? One possible answer to this criticism is that the competitive index is forward, rather than backward, looking in that it measures the conditions that would lead to higher national growth in the future rather than the reasons for its faster growth in the past. Viewed in this way, we could say that the UK's higher growth in 2002 reflects its higher competitive index in previous years, and that its higher competitive index in 2002 leads us to expect that it will grow faster than either Japan or Italy in the coming years.

Finally, the index has been criticized because it gives an overall index of the nation's international competitive position. It is well known that a nation may score low on its overall competitiveness index and still have some sectors in which it is more productive and efficient than its competitors. Although this is a valid criticism, there is some usefulness in such overall measures of international competitiveness. First, in the process of obtaining an overall competitive score, a great deal of data had to be collected and made available (for example, as was pointed out earlier, 314 individual indices were used in calculating the 2002 index), which can be extremely valuable in evaluating the efficiency of specific sectors of the economy. Second, entrepreneurs and managers from around the world do seem to rely on this type of overall index or general beliefs as to the relative efficiency and attractiveness of investing in various nations. This is the reason, for example, that multinationals prefer to invest in the UK rather than in Italy.

The IMD competitiveness index is also not the only one available. Displeased by how the world competitiveness index was measured, the World Economic Forum (WEF), which had previously collaborated with IMD in measuring the international competitiveness of nations, started to prepare its own index. WEF (2002), which is also based in Switzerland, defines international competitiveness as 'the ability of a country to achieve sustained high rates of growth in GDP per capita'. The most significant difference between the two competitiveness indices is that the WEF, unlike IMD, excludes such variables as GDP growth, export growth, and the inflow of foreign direct investments among the variables used in measuring international competitiveness because it regards these as the result or consequence, rather than the cause, of a country's level of international competitiveness. The WEF ordinal competitiveness ranking of the G-7 countries in 2002, however, is very similar to the IMD's results (with the United States leading the list of the G-7 countries and Canada in second place, but with the UK ahead of Germany in third place, followed by France, Japan and Italy). The same general results were obtained by the European Commission (1998).

5. MEASURING INTERNATIONAL COMPETITIVENESS BY LABOR PRODUCTIVITY

A third method of measuring the change in the international competitiveness of nations is by the change in their relative labor productivity over time. Table 3.7 shows the change in output per hour in manufacturing in the G-7 countries from 1979 to 2001. The time series starts in 1979, a year in which US manufacturing output reached its business cycle peak. Assigning a value of 100 to 1979, Table 3.7 shows that the output per hour in US manufacturing rose to 207.7 by 2001. This is much higher than for Canada, Italy and Germany, a little higher than for Japan, but less than for the UK and France.

The last column of the table shows the ratio of the index of output per hour in US manufacturing to the trade-weighted index of nine US trade partners (the other G-7 countries, as well as Belgium, Norway and Sweden). According to this measure, the international competitiveness of the United States remained about constant until 1985, it declined a little from 1990 to 1997, but then it increased continuously and reached 111.5 in 2001.

The bottom part of Table 3.7 gives the average yearly change in output per hour in manufacturing for sub-periods of the 1979 to 2001 period for each of

Table 3.7 *Output per hour in manufacturing, G-7 countries, 1979 = 100*

Year	US	Japan	Germany	France	UK	Italy	Canada	Ratio of US to trade partners
1979	100.0	100.0	100.0	100.0	100.0	100.0	100.0	100.0
1980	100.6	101.6	98.5	100.5	98.8	104.3	98.7	100.3
1985	122.7	122.9	113.6	119.4	129.4	122.9	123.3	100.2
1990	138.2	151.7	126.2	141.3	162.3	134.7	126.4	98.8
1995	162.3	178.4	148.4	171.5	190.8	151.9	152.1	97.9
1996	166.9	186.6	150.6	172.6	188.8	152.1	148.5	99.6
1997	173.0	194.5	157.9	183.5	191.4	154.5	153.7	99.3
1998	180.4	194.8	159.1	192.3	194.6	154.7	153.1	102.9
1999	193.0	203.9	159.2	199.8	203.0	154.5	157.0	106.7
2000	203.9	215.5	169.1	214.6	214.7	158.9	160.3	107.8
2001	207.7	205.8	170.8	220.4	218.0	161.6	157.2	111.5
1979–85	3.5	3.5	2.1	3.0	4.4	3.5	3.6	0.0
1986–90	2.4	4.3	2.1	3.4	4.6	1.9	0.5	−0.3
1991–95	3.3	3.3	3.3	4.0	3.3	2.4	3.8	0.0
1996–01	4.2	2.5	2.3	4.3	2.3	1.0	0.6	1.1
1979–01	3.4	3.3	2.5	3.7	3.6	2.2	2.1	0.5

Source: Bureau of Labor Statistics, US Department of Labor (2002).

the G-7 countries. The data show that over the 1979–85 period, the US did better than Germany and France, the same as Japan and Italy, and worse than the UK and Canada, but it held its own on average. Over the 1986–90 period, the United States outperformed Germany, Italy and Canada, but did worse than Japan, France and the UK, and on average lost some international competitiveness. The United States held its own, on average, over the 1991–95 period but did much better in the 1996–2001 period, outperforming all but France among the other G-7 countries. Over the entire 1979–2001 period, the United States outperformed (i.e., increased its international competitiveness) with respect to Japan, Germany, Italy and Canada but fell short of France and the UK, and managed to improve its position a little on an overall basis.

If improvements in labor productivity are entirely distributed to labor, then unit labor costs remain more or less constant. If wage increases exceed the growth in productivity, then unit labor costs rise, and if they rise more than abroad the nation loses international competitiveness. Figure 3.1 shows that manufacturing unit labor costs in the United States declined gradually from 1979 to 2001 when measured on a national currency basis. They rose sharply from 1979 to 1986 as a result of the sharp appreciation and overvaluation of the dollar. With the elimination of the overvaluation over the 1986–88 period, US unit labor costs declined even more sharply than they had previously risen.

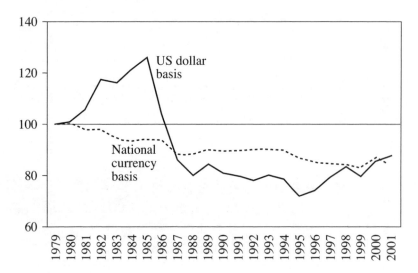

Source: Bureau of Labor Statistics, US Department of Labor (2002).

Figure 3.1   US manufacturing unit labor costs relative to competitors,
1979–2001 (1979 = 100)

They continued to decline a little until 1996, when they gradually rose as a result of a recurrence of the overvaluation of the dollar.

6. CONCLUSION

The concept and measurement of the international competitiveness of nations is a useful tool. Measuring the international competitiveness of a nation by its revealed comparative advantage can help in determining its sectoral competitiveness, but not when the nation's currency is misaligned. It then becomes very difficult to separate changes in underlying international competitiveness of the nation from exchange-rate effects. Although much maligned, measuring international competitiveness directly, as is done by the Institute for Management Development and the World Economic Forum, can be useful as a general indication of where the national economy is heading and also because of the useful data that are made available in the process of calculating the index. A very effective measure of the change in the international competitiveness of a nation is also provided by the change in its labor productivity in relation to that of its trade partners. This also permits us to separate and analyze the effect on labor costs, and hence on the international competitiveness of the nation, of changes in relative labor productivity and exchange-rate changes.

When used to measure the changes in international competitiveness of the United States over the past two decades, these three methods give somewhat conflicting results, but they seem to confirm that the United States did lose some international competitiveness during the 1980s, but seems to have regained it, and even improved on it, since the second half of the 1990s.

REFERENCES

Council of Economic Advisors (1986, 1987), *Economic Report of the President*, Washington, DC.

Crockett A. and M. Goldstein (1987), *Strengthening the International Monetary System: Exchange Rates, Surveillance, and Objective Indicators*, Washington, DC: International Monetary Fund.

Dunning, J.H. (1995), 'Think Again Professor Krugman: Competitiveness Does Matter', *The International Executive*, March–April, 315–24.

European Commission (1998), *The Competitiveness of European Industry – 1998 Report*, Luxembourg: Office of Official Publications of the European Communities.

Krugman, P. (1994), 'Competitiveness: A Dangerous Obsession', *Foreign Affairs*, March–April, 28–44.

McKibbin W. and D. Salvatore (1995), 'The Global Economic Consequences of the Uruguay Round,' *Open Economies Review*, April, 111–29.

Porter, M. (1990), *The Competitive Advantage of Nations*, New York: Free Press.

Rausch, L.M. (1995), *Asia's New High-Tech Competitors*, Washington, DC: National Science Foundation.

Salvatore, D. (1990), *The Japanese Trade Challenge and the US Response*, Washington, DC: Economic Policy Institute.

――― (ed.) (1992), *Handbook of National Trade Policies*, Amsterdam: North-Holland.

――― (ed.) (1993), *Protectionism and World Welfare*, New York: Cambridge University Press.

――― (1995), 'Can the United States Compete with Japan?' in M. Kreinin (ed.), *Contemporary Issues in Trade Policy*, New York: Pergamon Press, pp. 1–10.

――― (1998), 'Europe's Competitiveness Problems,' *The World Economy*, March, 189–205.

――― (2003), 'The New Economy and Growth in the G-7 Countries,' *Journal of Policy Modeling*, July, 531–40.

US Department of Labor (2002), *International Comparisons of Labor Productivity and Unit Labor Costs in Manufacturing*, Washington, DC: Bureau of Labor Statistics.

WEF (2002), *The Global Competitiveness Report*, New York: Oxford University Press.

4. Why does optimal currency area theory fail to predict changes in currency areas? Evidence from Europe and lessons for Asia

Richard Pomfret

The dominant theoretical framework for analysing currency domains has been the optimum currency area theory originating from Mundell (1961) and McKinnon (1963). Much of the applied literature on currency area formation has come from Europe, following steps towards monetary integration within the European Union (EU) since 1970. The appearance of euro banknotes in January 2002 was a highly visible sign of monetary union among EU members, and many commentators have drawn positive lessons from European monetary union for monetary integration in other parts of the world. Yet the process of currency union in Europe has not fitted in with the predictions of optimal currency area (OCA) theory. One of the few empirical studies using OCA theory to identify the most likely candidates for currency union (Kreinin and Heller, 1974, p. 137) concluded that among the OECD countries Italy, Sweden and Switzerland should be keenest to abandon their national currencies. From the post-euro perspective, a score of one out of three raises questions about the success of OCA theory in explaining changes in actual currency areas.

This chapter argues that the European experience of the 1990s is richer than a simple story of the inevitability of monetary integration. In Eastern Europe the number of currencies proliferated between 1991 and 1993 with the dissolution of the Yugoslav, Czechoslovak and Soviet currency areas, so that Europe had more independent currencies in 2002 than it did in 1991. The two main sections of the chapter analyse the experiences of the European Union (EU), Yugoslavia, Czechoslovakia and the former Soviet Union. Although political considerations are part of the story, I will argue that economic forces were critical for both monetary union and disunion, but they were not the economic factors identified in OCA theory. The crucial issues concerned who determines the conduct of monetary and fiscal policy, rather than the more technical issues emphasized in OCA theory of whether macro policy will be effective or not.

The issue of the economic arguments for currency union and the optimal size of a currency area is now being actively debated in several parts of the world.[1] Focusing on lessons from Europe's recent monetary experiences, the fourth section of this chapter addresses the prospects for monetary union among the independent currency areas in East Asia. Since September 1997, proposals have been floated to form an Asian Monetary Fund or create an Asian currency unit and some steps have been taken to increase regional monetary cooperation among the ASEAN (Association of South East Asian Nations) 10, China, Japan and South Korea, but these are far short of monetary union. Assessment of the relevance of OCA theory has implications for the prospects for monetary union in East Asia. Discussing the matter as a technical one of economic benefits versus economic costs misses the point of whether any of the independent countries, apart from the very small states, are willing to cede national autonomy over monetary and part of fiscal policy to a supranational institution.

1. THE THEORY OF OPTIMUM CURRENCY AREAS

The modern theory of optimum currency areas (OCAs) dates from the seminal papers by Mundell (1961) and McKinnon (1963). The timing is significant in that the early 1960s were the high-water mark for Keynesian macroeconomic policy. Both of these papers were concerned with analysing conditions under which macro policy could be effective in an open economy. Mundell emphasized breaks in factor mobility, while for McKinnon OCAs coincide with money illusion, which is related to degree of openness. For them, the emphasis was on establishing the geographical boundaries at which macro policy becomes effective, and hence the point at which abandoning currency independence becomes costly. Kreinin and Heller (1974) compared the costs of adjusting external imbalance via devaluation or via income policies; if the marginal propensity to import is high and demand elasticities for imports and exports are large, then income policies are likely to be the less costly approach and currency independence is less valuable. In their empirical section Kreinin and Heller (1974, p. 137) concluded that among the OECD countries Italy, Sweden and Switzerland should be keenest to abandon their national currencies.

Before the OCA literature, the emphasis had been on the benefits of a common currency, or fairly rigidly fixed exchange rates.[2] In the early twentieth century the gold standard provided, in principle at least, a common global means of exchange even if national currencies were issued in differing denominations. Attempts to restore the gold standard, or establish a gold exchange standard, in the 1930s and 1940s were based on deep beliefs in the need for stable means of exchange for both domestic and international transactions.

Through the 1950s and 1960s exchange rates among the major trading nations were generally stable.

The main economic benefit from a common currency (or fixed exchange rates) is lower transactions costs. This has long been accepted as the overwhelming argument for mini states (e.g. Luxemburg, San Marino, Monaco) not to have independent currencies, but the argument becomes less potent as the currency area becomes large enough to have well-functioning (foreign exchange – including forward) markets.[3] A second benefit is that in larger currency areas disturbances are more likely to be offsetting, so that exchange-rate changes are smaller, with less feedback on domestic prices.[4]

Following the move to generalized floating in the early 1970s, the choice of exchange-rate regime and related question of OCAs became much more policy-relevant. During the 1970s and 1980s the debate was most virulent in Western Europe, where some countries (e.g. Belgium and Luxemburg) already had monetary unions and where the prime international monetary issue was European economic and monetary union (EMU).

The main disadvantage of adopting a common currency is the loss of monetary independence. Economists (e.g. Eichengreen, 1990) compared the adjustment mechanism in US states to that in independent countries. If oil prices fall, for example, output will decline and unemployment increase in Texas or Alaska and these states would like to either (a) increase the money supply, in order to reduce interest rates and stimulate investment, or (b) devalue, in order to encourage non-oil exports and import-competing activities, but they cannot do either. The adjustment problem will be less if capital and labour are mobile, because the unemployed factors will move to other states, and in very open economies devaluation will not work because prices and wages immediately increase to wipe out any competitive advantage; hence the Mundell and McKinnon criteria for OCAs, respectively.

This approach remains essentially that of recent contributions, such as Alesina and Barro (2001, 2002). Although Alesina and Barro acknowledge a distinction between (a) 'client' countries seeking an anchor for their monetary policy and (b) a group of countries creating a new currency (for example, in Alesina, Barro and Tenreyo, 2002, p. 2), their analysis centres on the conditions under which an independent currency would permit the exchange rate to be a useful macroeconomic adjustment tool. The issue, as with Mundell, is the extent to which having this extra macroeconomic policy tool is worth giving up the transactions benefits of being in a larger currency area. Alesina and Barro argue that the trade-offs might be mediated by history and geography in the real world, so that the type of country most likely to give up its own currency is a small open economy heavily trading with a particular large country and with a history of high inflation and a business cycle highly correlated with that of the potential anchor.[5]

The outcome of the Western European policy debate was the establishment of a common currency, the euro, around the turn of the century, but the process did not parallel predictions of the OCA literature. Although the EU did become more integrated with greater factor mobility and more open national economies, the pace of monetary integration did not follow these trends, and in the endgame capital controls were abolished as a step towards monetary union rather than monetary union being driven by greater factor mobility. Meanwhile, during the 1990s Eastern Europe witnessed substantial monetary disunion as several currency areas disintegrated, despite high levels of economic integration (including factor mobility and the absence of money illusion) among their members. The next two sections analyse these divergent trends in Europe, prior to analysis in Section 4 of their relevance to monetary integration in East Asia.

2.   EUROPEAN MONETARY UNION

Starting with the European Coal and Steel Community in 1951 and more significantly the Treaty of Rome in 1957, Belgium, France, Germany, Italy, Luxemburg and the Netherlands set out on a process of Western European economic integration. During the 1960s these six countries completed a customs union and introduced common policies, including the Common Agricultural Policy (the CAP). In the Treaty of Rome there was, however, no mention of monetary integration and with more or less fixed exchange rates among the six signatories for most of the 1960s this remained a non-issue.

The first major step towards monetary integration, following large currency realignments in 1969 (the French franc was devalued by 11 per cent; and the German mark (DM) revalued by 9 per cent), was the 1970 Werner Report. The Werner Report provided a blueprint for EMU by 1980 in two steps: three years of narrower limits to exchange-rate fluctuations, followed by the operation of rigidly fixed exchange-rates and eventual withdrawal of national currencies. The programme was adopted in June 1971, which was an inopportune moment as it coincided with the collapse of the Bretton Woods system of quasi-fixed exchange rates. In the new international monetary context, the member countries' currencies operated within narrow bands *vis-à-vis* one another and within a wider band *vis-à-vis* other currencies, of which the US dollar was the most important; because the European currencies as a group slithered together within the wider band, when this arrangement was launched in April 1972 it was christened the Snake. Within weeks the large member countries started to exit the Snake; the UK left in June 1972,[6] Italy in February 1973, and France in January 1974. France returned in July 1975, but after France's second exit in March 1976 the Snake had clearly collapsed into a DM zone with Germany plus some small countries.

Why did the Snake fail? The larger countries were unwilling to accept the constraints on their monetary policy independence that were imposed by the fixed exchange rates. The defectors faced a choice between deflation and quitting the Snake, and all took the latter option. The small countries' currencies (Denmark, Belgium, Luxemburg and the Netherlands) remained pegged to the DM. This division could be explained by OCA theory in so far as the small countries were highly open with little macro-policy independence under any exchange-rate regime, but it could equally be explained by the benefits from lower transactions costs or greater policy credibility with a DM anchor.

More surprising than the Snake's demise was the brevity of the period before the European countries embarked on a second attempt at EMU. In 1977, the idea of reviving EMU was floated publicly by the President of the European Commission, Roy Jenkins, and was endorsed by the French President, Giscard d'Estaing, and the German Chancellor, Helmut Schmidt. With such support, the next step was inevitable, although ironing out technical details and bringing other large countries on board (notably Italy) took over a year.

Why did these key politicians address the post-Snake situation so quickly? An important consideration was that the Community's common policies, notably the CAP, were difficult to administer with fluctuating exchange rates (Pomfret, 1991). With fluctuating bilateral exchange rates and a free internal market, the CAP support price system meant that the price of a commodity in francs or in DM could diverge daily with politically undesirable effects on producers or consumers. To avoid such volatility in national-currency food prices, a system of artificial exchange rates (so-called 'green currencies') was implemented with monetary compensation paid to cover unanticipated costs of divergence between green and market exchange rates. In 1977 the net monetary compensation payments accounted for 11 per cent of CAP spending, and the CAP took up over three-quarters of the Community's total budget.[7] Moreover, the system's complexity offered opportunities for fraud, corruption and niggling political disagreements (about when to adjust green exchange rates), as well as involving border measures which were incompatible with the principle of a common market. Some evidence of the relationship between CAP and the EMS is that those states benefiting most from the CAP tended to support the EMS, while the UK, Portugal and Greece were more sceptical.

The European Monetary System (EMS) was established in March 1979, with eight of the then nine European Community members participating (the UK was the exception). The new features (a new unit of account called the *ecu* and formal divergence indicators, which were christened the 'rattlesnake') were cosmetic, but contrary to pessimistic predictions by many economists the EMS survived the 1980s unscathed. The EMS passed through three phases:

1. March 1979–March 1983 – many realignments,
2. March 1983–January 1987 – less frequent (and smaller) realignments,
3. January 1987–September 1992 – no realignments.

Unlike the 1970s, the 1980s were favourable to monetary integration due to policy convergence, as all members accepted low inflation as a target.[8] Even beyond this, however, there was a greater willingness to subsume macro policy to the EMS constraints. The key episodes concerned France in 1981–82, where the new Socialist government espoused expansionary macro policies but fairly quickly accepted the primacy of maintaining the EMS intact.

Why did the EMS not follow the Snake into oblivion? OCA theory would point to increased integration of factor markets and greater openness, but the 1980s were a decade of Eurosclerosis when little progress was made until the '1992' project for completing the internal market was adopted and implemented in the late 1980s and early 1990s.[9] A common explanation during the 1980s was that EMS members sought to take advantage of the German central bank's reputation by anchoring their currencies to the DM, but this too is an unconvincing explanation, because France and Italy had poorer inflation records in 1979–83 than the UK (which had a floating exchange rate) and because by the early 1990s France, not Germany, was the low-inflation country of the EMS.

A more convincing argument is that EMU was perceived by the more federalist-minded EU members as necessary to prevent exchange-rate fluctuations from undermining the policy consensus on the common market by accentuating adjustment pressures on inefficient national industries (Eichengreen, 1993, p. 1332). As mentioned above, the most salient of the sectors affected by the EU's common policies was agriculture, and the CAP had immediately become more difficult to administer with fluctuating exchange rates (Basevi and Grassi, 1993). This argument could be extended to the entire budget process; if the EU were to move to a more federal entity with a larger and more politically contentious budget, then it would be awkward to set contributions and benefits in a common currency when national currencies' relative values were changing daily by possibly substantial amounts. When the currency area literature refers to the benefits of reduced transactions costs with a common currency, this is typically interpreted as the costs facing private-sector traders, but it also applies to the transactions costs within the public sector of a political entity covering multiple currency areas.

The success of the EMS encouraged European leaders to consider how to move from the EMS fixed exchange rates to full monetary union. The 1988/9 Delors Committee set out a timetable for EMU, by which:

- all EU members would join the EMS exchange rate mechanism (Spain entered the EMS exchange-rate mechanism in June 1989 and the UK in October 1990);
- restrictions on movement of capital and on financial transactions within the EU would be abolished in 1990, with a two-year extension for poorer countries;
- a European Monetary Institute, forerunner of a European Central Bank, would be created in 1994 to coordinate monetary policy. National central banks would continue to exist but be independent of their governments and not grant credit to public corporations. Governments were to avoid excessive budget deficits;
- full monetary union with a common currency.

The December 1991 Maastricht conference set targets for policy convergence, which were formalized in a treaty signed in February 1992. The important point about giving the Maastricht agreement treaty force was that it indicated the political will in the majority of EU members to move to EMU.[10]

The biggest challenge to the EMS exchange rate mechanism arose after German economic and monetary union occurred in 1990.[11] German interest rates rose as the government borrowed to finance reunification, and pressure to follow the German interest rate increases led to a major crisis in other EMS members in September 1992. The UK and Italy left the exchange-rate mechanism, although Italy returned. Spain and Portugal introduced capital controls, but they were temporary; their currencies were devalued, and then the controls were removed. Sweden left the exchange-rate system after raising interest rates to 500 per cent. The lesson drawn from this episode was that fixed but adjustable exchange rates are unsustainable without capital controls. Given the agreement to abolish capital controls within the EU as part of the 1992 programme, only two alternatives remained: the UK, Sweden and Denmark have opted for floating exchange rates, and the other EU members have given up monetary policy. Establishment of the European Monetary Institute on schedule in 1994 effectively terminated independent monetary policy for the participating countries. A currency crisis in 1995, following depreciation of the US dollar which increased demand for DM, was far less significant than that of 1992.

The final stage of EMU began in January 1999 with the introduction of the euro for transactions. The European Central Bank (successor to the European Monetary Institute) in Frankfurt now conducts monetary policy for the euro region. In January 2002 the new banknotes were introduced and by July the old currencies ceased to be legal tender in the 12 participating countries. Of the OECD countries covered by the Kreinin and Heller analysis, Italy is indeed in the monetary union, but the two other 'most likely members' are not, because Switzerland is outside the EU and Sweden is sceptical about union. Ten of Kreinin and Heller's less likely members are inside the eurozone, but the UK and Denmark are not; again the division between insiders and outsiders has nothing to do with OCA-style criteria and everything to do with attitudes towards European political union.

3. MONETARY FRAGMENTATION IN EASTERN EUROPE AND THE COMMONWEALTH OF INDEPENDENT STATES

While Western Europe was moving towards EMU, in the rest of Europe the trend during the 1990s was towards an increase in currency areas. The dissolution of Yugoslavia in 1991 was accompanied by the appearance of new national currencies in the five successor states. The velvet divorce in Czechoslovakia was followed by the emergence of separate Czech and Slovak currencies. After the dissolution of the Soviet Union in December 1991, the majority of the successor states attempted to retain a common currency, but by November 1993 the ruble had been replaced by 15 national currencies.

In some of these cases, the issue of a national currency had a symbolic element driven by national pride, but in practically all cases there were pressing economic considerations. A key problem for currency unions embracing several countries is who controls monetary policy? The issuer of money gains the seigniorage, but the costs in terms of higher inflation are spread across the currency union.

A single issuer has an incentive to print money to solve its financial problems. This happened after the break-up of the Austro-Hungarian Empire in 1919 tempted Austria to solve its financial problems by printing money; Czechoslovakia and Hungary left the currency union. The dissolution of Yugoslavia after 1991 had the same result, as the government in Belgrade pursued an inflationary monetary policy. Slovenia and Croatia enjoyed no benefit from the expenditure (and in the latter case was being attacked by military forces funded out of the inflationary finance) and immediately delinked themselves from the Yugoslav dinar. Even with a peaceful and reasonably amicable political separation, disagreement over monetary policy may make joint decision-making infeasible. One reason for the Czech and Slovak Republics to issue separate national currencies in 1993 was that they wanted to pursue differing monetary policies, with the former placing greater emphasis on price stability and the latter wishing to use deficit financing to alleviate the costs of transition from central planning.

Having several centres of money creation is unsustainable because of the free-rider problem. Casella and Feinstein (1989) had made this point in the

EMU context, but it was most clearly illustrated by the experience of the Soviet successor states.[12] Even after the dissolution of the USSR in December 1991, the ruble continued to be used as a common currency by the successor states. In 1992 the Baltic countries and Ukraine issued national currencies, because they wanted to pursue differing monetary policies to Russia.[13] The other 11 successor states exerted no real pressure for change, and indeed often stressed the benefits of retaining the common currency, fearing that the increased transactions costs associated with proliferating currencies would exacerbate the already substantial decline in output. Nevertheless, by the end of 1993 the currency union had disintegrated, mainly because the free-rider problem was fuelling inflation (Pomfret, 1996, pp. 118–29).

By traditional arguments the Soviet Union was an OCA, and this remained true of the successor states as a group. Initially, the International Monetary Fund supported retention of the ruble zone and, on occasion, even cited OCA theory as justification.[14] By late 1992 and early 1993, however, it was apparent that the institutional situation was not conducive to the ruble zone's survival. Even though Russia had sole control over the supply of banknotes, it was unable to control credit creation. Every member of the zone could create ruble credits and use them for its national expenditure, while the costs of credit expansion (in terms of increased inflation) were spread across all members of the ruble zone. When, in the second half of 1993, Russia took firmer measures to gain full control over monetary policy, this was unacceptable to the other ruble zone members. In November 1993 the remaining members introduced national currencies.[15]

The key issue in the collapse of the ruble zone was control over monetary policy. The ruble zone might have been an OCA, as defined by factor mobility or openness, and the replacement of the ruble by national currencies imposed substantial increases in transactions costs on the small open economies in the zone. Nevertheless, abandoning the common currency was ultimately in everybody's interest, given that the existing monetary arrangements were producing hyperinflation and that no alternative monetary institutions were acceptable to all members.

4. MONETARY INTEGRATION IN EAST ASIA

The emergence of Asian regionalism can be dated from the aftermath of the 1997 Asian crisis and started in the area of monetary cooperation, involving the so-called ASEAN+3 group of the ten ASEAN countries plus China, Japan and South Korea. That was partly in reaction to dissatisfaction with the IMF's role in the international monetary system, but the collapse of the 1999 WTO (World Trade Organization) meetings in Seattle and the diminishing significance of

APEC (including the half-hearted attempt by the USA to kick-start further trade liberalization at the 1999 APEC summit through its P5 initiative with Australia, Chile, New Zealand and Singapore) led to new approaches to trade liberalization in the Asia-Pacific region.[16] Bilateral negotiations were begun in 1999/2000 by Japan with Singapore, South Korea, Canada and Mexico, by South Korea with New Zealand and Chile as well as with Japan, and by Singapore with New Zealand (concluded in 2000), Australia, Canada and other countries.[17]

Although the heads of some Asian central banks had met on a fairly structured basis before 1997, the Asian crisis provided the stimulus for new proposals.[18] In particular, the International Monetary Fund's handling of the Asian crisis came under criticism in the region for the amount and timing of IMF assistance and for inappropriate conditionality. The lead in proposing new institutional responses was taken by Japan, which floated the idea of an Asian Monetary Fund (AMF) at the Asia–Europe Meeting (ASEM) Finance Ministers' meeting in Bangkok in September 1997. Subsequently, Hong Kong and the Philippines have gone further and proposed creating an Asian currency unit (Lloyd and Lee, 2001, p. 215).[19]

The Japanese arguments in support of the AMF have been fourfold. First, the IMF financial support for the crisis-hit countries was too little and too late. For Thailand and Indonesia in August and November 1997, the IMF loans were limited to around 500 per cent of the countries' IMF quotas. This was viewed as inadequate, and packages had to be put together with other contributors, in which the IMF's contribution was about a quarter (Table 4.1). Although this limit was relaxed in the December 1997 loan to South Korea and the second loan to Indonesia, in August 1998, came from the Extended Fund Facility which was not subject to quota-linked maxima, these last two IMF loans also fell far short of the total loan package, which may in turn have been inadequate. Of course, the validity of the argument that the IMF supplied too

Table 4.1   Financial support to Thailand, Indonesia and South Korea following the 1997 crisis (billion US dollars)

		IMF	World Bank + ADB	Bilateral support	Total
Thailand	20 Aug. 1997	4.0	2.7	10.5	17.1
Indonesia	5 Nov. 1997	10.1	8.0	18.0	36.1
Indonesia	29 July 1998	11.2	10.0	21.1	42.3
South Korea	4 Dec. 1997	21.1	14.2	23.1	58.4

Source: Ogawa (2001, p. 233).

little from its own resources depends upon some assessment of what was necessary. Malaysia weathered the crisis without any IMF assistance at all.

Second, East Asian countries are underrepresented in the IMF. Japan, China, South Korea and the five original ASEAN members accounted for 20.9 per cent of world GDP in 1996, but their IMF quotas only gave them 11.6 per cent of the votes in the IMF and, even when these quotas were revised in February 1999, the share of the eight Asian countries only went up to 12.7 per cent (Ogawa, 2001, p. 240). This apparent inequity is, however, solely a Japanese issue. The other seven countries listed by Ogawa had a combined GDP share of 6.3 per cent and a post-1999 quota share of 6.2 per cent.[20]

Third, an AMF could help prevent regional contagion in future crises. This argument is related to criticisms of the tardiness of the IMF's responses in 1997. According to Ogawa (2001, p. 235):

> A 'currency meltdown' occurred on July 24 when all of the countries faced severe speculative attacks. Thus, the Thai baht crisis had the contagion effects on the other ASEAN countries before the IMF decided its financial support to Thailand.

The weight to be placed on this argument depends on the extent to which one accepts the contagion hypothesis, as well as on whether one believes that faster or bigger or better directed assistance could have forestalled contagion.

Fourth, an AMF could better conduct regional surveillance and muster peer pressure to forestall crises than could an institution based in Washington, DC. This argument is closely connected to deeper resentment about the insensitivity of the IMF to local conditions during the 1997 crisis, especially in its treatment of Indonesia, where the IMF's managing director was seen as publicly imposing conditions on Indonesia's president and these included measures, such as reduced food and energy subsidies, which directly hurt the poor and contributed to social upheaval. Whether the conditions were inappropriate depends upon the causes of the crisis, which clearly included the president's recent economic management.

The four arguments have some merit and struck chords with policy-makers outside Japan, but they are not conclusive arguments for a new institution. Some of the suggestions could be handled within existing institutions. For example, in 1998 the Southeast Asian countries proposed an ASEAN Surveillance Process and requested ADB technical support, and the ADB has subsequently taken on a regional surveillance role through its Asia Recovery Information Center.[21] The fundamental reason for the AMF's lack of progress has been the opposition from other IMF members, notably the USA, to duplication of roles. Support within the region has also been lukewarm, although the episode has generated new initiatives and thinking about Asian monetary arrangements.[22]

A weaker version of the AMF proposal emerged at a meeting of Asia-Pacific finance ministers and central bankers in Manila in November 1997.[23] The Manila Framework called for a regional surveillance mechanism, enhanced economic and technical cooperation in strengthening domestic financial systems and their regulation, and measures to strengthen the IMF's response to financial crises. Although the topics are reminiscent of the AMF proposals, the tone is in terms of supplementing the central role of the IMF.

A more important forum for regional financing arrangements emerged out of meetings begun in March 1999 among the ASEAN +3 countries (the three being China, Japan and South Korea).[24] The most significant of these meetings was that of the 13 countries' finance ministers in Chiang Mai in May 2000, when a regional financing arrangement was established with US$1 billion in commitments. The Chiang Mai Initiative (CMI), which became effective in November 2000, allows countries to swap their local currencies for major international currencies for up to six months and for up to twice their committed amount.[25] The CMI is framed in terms of supplementing the IMF's role in so far as countries seeking liquidity support must also look for IMF assistance although bilateral swaps under the CMI are not conditional on IMF negotiations being completed. By March 2002 six bilateral swaps, worth $14 billion, had been concluded under the CMI (Manupipatpong, 2002, p. 118). The CMI has the potential to evolve into the role foreseen for the AMF as lender of last resort in crises, and, with combined forex reserves of around $800 billion, the ASEAN +3 countries have resources which dwarf the assistance given in 1997–98 (Table 4.1).[26]

Monetary coordination is less advanced. A case is often made for exchange-rate fixity to forestall competitive devaluations by countries competing with one another across a range of traded goods and also to encourage direct foreign investment. The simplest solution would be region-wide pegs to the dollar, or even dollarization; McKinnon and Schnabl (2002), for example, conclude that East Asia is a 'natural dollar zone'. In the years up to 1997 such an arrangement was more or less maintained among the ASEAN countries, China, Hong Kong, South Korea and Taiwan by their *de facto* pegs to the US dollar, but this led to, disastrous in some cases, swings against the yen. Including the yen in an Asia-wide dollar bloc, as with a yen bloc, is a political non-starter.[27]

Proponents of a common currency see that as the best solution to the competitive devaluation threat. In addition, a larger currency area could reduce the required level of forex reserves, because offsetting shocks would reduce the need for a lender of last resort (Stockman, 2001). A single currency is also advocated as allowing the East Asian countries to speak with a single voice in international financial fora.[28] The advocates of a common currency have, however, not addressed the institutional question of how the common exchange rate is determined (and hence how monetary policy is conducted for the entire currency area), who would determine when the lender of last resort acts, and who would speak with the single voice.

5.   CONCLUSIONS

What can we learn from the recent history of monetary union and disunion in Europe that might be relevant to the embryonic East Asian financial integration? One negative lesson is that the optimum currency area literature provides little practical guide. The OCA literature assumes a background of optimum monetary policy.[29] The Eastern European and former Soviet Union experience indicated that a currency union without appropriate monetary policy instruments is a far worse evil than the higher transactions costs from independent currencies, even when the independent currency covers a small national economy. Western European monetary union also stalled on the monetary policy hurdle in the 1970s and only overcame the hurdle when in the 1990s most, but not all, of the EU members accepted the loss of sovereignty inherent in a common central bank.

Monetary union also tends to embed some degree of fiscal policy cooperation. Kenen (1969) argued that in federal states such as the USA or Canada regional idiosyncratic shocks generate automatic and prompt redistribution via fiscal rules, and other federal systems all embody some degree of fiscal insurance. In the EU the problems of operating common fiscal policies when members' contributions and benefits fluctuated with volatile bilateral exchange rate changes were a critical reason for maintaining the momentum for monetary union in 1977–78 and in 1992, when member states appeared to be abandoning the project due to the costs of lost monetary independence.

The close nexus between currency union and both monetary policy and fiscal policy highlights the distance that East Asia has to go before an Asian currency union is seriously on the political agenda. Monetary policy has to be ceded to a single central bank (or equivalently to a rigid rule such as the principle which the gold standard embodied). Moreover, some degree of fiscal insurance may be necessary to convince all countries of the benefits. Yet, in East Asia the political will to give up national autonomy over macro policies is far away.[30]

On the other hand, many scoffed at the prospects for EMU in the 1970s (and some still failed to recognize its likelihood right up until the introduction of the euro). There are obviously pressing arguments for currency union. In the EU, these are associated with the project for economic and political integration. As many have started to observe in recent years, the relationship between monetary integration and economic integration (and political integration) is two-way and mutually reinforcing. There remains, moreover, a lingering feeling that economic forces for currency union may be gathering pace in an era of increasing globalization. What are those forces?

What seem to be absent from the existing literature are convincing empirical estimates of the benefits of currency union in reducing transactions costs. The Commission of the European Communities (1990), in measuring the 'costs of non-Europe', estimated large benefits from completing the internal market and from monetary union, but the exercise was clearly biased in the direction of finding such benefits in order to justify the policies. Krugman (1993) drew attention to the absence of serious consideration of the nature or magnitude of transactions costs in debates over the international financial system. Frankel and Rose (1998) further analysed the two-way causality between economic integration and monetary union, and one aspect of that paper was addressed in greater depth by Rose (2000), who found that the impact of monetary union on trade was much larger than the impact of fixed exchange rates.[31] Although this indicates movement towards investigating the nature and extent of the reduction in transaction costs, the literature is still at an early stage. Some authors have suggested that globalization and factors such as the growth of e-commerce have reduced the usefulness of minor currencies to their holders (von Furstenberg, 2002), but there has been no attempt to determine whether the transactions costs of small currency areas have been rising.

To conclude, the main determinant of currency area size is transactions costs. Micro states often do not have independent currencies, whether they use a foreign currency (as in San Marino or East Timor) or have an asymmetric union (as in Belgium–Luxembourg or Brunei–Singapore). Large states have a single currency, even though the regions of the USA or Canada or China are diverse. For the micro states, the transactions costs for private-sector agents would be too high with a separate currency. For the large states the transactions costs for the public sector's economic decision-making would be too great with multiple independent currencies. For East Asia's medium-sized and large states, the reduction in private-sector transactions costs are insufficient to compensate for renouncing macroeconomic policy independence, while the prospects for federalism or other political union are too distant to make the public-sector transactions costs relevant.

NOTES

1. In the Americas, since the December 2001 collapse of Argentina's currency board, the debate has centred on the costs and benefits of dollarization as practised by Panama and recently introduced by Ecuador. Full currency union has been the subject of academic discussion in Canada, but a Canada–US currency union is a non-starter given Canadian desire to maintain political independence. In Australasia there have been some discussions

of an Australia–New Zealand currency union, but again they seem distant from actual policy-making as long as the two countries remain independent.

2. In much of the international economics literature a single currency is viewed as the extreme case of fixed exchange rates – the only differences are transactions costs or petty inconveniences of acceptability and seigniorage; see Corden (2002) for a careful analysis which specifically sets the issues in the OCA context in his ninth chapter. Rose (2000, p. 31), however, argues that empirically the impact of a common currency is an order of magnitude larger than the effect of reducing moderate exchange rate volatility to zero but retaining separate currencies.

3. Rose (2000, pp. 11n. and 41) lists 82 countries and territories which used another country's currency or were in a currency union between 1870 and 1990. They are all small, with the most populous being the African CFA countries and Panama and Liberia.

4. The greater price stability is usually ascribed to random shocks being offsetting. Other mechanisms include reduction in weights of outliers in the CPI and reduction in the ratio of trade (or rather transactions denominated in, potentially volatile, foreign currencies) to GDP.

5. This list is similar to the criteria identified in the survey of the original OCA literature by Tower and Willett (1976). With several criteria it is difficult to find a unique ranking of suitability for currency union; e.g. a small open economy has the most to gain from reduced transactions costs, but may also be most exposed to external shocks and hence has the most to lose from giving up the exchange rate as a macro-policy instrument. Kreinin and Heller's solution was to synthesize the various criteria into the single question of whether a country could better deal with external imbalance through devaluation or through adjustment of domestic demand (i.e. by expenditure switching or by expenditure reduction).

6. Denmark and Ireland also exited with the UK, but Denmark rejoined in October 1972. Ireland broke its *de facto* union with sterling when the Irish punt joined the EMS in 1979, and the British pound did not.

7. Although the system was supposed to be symmetrical, countries paying into the common budget brought their green exchange rates into line with market exchange rates more quickly than countries receiving payments from the common budget, so that the net effect on the Community's budget was negative.

8. Initial conditions in 1978–79 could, however, have provided a plausible explanation of failure if the EMS had collapsed quickly; the 1979–80 oil shocks had differential impact on EMS participants, as did the monetary policy change in the UK following Mrs Thatcher's 1979 election victory.

9. In 1982, on the twenty-fifth anniversary of the Rome Treaty, the (London) *Economist* newspaper had a cover picture of a tombstone dedicated to the death of the European Community. Although the *Economist* was a long-time Eurosceptic, this dismal view was widely held at a time when the Community appeared to be having trouble both in absorbing new members and in finding new initiatives. Even under these adverse conditions, the EMS had by 1982 survived three years, already outstripping the Snake's effective longevity.

10. Gros and Thygesen (1990) set out the case for the institutional approach, based on establishing a European Central Bank, as a necessary and feasible method of attaining EMU. Many academic economists underestimated the importance of political will in making EMU happen. A widely read article by de Grauwe (1994) contained a section entitled 'The Maastricht road does not lead to EMU' and, given that the strategy devised in the Maastricht Treaty had proven impracticable, he proposed an alternative road. Similar dismissal of the Maastricht approach was voiced by many other European economists (cited by de Grauwe) and prominent US macroeconomists (e.g. Feldstein, 1992).

11. Although not well integrated into the currency area literature, German economic and monetary union clarified some issues. Technically, monetary union was not difficult. There were associated costs of increased unemployment in East Germany and higher interest rates in West Germany, but the extent to which these costs were due to monetary union and the extent to which they were due to other policies, especially the imposition of uniform wages, is debatable.

12. Flandreau (1993) has documented the same problem as the major cause of failure of the Latin currency union in the nineteenth century.

13. The Baltic countries were the most committed to re-establishing market economies and, more than other parts of the Soviet Union, recognized aggregate price stability as a precondition for relative prices to play their signalling role. The Ukrainian leadership, on the other hand, was the most committed to using monetary expansion to alleviate the costs borne by those hurt by the end of central planning, with little regard for any inflationary consequences. These differing views reinforced the fact that these four republics had been the most independent-minded in the final year of the Soviet Union, so that there was also a political desire for monetary independence as a symbol of nationhood. In a little-noticed paper, Goldberg, Ickes and Ryterman (1994) characterized the situation in public finance terms: 'participation in a currency union may facilitate the continuance of a pattern of fiscal transfers and political influence within a region that otherwise would be sharply altered.' For them, the argument for leaving the ruble zone was to free a country from the inherited patterns of fiscal transfers so that they could conduct new policies or, in other words, reduce the transactions costs of policy reform.

14. The IMF was particularly influential in a situation where policy-makers were unfamiliar with macroeconomics, which had been irrelevant in the centrally planned economies. The role of the IMF is debated in Pomfret (2002) and other papers in that special issue of *Comparative Economic Studies*.

15. The official timing of the introduction of national currencies was complicated by the fact that some countries issued coupons and other quasi-currencies before formally adopting a national currency. War-torn Tajikistan continued to use the Soviet ruble until it introduced its own currency in 1995, but after November 1993 the Soviet ruble was not accepted in any other country.

16. With respect to regional trading arrangements, a third wave of regionalism was gathering force in the closing years of the twentieth century. This was led by Asian countries, which had thus far been the strongest bulwarks of non-discrimination – Japan and South Korea within the WTO and China and Taiwan outside the WTO (Pomfret, 2001, pp. v–vii). Lloyd and Lee (2001) analyse the forces behind the new regionalism in Asia.

17. On the new bilateral agreements see Rajan, Sen and Siregar (2001) and Scollay and Gilbert (2003).

18. Fukasaku and Martineau (1996) provide a pre-1997 perspective on monetary cooperation and integration in East Asia.

19. More limited currency union has also been considered, especially within Southeast Asia, e.g. at Hanoi in 1998 ASEAN heads of state directed the secretariat to study the feasibility of an ASEAN currency (Bayoumi and Mauro, 1999; Madhur, 2002).

20. Indonesia, Malaysia, the Philippines and Singapore all have IMF voting weights greater than their share of world GDP, as calculated by Ogawa. The complaints about Japanese underrepresentation go back beyond 1997, and the suspicion is that the unpopularity of the IMF's response to the 1997 crisis provided an opportunity for Japan to cloak its dissatisfaction under a broader Asian mantle.

21. The IMF's surveillance mechanism is bilateral, so the regional nature of the ASEAN proposal was innovative. The ASEAN Surveillance Process became operational in March 1999 with a coordinating unit at the ASEAN Secretariat in Jakarta and national units in the ten member countries (Manupipatpong, 2002, pp. 112–15). At a meeting in Sydney in March 1999 the Australian government proposed that a regional surveillance information facility be based at the ADB in Manila, and provided financial assistance through AusAID. Staff of the ADB's Regional Economic Monitoring Unit now prepare the *Asia Recovery Report* twice a year and maintain a website at http://www.adb.org/REMU/aric.asp.

22. The following paragraphs draw on Manupipatpong (2002) and Murase (2002) for information about the various developments and on Bird and Rajan (2002) for policy options raised in the process.

23. The 14 economies represented in Manila were the first six ASEAN members, China, Hong Kong, Japan, South Korea, Australia, New Zealand, Canada and the USA.

24. China had supported the IMF's approach to the 1997 crisis and its 'mainstay' role was acknowledged at the December 1998 APEC summit in Kuala Lumpur. China, however, felt that it received little practical reward and relations with the USA soured in the first half of

1999 over the US intervention in Kosovo and bombing of the Chinese embassy in Belgrade. Bowles (2002) contrasts the coolness of Jiang Zemin's visit to Japan in December 1998 with the conciliatory nature of Zhu Rongji's visit in October 2000.

25. The CMI superseded the ASEAN swap arrangement, which had been in place since 1977 but at its maximum the facility only amounted to $200 million.

26. Henning (2002) provides fuller documentation of East Asian monetary cooperation and the CMI.

27. Dollarization is also politically implausible apart from extreme cases. The only example in the region is East Timor, whose new independent government decided not to introduce a national currency, but the obvious foreign currencies (of Indonesia or of Australia) were politically unacceptable.

28. This point, which addresses the Japanese concern about its low voting weight in the IMF, has also been raised by Korean economists (Oh and Harvie, 2001, p. 261).

29. With this assumption the OCA literature was hijacked by monetary theorists, and discussion (e.g. of EMU) tended to revolve around monetary policy conflicts among potential members of a currency union. The argument of this chapter is that monetary policy is not why currency union (as opposed to currency boards or other hard pegs) occurs, although monetary policy disputes may trigger currency disunion (as they did in the ruble zone). The eurozone was not constructed around an anchor currency and the EU's non-euro countries show no common pattern of being, say, the least open or having less synchronized cycles with Euroland; indeed, Denmark or Sweden would, on OCA-theoretical grounds, appear to be better candidates for currency union with the six original EU members than would the Iberian countries or Greece.

30. Smaller currency unions, such as a Thai–Lao baht zone or a Greater Chinese monetary union (combining the RMB, Taiwan and Hong Kong dollars), may be politically more viable even though monetary policy authority is derogated to Bangkok or Beijing. This already happens in the Singapore–Brunei monetary union (Ngiam and Yuen, 2001), which has lasted since 1967 in a similar fashion to the Belgium–Luxemburg economic union (BLEU) in Europe; as the BLEU illustrated, this is not necessarily a stumbling block to wider monetary integration. The ASEAN members' 2002 proposal to study an ASEAN Economic Community may be a step towards political supranationalism, but still a very cautious one.

31. This finding has already been mentioned (note 3 above). Rose's results have been criticized for being based on a small and unrepresentative sample; his panel data contain 33 903 bilateral trade observations, of which only 320 are classified as within currency union trade, and most of these involved a tiny economy and a much larger neighbour. Later studies have generally found smaller, but still statistically significant, impacts of currency union on trade (see, for example, the debate between Nitsch, 2002 and Rose, 2002). Alesina, Barro and Tenreyro (2002, Table 8) summarize the empirical studies.

REFERENCES

Alesina, Alberto, and Robert J. Barro (2001), 'Dollarization,' *American Economic Review 91(2)*, May, 381–5.

Alesina, Alberto, and Robert J. Barro (2002), 'Currency Unions,' *Quarterly Journal of Economics*, May, 409–36.

Alesina, Alberto, Robert J. Barro and Silvana Tenreyro (2002), 'Optimal Currency Areas,' *Harvard Institute of Economic Research Discussion Paper No. 1958*, June.

Basevi, Giorgio, and Silvia Grassi (1993), 'The Crisis of the European Monetary System and its Consequences for Agricultural Trade.' *Review of Economic Conditions in Italy*, June, 81–104.

Bayoumi, Tamim, and Paolo Mauro (1999), 'The Suitability of ASEAN for A Regional Currency Arrangement,' *IMF Working Paper 99/162*, Washington DC, December.

Bird Graham, and Ramkishen Rajan (2002), 'The Evolving Asian Financial Architecture,' *Essays in International Economics No.226* (International Economics Section, Princeton University NJ), February.

Casella, Alessandra, and Jonathan Feinstein (1989), 'Management of a Common Currency' in Marcello de Cecco and Alberto Giovannini (eds.) *A European Central Bank? Perspectives on Monetary Unification after Ten Years of the EMS.* (Cambridge UK, Cambridge University Press) 131–56.

Commission of the European Communities (1990): 'One Market, One Money,' *European Economy 44*, October.

Corden, W. Max (2002), *Too Sensational: On the choice of exchange rate regimes,* (Cambridge MA, MIT Press).

De Grauwe, Paul (1994), 'Towards European Monetary Union without the EMS,' *Economic Policy 18*, 149–85.

Eichengreen, Barry (1990), 'One Money for Europe? Lessons from the US Currency and Customs Union,' *Economic Policy 10*, April, 117–87.

Eichengreen, Barry (1993), 'European Monetary Unification,' *Journal of Economic Literature 31(3)*, September, 1321–57.

Feldstein, Martin (1992), 'Europe's Monetary Union: The Case against EMU,' *The Economist* (London), 13th June.

Flandreau, Marc (1993), 'On the Inflationary Bias of Common Currencies: The Latin Union Puzzle,' *European Economic Review 37(2–3)*, April, 501–06.

Frankel, Jeffrey, and Andrew Rose (1998), 'The Endogeneity of the Optimum Currency Area Criteria,' *Economic Journal 108*, July, 1009–25.

Fukasaku, Ki, and David Martineau (1996), 'Monetary Co-operation and Integration in East Asia', paper presented at the Japan-Europe Symposium, OECD Development Centre, Paris, 7–8 October.

Goldberg, Linda, Barry Ickes and Randi Ryterman (1994), 'Departures from the Ruble Zone: The Implications of Adopting Independent Currencies,' *World Economy 17(3)*, May, 293–322.

Gros, Daniel, and Niels Thygesen (1990), 'The Institutional Approach to Monetary Union in Europe' *Economic Journal 100*, September, 925–35.

Henning, C. Randall (2002), 'East Asian Financial Cooperation,' *IIE Policy Analyses in International Economics 68*, Institute for International Economics, Washington DC, October.

Kenen, Peter (1969), 'The Theory of Optimum Currency Areas: An Eclectic View' in Robert Mundell and Alexander Swoboda, (eds.), *Monetary Problems of the International Economy.* (Chicago, University of Chicago Press) 41–60.

Kreinin, Mordechai, and H. Robert Heller (1974), 'Adjustment Costs, Optimal Currency Areas, and International Reserves', in Willy Sellekaerts (ed.), *International Trade and Finance: Essays in Honour of Jan Tinbergen.* Macmillan: London, 127–40.

Krugman, Paul (1993), 'What Do We need to Know about the International Monetary System?' *Essays in International Economics No.190* (International Economics Section, Princeton University NJ), July.

Lloyd, Peter, and Hyun-Hoon Lee (2001), 'Subregionalism in East Asia and its Relationship with APEC,' *The Journal of the Korean Economy 2(2)*, Fall, 211–27.

McKinnon, Ronald (1963), 'Optimum Currency Areas,' *American Economic Review 53*, 717–25.

McKinnon, Ronald, and Gunther Schnabl (2002), Synchronized Business Cycles in East Asia: Fluctuations in the Yen/Dollar Exchange Rate and China's Stabilizing

Role, unpublished ms available at http://www.stanford.edu/~mckinnon/ or at http://uni-tuebingen.de/uni/wwa/homegs.htm

Madhur, Srinivasa (2001), 'Costs and Benefits of a Common Currency for ASEAN,' *ERD Working Paper No.12*, Asian Development Bank, Manila, May.

Manupipatpong, Worapot (2002), 'The ASEAN Surveillance Process and the East Asian Monetary Fund,' *ASEAN Economic Bulletin 19(1)*, April, 111–22.

Mundell, Robert (1961), 'Theory of Optimum Currency Areas,' *American Economic Review 51*, 657–65.

Murase, Tetsujui (2002), *A Zone of Asian Monetary Stability* (Asia Pacific Press, Canberra).

Ngiam, Kee Jin, and Hazel Yuen (2001), 'Monetary Cooperation in East Asia: A Way Forward', *Singapore Economic Review 46(2)*, 211–46.

Nitsch, Volker (2002), 'Honey, I Shrunk the Currency Union Effect on Trade' *World Economy 25(4)*, April, 457–74.

Ogawa, Eiji (2001), 'A Regional Monetary Fund and the IMF', *The Journal of the Korean Economy 2(2)*, Fall, 229–48.

Oh, Junggun, and Charles Harvie (2001), 'Exchange Rate Coordination in East Asia', *The Journal of the Korean Economy 2(2)*, Fall, 249–96.

Pomfret, Richard (1991), 'The Secret of the EMS's Longevity', *Journal of Common Market Studies 29*, December, 623–33.

Pomfret, Richard (1996), *Asian Economies in Transition: Reforming Centrally Planned Economies* (Edward Elgar, Cheltenham UK).

Pomfret, Richard (2001), *The Economics of Regional Trading Arrangements* (Clarendon Press, Oxford, 1997; paperback edition with new Preface, Oxford University Press, Oxford, 2001).

Pomfret, Richard (2002), 'The IMF and the Ruble Zone', *Comparative Economic Studies 44*, Winter, 37–48.

Rajan, Ramkishen, Rahul Sen and Reza Yamore Siregar (2001), *Singapore and Free Trade Agreements: Economic Relations with Japan and the United State.* (Singapore, ISEAS Publications).

Rose, Andrew (2000), 'One Money, One Market: The Effect of Common Currencies on Trade', *Economic Policy 30*, April, 9–45.

Rose, Andrew (2002), 'Honey, the Currency Union Effect on Trade Hasn't Blown Up', *World Economy 25(4)*, April, 475–79.

Scollay, Robert, and John Gilbert (2003), Assessing New Preferential Trading Developments in the Asia-Pacific Region, paper presented at the conference on 'Empirical Methods in International Trade', held in honor of Max Kreinin at the Johns Hopkins University School of Advanced International Studies in Washington DC on 5–6 January.

Stockman, Alan (2001), Optimal Central Bank Areas, Financial Intermediation, and Mexican Dollarization, *Journal of Money, Credit and Banking 33(2)*, 648–66.

Tower, Edward, and Thomas Willett (1976), The Theory of Optimum Currency Areas and Exchange-Rate Flexibility, *Princeton Special Papers in International Economics, No.11* (International Finance Section, Princeton University), May.

von Furstenbeg, George (2002), 'One Region, One Money: The Potential Contribution of Currency Consolidation to Financial Stability in the Developing World' in Michele Fratianni, Paolo Savona and John Kirton, (eds.), *Governing Global Finance: New Challenges, G7 and IMF Contributions*, (Ashgate, Aldershot UK).

5. Labor market structure and its influence on trade-related outcomes: some initial findings

Carl Davidson and Steven J. Matusz

1. INTRODUCTION

The fact that international trade affects labor market outcomes is never debated. It is generally accepted that the pattern of trade influences the composition of employment within a country as well as its wage structure. However, the exact nature of the link between trade and labor market outcomes is often the center of debates. Does trade create or destroy jobs? Does it affect overall employment? Have changes in trade and/or trade policies had a significant impact on the distribution of income? If so, what is the nature of the impact? While tremendous resources have been devoted to these questions, none of them have been truly resolved. There is significant disagreement in the public about trade's impact on job opportunities and in academic circles there are several recognized theories about the link between trade and wages. Thus the debates continue.

In contrast, there has been very little attention paid to the manner in which the structure of the labor market itself affects trade-related outcomes. This is somewhat surprising given that labor market institutions vary greatly across countries. Jobs last longer in Europe and Japan than they last in the United States (Freeman, 1994) and the average duration of unemployment is lower in the US than it is in most European countries. The implication is that labor markets in the US are characterized by greater turnover than their European counterparts (see, for example, Nickell, 1997; Haynes, Upward and Wright, 2000; or Greenaway, Upward and Wright, 2001). In addition, unions are much more influential in Europe than they are in the US and many European firms face greater restrictions on their hiring and firing practices than do US firms. As a result, labor markets in the United States are viewed as 'more flexible' than the labor markets in most European countries. Macroeconomists and labor economists have emphasized that this fundamental difference in labor market structure has important implications for a wide variety of issues including macroeconomic performance, trends in income inequality, problems associated with long-term unemployment and the willingness of firms to pay for worker training. In international economics, these differences have received very little attention.[1] Part of the reason for this may be the field's continued reliance on full employment models – in the absence of equilibrium unemployment, the structure of the labor market becomes much less important.

There is also considerable evidence that internal labor markets vary greatly across industries within countries, especially when they are characterized by their turnover rates. For the United States, Davis, Haltiwanger and Schuh (1996) were among the first to document the surprisingly high amount of job turnover in manufacturing. By examining establishment-level data they found that even during periods of relative stability in terms of overall industry-wide employment, there is a great deal of job creation and job destruction taking place at the plant level. Furthermore, these rates vary dramatically across industries and across time. Davis, Haltiwanger and Schuh's work created a whole new area of research, with papers emerging about job creation and destruction rates in labor markets in the United Kingdom, France, Ireland, Italy, Japan, Canada, Denmark, Australia, Taiwan, Russia, China, Estonia, Bulgaria, Hungary, Romania and the Netherlands. In each case, the findings were similar – there is a great deal of variability in turnover across sectors within any given economy.

One would expect trade economists to sit up and take notice of these findings. After all, international trade is all about exploiting differences across countries and industries. The Heckscher–Ohlin–Samuelson (HOS) model explains trade as the result of differences in factor endowments across countries coupled with differences in technologies across sectors. The Ricardian model explains trade as a result of differences in technologies across countries and industries. It is hard to believe that such dramatic differences in labor market structure have no implications for trade-related issues.

Over the last few years, we have written several papers devoted to the issue of the impact of labor market structure on trade-related outcomes. We have argued that the link between trade and the labor market goes both ways – the underlying structure of the labor market can influence trade patterns. Moreover, we have also argued that when trade affects labor market outcomes; the nature of the link depends on the underlying structure of the labor market. The purpose of this chapter is to provide a general overview of our most recent work in this area.

We shall focus on three papers. The first, Davidson, Martin and Matusz (1999), provides the basic theoretical framework. In that paper we extended the traditional HOS model by introducing search-generated equilibrium unemployment and examined how the model's basic structure was altered. For what follows, two results are particularly important. First, we showed how differences in labor market structure, as characterized by job break-up rates and the efficiency of the matching process, could alter the pattern of comparative advantage. Thus we showed how labor market structure could influence trade patterns. Second, we showed that the manner in which changes in trade affect the distribution of income depends upon the underlying structure of the labor market. In two subsequent papers, Davidson and Matusz (2004) and Magee, Davidson, and Matusz (2004) we used data on turnover rates, trade patterns and political lobbying activity to test these two predictions. Our conclusion is that there is considerable empirical support for both predictions of the model.

We provide a heuristic summary of our theoretical arguments in the next section of this chapter. Section 3 is devoted to a summary of our empirical work. The chapter concludes in Section 4 with suggestions for future research in this area.

2. THE THEORY

2.1 Labor Market Structure and Comparative Advantage

The HOS model of international trade assumes that factors are perfectly mobile across sectors and that factor markets are perfectly competitive and frictionless. As a result, equilibrium is characterized by full employment. Autarkic prices (and hence the pattern of trade) then depend upon issues such as relative endowments of inputs and the sectoral factor intensities of the various production processes. When factor markets are imperfect, giving rise to equilibrium unemployment, additional issues emerge which can help shape the pattern of comparative advantage.

This point was made explicit in our (1999) paper with Lawrence Martin in which we extended the traditional $2 \times 2 \times 2$ HOS model to include equilibrium search-generated unemployment. The basic idea is straightforward. Suppose that it takes time and effort for unemployed workers to meet firms with idle capital. Suppose further that once they do meet, the length of the subsequent employment relationship is uncertain (this could be due to, say, random fluctuations in demand). This creates an environment in which workers cycle between periods of employment and unemployment with the length of time spent in each labor market state a function of the job acquisition and break-up rates in each sector (i.e., the sector-specific turnover rates). The implication is that the employment process will be risky; and, when workers choose an occupation, they will take the risk associated with each occupation into account. Firms attempting to hire workers in riskier industries will be forced to offer higher wages in order to entice workers to search for such jobs. These higher wages will push up autarkic prices and can influence the pattern of trade.

To be more specific, let's suppose that a particular industry (denoted by X)

in a particular country (denoted by A) has a job acquisition rate that is high relative to similar industries in other countries (this could be due to an unusually efficient search process or a superior matching technology in that country). Then sector-X firms in country A will be able to entice workers to search for their jobs with lower wage offers than their counterparts in other countries. As a result, wages and production costs will be relatively low in country A, making it more likely that country A will export good X.

A similar argument holds for job break-up rates. Suppose that the US has an industry in which the job destruction rate is high relative to the same industry in other countries. Then compared with other countries, US firms in that industry will have to pay relatively high wages in order to entice workers to seek employment in that sector (since workers know that jobs obtained in that industry are not very secure). These firms essentially pay their workers a compensating differential in order to make up for the industry's relatively high turnover rates. This compensating differential pushes up the autarkic price, making it more likely that the US will import that good.

The bottom line is this – in the presence of equilibrium unemployment, job turnover rates ought to influence the cost of production and this ought to affect the pattern of trade. All else equal, a country should be more likely to export goods produced in industries with (1) job acquisition rates that are high relative to similar industries in the rest of the world and (2) low break-up rates relative to the rest of the world. For such propositions to hold and be relevant there must be differences in turnover rates across industries and across countries. As we noted in the introduction, there is substantial evidence that this is indeed the case.

To test these predictions, it would be reasonable to start by asking whether or not there is a link between industry-specific employment risk and wages. It turns out that there is some empirical evidence that such a link exists. Abowd and Ashenfelter (1981) tested the proposition that inter-industry wage differentials at least partially compensate workers for the differences in industry-specific employment risk. They use data from the Panel Study of Income Dynamics (1967–75) to estimate the impact of employment risk on the wage differential. They conclude that the compensating differentials range from quite low in industries characterized by relatively little anticipated unemployment (less than 1 per cent) to quite high in industries with a relatively large amount of anticipated unemployment (as much as 14 per cent).

Given the Abowd and Ashenfelter (1981) results, we follow a different approach to test our theory and look for a direct link between turnover rates and the pattern of trade. In Section 3, we report the results from Davidson and Matusz (2004) in which we use two sources of data on labor market turnover and data on trade patterns to test the proposition that differences in industry-specific turnover rates can influence the pattern of trade.

2.2   Trade and the Distribution of Income

We begin by briefly reviewing the logic behind the results linking trade and the distribution of income that are derived in the traditional HOS and RV (Ricardo–Viner) settings. We then provide a heuristic description of how these results are altered by the presence of equilibrium unemployment. Readers interested in the detailed proofs of these propositions are referred to the appropriate articles below.

We start with the traditional two-good, two-factor HOS model in which all factors are perfectly mobile across sectors. In such a setting, labor has no reason to prefer one sector over another, except if that sector offers higher compensation than the other. Similarly, capital flows to the sector that offers the highest profit rate. The fact that factors can react instantly to changes in compensation has strong implications for the link between trade patterns and the distribution of income. For example, suppose that the world price of a good that is produced using a relatively labor-intensive production process rises. This will cause domestic firms to increase production of that good, leading to an increase in the demand for *all* factors used in that sector. However, the other sector uses a less labor-intensive production process. Thus, as factors flow out of the other sector towards this sector, the labor intensity of the factors being released will be lower than the labor intensity of the factors being absorbed. As a result, the aggregate demand for labor will rise while the aggregate demand for capital will fall. When the dust has settled, all labor benefits, regardless of where it is employed, while all capital suffers.

Now, turn to the RV model in which some factors may be tied to a specific sector. For example, machinery used to produce automobiles and computers cannot be substituted for each other all that easily. If the return to capital increases in Silicon Valley, we would not expect an immediate outflow of capital from the automobile industry to the computer industry. Likewise, when workers make an occupational choice they often acquire skills that are sector-specific. If the average wage paid to engineers increased, we would not expect lawyers or economists to immediately quit their jobs and switch occupations. Instead, over time, we might see an increase in the number of students majoring in engineering and a decline in other areas. As a result, over time the number of engineers will grow and the number of economists may shrink. The RV model stresses that these short-run attachments create an environment in which the fortunes of each factor are intertwined with the fortunes of the sector in which that factor is employed. If the world price for automobiles increases at the same time that the world price for computers falls, any factor that is tied to the automobile sector will gain while factors specific to the computer sector will lose.

Now, suppose that we take the standard two-good, two-factor HOS model and assume that search is required to find employment in either sector. Thus, when a new worker enters the labor force (or when an employed worker loses her job), that worker will have to choose a sector in which to seek employment. Naturally, unemployed workers will be drawn to the sector offering the highest expected lifetime reward. That is, if we let V_{js} denote the income that a worker searching in sector j can expect to earn over her lifetime and let V_{is} represent the same for sector i, then that worker will choose to search in sector j if $V_{js} > V_{is}$. It follows that in a diversified equilibrium unemployed workers will distribute themselves across the two sectors so that $V_{js} = V_{is}$. A model with this feature was developed and analyzed in Davidson, Martin and Matusz (1988) and Hosios (1990). In both papers the authors show that under certain conditions the returns to *searching* factors vary according to the Stolper–Samuelson Theorem (provided that factor intensities take into account the number of active searchers in each sector).[2] Thus, if a tariff is instituted in a relatively labor-intensive industry, all *unemployed* labor will benefit while all *idle* capital will be harmed (in terms of expected lifetime income and profit). The reasoning is much like the logic behind the Stolper–Samuelson Theorem. An increase in the price of a good will draw unemployed factors toward that sector (unless the price increase is large, factors *employed* in other sectors will be unwilling to give up their secure jobs and switch sectors). If the growing sector is more labor-intensive than the sector that is shrinking, the aggregate demand for labor will rise while the aggregate demand for capital falls. Consequently, the return to searching labor will increase while the return to idle capital falls. The key here is that in a setting with equilibrium unemployment it is the idle factors that are perfectly mobile across sectors and they are the factors that respond immediately to changes in product prices. These factors and their returns act exactly in the manner predicted by the HOS model and the Stolper–Samuelson Theorem.

The analysis in these two papers was somewhat incomplete, since neither one addressed the issue of how changes in trade patterns or trade policy would affect the returns to *employed* factors. This issue was addressed in Davidson, Martin and Matusz (1999), where we showed that search costs create an attachment to a sector that makes employed factors much like the specific factors in the RV model. Because it takes time and effort for jobless workers and firms with vacancies to find each other, once a job match is created both parties are reluctant to sever the ties unless they are convinced that they can earn significantly more by searching for a different production opportunity elsewhere. To make this argument a bit more formal, let V_{je} denote the income that a worker who is currently employed in sector j expects to earn over her lifetime. If this value falls below V_{is}, then this worker will quit her job and seek a new job in sector i. However, as long as V_{je} remains above V_{is}, this worker will want to continue to work in sector j. But, in equilibrium, unemployed workers allocate themselves such that $V_{is} = V_{js}$ and both of these values are strictly below V_{je}. It follows that small changes in product prices will not cause employed factors to switch sectors. The implication is that the reward earned by employed factors will be tied to the overall success of the sector. If an export sector is growing, this will tend to increase the reward to labor and capital employed in that sector.

But, at some point, most jobs break up for one reason or another. When that happens, the firm must recruit a replacement for the lost employee and the worker must search for a new job. Thus, the expected lifetime income for employed factors includes what those factors expect to earn when they become unemployed (for labor) or idle (for capital). We have already argued that this component of expected lifetime income varies according to the Stolper–Samuelson Theorem. It follows that the overall return to each *employed* factor is driven both by Stolper–Samuelson *and* Ricardo–Viner forces. Moreover, the force that dominates depends upon the turnover rates in that sector. If jobs last for a long time or are difficult to find, then the attachment to a sector caused by search costs will be strong. This makes it more likely that the Ricardo–Viner force will dominate. On the other hand, if jobs are easy to find and/or do not last long, then employed factors will not feel a strong attachment to their sector. In this case, it is more likely that the Stolper–Samuelson forces will dominate.

To summarize, in the presence of equilibrium unemployment, the returns to employed factors are driven by two forces. The Stolper–Samuelson force, which dictates that an economy's abundant factor gains from trade liberalization while its scarce factor loses, and the Ricardo–Viner force, which dictates that a factor that is specific to an export sector gains from trade liberalization while a factor that is specific to an import sector loses from trade liberalization. While these are the two traditional channels that link factor rewards to trade patterns, they do not emerge simultaneously in full employment models. The Stolper–Samuelson force is present only when all factors are perfectly mobile across all sectors, while the Ricardo–Viner force emerges only in full employment models with specific factors. The key insight that is gained by allowing for unemployment is that market imperfections (like the transaction costs associated with search) generate an environment in which the returns to employed factors are determined by a weighted average of these two forces. In addition, it is the labor market turnover rates of each sector that determine which force is given more weight. In the next section we combine data on turnover rates across sectors with data on PAC contributions made by groups representing the interests of labor and capital in different sectors to see if there is any empirical support for these predictions.

3. EVIDENCE

In this section we summarize some of the results that can be found in Davidson and Matusz (2004) and Magee, Davidson and Matusz (2004) in which we test the two theories described above. We do not intend to describe all the results, but rather to provide a flavor of the type of evidence that supports our theories linking the structure of the labor market to trade-related issues. Our focus will be on the most elementary analysis. Interested readers are referred to the papers for the more detailed econometric analysis.

3.1 Turnover and Trade Patterns

To test our first theory we need data on trade patterns and labor market turnover. As mentioned in the introduction, Davis, Haltiwanger and Schuh (1996) have provided extensive data on job destruction and job creation rates for manufacturing industries in the United States. This is our main source of data on turnover. For information on trade patterns, we rely on the NBER trade data.

One of the goals of the Davis, Haltiwanger and Schuh (DHS) project was to analyze turnover in manufacturing industries in the US. To do so, they analyzed plant-level data in order to get a measure of the amount of job destruction and job creation that was taking place each year. For each plant, they looked at the change in total employment from one year to the next (measured in March of each year).[3] Plants in each 4-digit SIC industry were then put into three categories – those with an increase in total employment, those with a decrease in total employment and those with no change in total employment. The first group was said to have 'created jobs' while the second group was said to have 'destroyed jobs.' To find the job creation rate, the authors summed over all jobs created in a given industry and then divided by total employment. The job destruction rate was calculated in an analogous manner. The data covered 447 4-digit SIC industries for the period 1973–86.

In our theoretical model, the job acquisition rate measures how difficult it is to obtain a job in a given sector. A true measure of this variable could be obtained by calculating the number of workers who find employment in an industry in a given time period and then dividing by the total number of workers seeking such jobs. The job break-up rate is a measure of job security – how likely is it that a worker who is currently employed in a given sector will lose his or her job? A true measure of this variable could be obtained by calculating the total number of workers terminated in an industry in a given time period and then dividing by total employment. The DHS measures of turnover are not perfect proxies for these rates. To begin with, the DHS measures are measures of net changes in employment. A plant that fires ten employees and then hires nine new workers will show up with a net change in employment of only −1. This clearly understates the amount of turnover in this plant. Second, the DHS measures focus on job turnover, not worker turnover. Finally, the DHS measure of job creation suffers from one additional flaw – it uses total employment in the industry as its base rather than the total number of workers seeking employment in that sector.

We do two things in order to deal with these shortcomings. First, in order to get a better measure of the job acquisition rate we replace the DHS measure of job creation with a slightly different measure – we use the DHS data to calculate the fraction of all new jobs created that can be attributed to a specific sector. That is, for each industry we divide the total number of jobs created in that industry by the total number of jobs created in *all* industries. Although not a perfect measure of the job acquisition rate, this alternative measure gives us a better sense of the relative difficulty workers face when trying to find a job in a specific industry.[4]

The second action that we take is that we re-run all of our analyses using a second source of data on turnover to check for robustness. This second source provides measures of worker flows that are very good proxies for the job acquisition and break-up rates in our theoretical model. These data, which come from the United States Bureau of Labor Statistics (BLS), focus squarely on worker accessions and separations. In particular, the labor market turnover rates reported by the BLS measure the gross movement of workers into and out of employment at the establishment level in 4-digit SIC industries. While the BLS measure of worker separations is exactly the right proxy for the job break-up rate in our theoretical model, the measure of worker accessions suffers from the same shortcoming as the DHS measure of job creation – it uses the wrong base. Thus, we handle this variable in exactly the same manner as we handle the DHS measure of job creation. The main problem with the BLS data is that few such data are available. Collection of these data was stopped for budgetary reasons in 1981. Thus, while the DHS data covers 1973–86, we only have BLS data for 1978–81. In addition, while the DHS data encompass 447 4-digit SIC industries, the BLS data cover only 106 such industries. For this reason, we use the DHS data to obtain our primary proxies for turnover rates. However, the fact that we obtain remarkably similar results when we use the BLS data provides us with some comfort that our results are robust to other ways of measuring turnover.

Turn next to our trade data. To explore the relationship between turnover and trade patterns we must find a way to measure the degree to which each industry is engaged in international trade. We accomplish this by introducing the following variable, T_{it}, where the i subscript refers to the industry and the t subscript refers to time:

$$T_{it} = \frac{E_{it} - M_{it}}{Q_{it} + M_{it}} \times 100,$$

where E_{it} represents gross exports, M_{it} denotes gross imports and Q_{it} represents domestic production. This variable ranges from −100 to 100. It takes on the minimum value if none of the industry i good is produced domestically and it takes on its maximum value if everything produced domestically or imported is subsequently exported. Thus higher values of T_{it} represent more net exports for industry i. We use trade and shipments data from the NBER for the period 1973–86 to calculate our trade variable.[5] For each year, we match our measures of turnover (calculated using the DHS measures of job destruction and job creation) with the trade data for 447 4-digit SIC industries.

Our theoretical model predicts that, all else equal, the US should have a comparative advantage in industries with relatively high job acquisition rates and relatively low job break-up rates.[6] This suggests that we should look for a positive correlation between our proxy for the industry-specific job acquisition rate and T_{it} and a negative correlation between our proxy for the industry-specific job break-up rate and T_{it}. To explore this issue, we start by running the following simple regression:

$$T_{it} = \hat{\beta}_0 + \hat{\beta}_1 b_{it} + \hat{\beta}_{it} e_{it},$$

where b_{it} is our proxy for the job break-up rate and e_{it} is our proxy for the job acquisition rate. The results for each year and for the pooled sample are reported in Tables 5.1 and 5.2 (these are Tables 2 and 4 in Davidson and Matusz, 2004). The results are striking. Consider Table 5.1, which reports the results using the DHS data. Every coefficient has the predicted sign and almost all of them are statistically significant at the 5 per cent (or better) level. Remarkably similar results hold for the BLS data reported in Table 5.2.

Of course, in these simple regressions we have made no attempt to control for other factors influencing comparative advantage that might also affect labor market turnover. Moreover, there is more than one theory that could explain this relationship. The one that surely springs to mind has the causality running in the opposite direction – instead of turnover rates causing trade, changes in trade patterns could be driving turnover. We may be picking up nothing more than an old story about workers in more open industries facing more job insecurity. According to this alternative theory, a surge of imports could destroy domestic jobs (pushing up job destruction) while an increase in the demand for domestically produced goods by foreign consumers could create new domestic jobs (pushing up job creation).

There is, however, an important distinction between this alternative theory

Table 5.1   *Results for each year (dependent variable = T, results based on 4-digit SIC)*

Year	Independent variables (DHS turnover data)		$\bar{R}^2$
	e_{it}	b_{it}	
1973	2.388	-0.441	0.029
	(1.36)	(−3.48)	
1974	4.433	−0.400	0.047
	(2.23)	(−4.09)	
1975	3.056	−0.258	0.042
	(1.73)	(−4.05)	
1976	0.165	−0.005	−0.004
	(0.10)	(−0.04)	
1977	2.554	−0.366	0.030
	(1.32)	(−3.72)	
1978	4.420	−0.786	0.089
	(2.27)	(−6.42)	
1979	3.012	−0.829	0.085
	(1.68)	(−6.16)	
1980	3.127	−0.412	0.039
	(1.68)	(−3.95)	
1981	3.250	−0.358	0.027
	(1.75)	(−3.26)	
1982	2.954	−0.389	0.072
	(1.73)	(−5.63)	
1983	2.066	−0.138	0.008
	(1.24)	(−1.89)	
1984	1.884	−0.550	0.044
	(0.975)	(−4.55)	
1985	3.240	−0.796	0.139
	(1.90)	(−8.162)	
1986	3.957	−0.716	0.084
	(2.017)	(−6.076)	
1973–86	2.941	−0.360	0.042
	(5.93)	(−15.13)	

Notes: Estimated coefficients are listed in the body of the table, with *t*-statistics in parentheses. There are 20 observations in each year.

Table 5.2 Results for the pooled sample (dependent variable = T, results based on 4-digit SIC)

Year	Independent variables (BLS turnover data)		$\bar{R}^2$
	e_{it}	b_{it}	
1977	1.258	−2.641	0.201
	(1.00)	(−5.24)	
1978	1.809	−2.836	0.263
	(1.42)	(−6.05)	
1979	2.641	−3.053	0.264
	(2.08)	(−6.29)	
1980	2.180	−3.510	0.238
	(1.79)	−(5.90)	
1981	2.285	−3.236	0.177
	(1.72)	(−4.95)	
1977–81	2.029	−3.013	0.233
	(3.61)	(−12.76)	

Notes: Estimated coefficients are listed in the body of the table, with *t*-statistics in parentheses. There are 106 observations in each year.

and ours that can be exploited to shed some light on the direction of causation. In our theory, workers choose an occupation based, in part, on the turnover rates associated with each industry. In making such a decision it is likely that the worker focuses on the average turnover rate in each sector, ignoring short-run fluctuations in turnover rates that might be caused by temporary shocks. In contrast, the alternative theory is consistent with short-run fluctuations (caused by sudden changes in the pattern of trade) driving turnover rates.

To control for other factors that might influence the pattern of trade and to try to sort out the direction of causality, we therefore estimated the following empirical model of net trade:

$$T_{it} = \beta_0 + \beta_1\bar{b}_i + \beta_2\Delta b_{it} + \beta_3\bar{e}_i + \beta_4\Delta e_{it} + \theta Z_t + \varepsilon_{it}, \qquad (5.1)$$

where $\bar{b}_i(\bar{e}_i)$ is the average value of our proxy for the job break-up (acquisition) rate in industry i over the sample period, Δb_{it} (Δe_{it}) is the percentage deviation of the job break-up (acquisition) rate from its long-run average rate in industry i in year t, Z_t is a vector of industry-specific variables that may influence trade patterns, θ_i is a vector of coefficients and ε_{it} is a random disturbance. In estimating (5.1) we included a proxy for the capital intensity of the industry, a proxy for the skill mix of labor in the industry, a measure of the size of the industry (in terms of employment) and the value of the dollar as controls.[7] The key questions are whether or not β_1–β_4 have the correct signs as predicted by the two theories and whether or not these coefficients are significantly different from zero. Once again, the results are striking. Using the pooled data from DHS to estimate (1) yields estimates of $\beta_1 = -1.144 < 0$ and $\beta_3 = 2.496 > 0$ just as our theory predicts. Moreover, the t-statistics for both coefficients are quite high (23.04 for β_1 and 4.94 for β_3). In contrast, the alternative theory in which changes in trade patterns affect turnover does not fare as well. While the estimates for β_2 and β_4 have the right signs ($\beta_2 = -0.001 < 0$ and $\beta_4 = 0.006 > 0$), only the estimate for β_4 comes close to having a reasonably high t-statistic (the t-statistics are 0.27 for β_2 and 1.72 for β_4) indicating that we cannot reject the hypothesis that $\beta_2 = 0$. Similar results are obtained when we use the BLS data: the estimated coefficients are $\beta_1 = -2.572 < 0$, $\beta_2 = -0.004$, $\beta_3 = 1.906 > 0$ and $\beta_4 = -0.013$. Thus, β_1–β_3 have the predicted sign while β_4 has the wrong sign. The t-statistics are 8.34 for β_1 and 3.40 for β_3, providing strong support for our theory; and 0.12 for β_2 and 0.37 for β_4, indicating that the BLS data provide no support for the theory that trade causes turnover.

We close this subsection by addressing one other flaw in this analysis. Our theory about trade and turnover is one of comparative advantage – a country has a comparative advantage in a good because workers in that industry face *relatively* high job acquisition rates and/or *relatively* low job break-up rates. As with any theory of comparative advantage, the term 'relative' refers to the rest of the world. It is not possible to test such a theory with data from just one country. But, up to this point, we have only reported results from statistical analyses using US data. These results are, at best, provocative. A proper test of the theory requires a cross-country analysis of intersectoral differences in labor market turnover and trade patterns. This is not an easy task. While it is true that there are many data now available on turnover for a wide variety of countries, there are many serious obstacles to carrying out such an analysis. In particular, there is the issue of industry concordance.

Fortunately, we were able to offer an initial analysis along these lines that yielded promising results. We did so by making use of data on US and Canadian labor market turnover provided in Baldwin, Dunne and Haltiwanger (1998). In that paper, the authors report average job creation and job destruction rates for 1974–92 for 19 2-digit SIC industries. We combined these data with data on bilateral trade between the US and Canada to get a better test of our theory. If our theory is correct, then, all else equal, US exports to Canada should be highest in industries in which US job destruction rates are lowest relative to those in Canada. To make this operational, we defined a new bilateral trade index of the form

$$TC_{it} = \frac{EC_{it} - MC_{it}}{X_{it} + M_{it}} \times 100,$$

where EC_{it} measures industry-i US exports to Canada in year t and MC_{it} measures industry-i US imports from Canada in year t. This natural extension of our trade index T_{it} measures the industry-i net exports to Canada in year t normalized by the total amount of trade between the US and all countries. Our theory suggests that TC_{it} should be negatively correlated with the ratio of the industry-specific US job destruction rates relative to the comparable Canadian job destruction rates.

The Baldwin, Dunne and Haltiwanger (1998) data provide us with 399 observations of job destruction rates and our bilateral trade index. Regressing TC_{it} against the ratio of job destruction rates yields an estimated coefficient that is negative and highly significant (the t-statistic is 13.10). The simple bivariate regression line also fits the data rather well ($\bar{R}_2 = 0.30$). We conclude that the limited amount of data available tends to provide further support for our theory linking labor market turnover rates to trade patterns.

It is also worth noting that the results reported by Baldwin, Dunne and Haltiwanger do not seem to be consistent with the theory that changes in trade patterns cause turnover. One of their main findings is that 'the Canadian and U.S. industry-level job creation and destruction data are remarkably similar.' This is not at all what one would expect to see if trade causes turnover. After all, trade is a much more important component of the overall economy in Canada than it is in the US – for the US, the combined values of imports and exports makes up less than 30 per cent of GDP, whereas the comparable figure for Canada is close to 80 per cent! If exposure to international trade really causes labor market turnover, we would expect to see much more turnover in Canada than we see in the US. But, as Baldwin, Dunne and Haltiwanger emphasize, this is not the case.

3.2 Trade Policy Preferences and Turnover

In order to test our theory that turnover affects the link between trade and wages, we make use of Magee's (1980) insight that it is possible to exploit the fact that preferences over trade policy influence lobbying behavior to test the predictions of the Stolper–Samuelson Theorem and the Specific Factors model. Magee noted that according to the Stolper–Samuelson Theorem preferences over trade policy should be split along factor lines while the Specific Factors model predicts that such preferences should be tied to industry affiliation. He then examined lobbying behavior with respect to the 1973 Trade Reform Act to see which theory did a better job of explaining the data. Our theory predicts that when search-generated unemployment is present, factor abundance and industry affiliation should both matter, with the industry's turnover rates determining which factor dominates. In Magee, Davidson and Matusz (2004) we tested this theory by combining the DHS data on turnover with data on Political Action Committee (PAC) contributions to candidates voting on trade-liberalizing legislation in the early 1990s.

The Federal Election Commission provides data on contributions to candidates for the House of Representatives and identifies whether the PAC represents corporate or labor interests. We were able to link the PACs to their 4-digit SIC industries based on data from the Center for Responsive Politics. The PACs were classified as representing an import-competing or exporting industry based on its net trade position for the years 1988–92 (based on the NBER trade data). We used data on 419 PACs in total: 42 represented the interest of labor; 377 represented capital; 226 were linked to import-competing industries; and 193 were linked to exporting industries.

Our goal was to examine the fraction of PAC contributions given to supporters of trade-liberalization policies to see if the fractions differed based on factor abundance (capital versus labor) and/or industry affiliation (import-competing versus exporting). The two trade-liberalizing pieces of legislation that we focused on were the North American Free Trade Agreement (NAFTA) and the ratification of the agreement reached during the Uruguay Round of GATT. A candidate was considered a supporter of trade liberalization if he or she voted in favor of NAFTA, in favor of GATT, or in favor of both. Our model predicts that in high-turnover industries (where Stolper–Samuelson effects should dominate), capital and labor should differ in their preferences toward free trade. In contrast, capital and labor employed in the same industry should have the same preferences towards trade policy if the industry is characterized by low turnover (so that the Specific Factor effects dominate).

The results of the most basic test of this theory are provided in Table 5.3 (which is Table 2 in Magee, Davidson and Matusz, 2004). Once again, the results are striking. Consider first the top half of the table. Note that in low-turnover industries the fraction of contributions given to supporters of NAFTA, GATT, or both by PACs representing capital is not statistically different from the fraction given by PACs representing labor.[8] Thus we cannot reject the hypothesis that capital and labor have the same preferences towards trade policy in low-turnover industries. The story is quite different for high-turnover industries. In all three cases, the fraction of contributions given by PACs representing capital is statistically different from the fraction given by labor PACs at the 5 per cent (or better) level. Thus it appears that in high-turnover industries labor and capital have different views towards trade policy.

Consider next the lower half of Table 5.3, where we examine the role of industry affiliation. In low-turnover industries, where our theory predicts that

Table 5.3   *Fraction of total PAC contributions given to free-trade proponents*

	Capital	Labor	*t*-statistic
Low turnover			
NAFTA	0.609	0.531	1.188
GATT	0.728	0.672	1.021
Both	0.515	0.456	0.929
High turnover			
NAFTA	0.628	0.307	5.644
GATT	0.746	0.635	2.294
Both	0.534	0.265	4.955
	Export industry	Import industry	*t*-statistic
Low turnover			
NAFTA	0.624	0.577	1.286
GATT	0.748	0.692	1.867
Both	0.531	0.484	1.339
High turnover			
NAFTA	0.586	0.602	–0.381
GATT	0.759	0.718	1.248
Both	0.516	0.506	0.259

industry affiliation should matter, there is a significant difference between the fraction of contributions given to the supports of NAFTA, GATT, or both by PACs representing exporting industries and the fraction given by PACs representing import-competing industries. In contrast, industry affiliation seems to play no role whatsoever in high-turnover industries!

An alternative way to test our theory is to run the following regression:

$$S_i = A_1 K_i + A_2 X_i + A_3 b_i + A_4 K_i b_i + A_5 X_i b_i + A_6 UL_i, \qquad (5.2)$$

where S_i denotes the share of contributions from PAC i going to the supporter of the bill; $K_i = 1$ (0) if PAC i represents the interests of capital (labor); $X_i = 1$ (0) if PAC i is linked to an exporting (import-competing) industry; b_i is the DHS measure of job destruction for the industry that PAC i represents; and UL_i measures the extent of unskilled labor in the industry represented by PAC i.[9] Our theory predicts that factor abundance should matter most in high-turnover industries – thus, if our theory is correct, A_4 should be positive. In addition, industry affiliation should matter most in low-turnover industries – thus, if our theory is correct, A_5 should be negative.

We estimated (5.2) using the share of PAC contributions going to the supporters of NAFTA, the supporters of GATT, and those candidates who supported both pieces of legislation.[10] The results, although not as strong as those in Table 5.2, are consistent with our theory. In all three cases, our estimate for A_4 is positive and our estimate for A_5 is negative.[11] In addition, our estimate for A_4 is statistically significant at the 1 per cent level in the NAFTA regression and at the 5 per cent level in the regression using both bills. The estimate for A_5 is statistically significant at the 10 per cent level in the GATT regression. Similar results are obtained with and without industry fixed effects.

4. CONCLUSION

The gains from trade come from exploiting differences across countries. The manner in which those gains are distributed across society is likely to depend on the institutions that govern factor markets. It is well known that labor market institutions vary widely across countries. We have argued elsewhere that such differences might influence the pattern of trade and the way in which trade affects wages. We have also provided evidence that tends to support this theory. In this chapter, we have summarized both the theory behind these arguments and the evidence that supports it. Our results are encouraging, but it should be clear that there is much left to do. Most of the work involves the collection of data that would allow for more rigorous tests of our theories and the execution of such analyses. Our hope is that others will now join us in pushing the analysis of trade and labor markets further.

NOTES

1. There are, of course, exceptions. For recent examples see Krugman (1994) and Davis (1998).
2. It is worth noting that the two papers differ in their emphasis. Davidson, Martin and Matusz (1988) emphasize that the Stolper–Samuelson Theorem holds only if bargaining between workers and employers leads to an efficient outcome. Hosios (1990) assumes that bargaining is efficient and then stresses that the Stolper–Samuelson Theorem holds for searching factors.
3. The data underlying the DHS statistical analysis is the Longitudinal Research Database developed by the United States Census Bureau. A more detailed description of the data and the DHS construction of their job destruction and job creation rates can be found in Davis, Haltiwanger and Schuh (1996) or Davidson and Matusz (2004).
4. The shortcoming of this alternative measure is that it does not take into account the number of unemployed workers who are suitable for employment in each industry.

5. See Feenstra (1996, 1997) for a detailed description of these data.
6. Of course, the key word here is 'relative' – we really need to compare the turnover rates in the US with those in similar industries in other countries. We return to this issue at the end of this subsection.
7. For capital intensity we used the ratio of the total real capital stock to total employment within an industry at time *t*. For the skill mix of labor we used the ratio of production workers to total employment within the industry at time *t*. Data on industry-specific capital stocks and employment were taken from the NBER–CES manufacturing database. The value of the dollar was obtained from the *Economic Report of the President*.
8. Industries were categorized as high- or low-turnover industries based on their average job destruction rates over the period 1988–92. We obtained similar results when we used other measures of turnover suggested by Davis, Haltiwanger and Schuh (1996) so our results do not appear to be sensitive to this method of categorization.
9. We include the skill mix of labor as a control variable because skilled and unskilled labor may have different views with respect to trade policy. Moreover, turnover rates might be correlated with the skill mix of industries.
10. Since the dependent variable is limited to [0,1], we estimated (5.2) as a linear regression with censoring above and below.
11. In the NAFTA regression we obtain $A_4 = 0.055$ and $A_5 = -0.024$. In the GATT regression we obtain $A_4 = 0.004$ and $A_5 = -0.024$. Finally, in the regression using supporters of both bills we obtain $A_4 = 0.046$ and $A_5 = -0.020$.

REFERENCES

Abowd, John and Orley Ashenfelter (1981), 'Anticipated Unemployment, Temporary Layoffs, and Compensating Wage Differentials,' in Sherwin Rosen (ed.), *Studies in Labor Markets*, Chicago: University of Chicago Press, pp. 141–70.
Baldwin, John, Timothy Dunne and John Haltiwanger (1998), 'A Comparison of Employment Flows in the Canadian and U.S. Manufacturing Sectors,' *Review of Economics and Statistics*, 347–56.
Davidson, Carl and Steven Matusz (2004), 'Trade and Turnover: Theory and Evidence,' forthcoming in the *Review of International Ecomonics*.
Davidson, Carl, Lawrence Martin and Steven Matusz (1988), 'The Structure of Simple General Equilibrium Models with Frictional Unemployment,' *Journal of Political Economy*, **96**, 1267–93.
Davidson, Carl, Lawrence Martin and Steven Matusz (1999), 'Trade and Search Generated Unemployment,' *Journal of International Economics*, **48**, 271–99.
Davis, Donald (1998), 'Does European Unemployment Prop Up American Wages? National Labor Markets and Global Trade,' *American Economic Review*, **88** (3), 478–94.
Davis, Steven, John Haltiwanger and Scott Schuh (1996), *Job Creation and Destruction*, Cambridge, MA: MIT Press.
Feenstra, Robert (1996), 'U.S. Imports, 1972–1994: Data and Concordances,' NBER Working Paper 5515.
Feenstra, Robert (1997), 'U.S. Exports, 1972–1994, with State Exports and Other US Data,' NBER Working Paper 5990.
Freeman, Richard (1994), 'How Labor Fares in Advanced Economies,' in Richard Freeman (ed.), *Working Under Different Rules*, New York: Russell Sage Foundation, pp. 1–28.

Greenaway, David, Richard Upward and Peter Wright (2001), 'Sectoral Mobility in UK and US Labour Markets,' in Harry Bloch and Peter Kenyon (eds), *Creating an Internationally Competitive Economy*, New York: Palgrave, pp. 72–104.

Haynes, Michelle, Richard Upward and Peter Wright (2000), 'Smooth and Sticky Adjustment: A Comparative Analysis of the US and the UK,' *Review of International Economics*, **8** (3), 517–32.

Hosios, A. (1990), 'Factor Market Search and the Structure of Simple General Equilibrium Models,' *Journal of Political Economy*, **98**, 325–55.

Krugman, Paul (1994), 'Europe Jobless, America Penniless?', *Foreign Policy*, **95** (Summer), 19–34.

Magee, Christopher, Carl Davidson and Steven Matusz (2004), 'Trade, Turnover and Tithing,' forthcoming in the *Journal of International Economics*.

Magee, Steven (1980), 'Three Simple Tests of the Stolper–Samuelson Theorem,' in P. Oppenheimer (ed.), *Issues in International Economics*, London: Oriel Press, pp. 138–53.

Nickell, Steven (1997). 'Unemployment and Labor Market Rigidities: Europe versus North America,' *Journal of Economic Perspectives*, **11** (3), 55–74.

6. Trade pattern persistence

James Cassing and Steven Husted

1. INTRODUCTION

In 1979, Jimmy Carter was President of the United States, the Berlin Wall was intact, as was the Soviet Union, the Tokyo Round was not implemented and the Uruguay Round was a decade away. Between 1980 and 2000, about 125 free-trade arrangements were negotiated and implemented, the EU expanded twice and adopted a common currency, and there was a capital market disruption in 1997 of historic proportions involving the former Soviet Union and many countries of East Asia.[1] Through all of this the world economy grew by more than 70 percent and world trade grew by a remarkable 175 percent. Yet, in this chapter we provide evidence that the pattern of international trade for many countries appears to have remained relatively stable: principal trading partners do not change, and trade shares exhibit remarkable constancy.

This trade pattern stability over a long period of time is not what economists usually predict. For example, Yarbrough and Yarbrough (2000 p. 74) echo the intuition of many economists when they write in their popular textbook:

> The evolution of comparative advantage over time implies that production and trade patterns will change over time as well, creating changes in the distribution of income and some difficult dilemmas for policymakers. These changes are evident even over a fairly short period of time.

But examination of the market for aggregate imports for almost 100 countries over the last two decades of the twentieth century calls this fluidity of trade patterns into question.

Another way to think about the presumptions of the profession regarding trade pattern stability is the skepticism that has often met evidence of very low price and income elasticities in studies of trade behavior. Clearly, since 1980, relative prices have changed a lot and the terms of trade of most countries have fluctuated considerably (see Table 6.1). Yet again, we will demonstrate that trade shares have remained relatively constant. This would seem to support estimates of low trade elasticities found in studies such as Warner and Kreinin (1983).

Table 6.1   *Characteristics of annual terms of trade changes, selected countries, 1980–2000*

	Avg. % chg.	S.d. % change	Max % change	Min % change
United States	0.53	2.72	5.39	−5.14
Canada	−0.33	2.90	5.61	−6.34
Australia	−0.79	5.49	14.46	−9.60
Japan	3.50	8.68	33.71	−8.10
New Zealand	0.51	3.61	10.98	−5.23
Finland	0.57	4.45	12.45	−4.98
Germany	0.31	4.51	15.07	−6.59
Greece	−1.35	3.86	4.60	−9.55
Ireland	−0.09	2.59	4.39	−4.64
Italy	1.11	4.57	15.85	−7.59
Netherlands	0.24	1.85	3.09	−3.54
Spain	1.10	7.00	20.85	−17.74
Denmark	0.57	2.04	6.59	−2.56
Norway	1.37	11.60	35.28	−24.77
United Kingdom	0.01	1.77	2.67	−5.47
Kenya	−1.25	11.31	17.25	−18.22
China, P.R.: Hong Kong	0.00	1.45	3.20	−2.77
India	2.21	10.96	23.47	−12.95
Korea	−1.16	5.58	8.85	−13.63
Pakistan	5.34	29.43	122.64	−15.85
Singapore	−1.19	1.85	2.09	−4.50
Thailand	−1.91	5.23	10.83	−12.88
Israel	1.13	2.96	5.54	−3.52
Jordan	0.90	7.10	14.34	−11.53
Brazil	−1.08	13.17	24.67	−21.71
Colombia	−0.15	11.50	21.83	−22.87

Source: IMF, *International Financial Statistics* CD-ROM, December 2002. Terms of trade constructed as the ratio of export unit values to import unit values.

Furthermore, growth rates have varied substantially between countries, which should affect trade shares (see Table 6.2). Similarly, technological progress has made the world a different place and this should also impact trading patterns, especially to the extent that technology changes have not been uniform across countries. Finally, ocean freight and port charges per short ton of cargo have fallen 50 percent since 1945, air transport costs are down by even more, and communications costs have essentially disappeared. These changes, one would think, might have an effect on trade patterns, but the data are not so conclusive.

Table 6.2   Average annual growth rates, selected countries, 1990–2001

Algeria	2.0	Jordan	4.8
Argentina	3.7	Kenya	2.0
Australia	4.0	Korea	5.7
Austria	2.1	Madagascar	2.4
Bangladesh	4.9	Malawi	3.7
Belgium	2.1	Malaysia	6.5
Benin	4.8	Mali	4.1
Bolivia	3.8	Mauritania	4.2
Brazil	2.8	Mexico	3.1
Burkina Faso	4.9	Morocco	2.5
Burundi	−2.2	Mozambique	7.5
Cameroon	2.1	Nepal	4.9
Canada	3.0	Netherlands	2.8
Central African Rep.	2.1	New Zealand	2.9
Chad	4.6	Niger	2.6
Chile	6.4	Nigeria	2.5
China	10.0	Norway	3.5
Colombia	2.7	Pakistan	3.7
Congo, Rep.	−0.1	Panama	3.8
Costa Rica	5.1	Papua New Guinea	3.6
Côte d'Ivoire	3.1	Paraguay	2.0
Denmark	2.5	Peru	4.3
Dominican Rep.	6.0	Philippines	3.3
Ecuador	1.7	Portugal	2.7
El Salvador	4.5	Rwanda	0.8
Finland	3.0	Senegal	3.9
France	1.8	Singapore	7.8
Germany	1.5	South Africa	2.1
Ghana	4.2	Spain	2.6
Greece	2.3	Sri Lanka	5.1
Guatemala	4.1	Sweden	2.0
Guinea	4.1	Switzerland	0.9
Haiti	4.1	Tanzania	3.1
Honduras	3.1	Thailand	3.8
Hong Kong	3.9	Togo	2.2
India	5.9	Tunisia	4.7
Indonesia	3.8	Turkey	3.3
Ireland	7.6	Uganda	6.8
Israel	5.1	United Kingdom	2.6
Italy	1.6	United States	3.5
Jamaica	0.6	Uruguay	2.9
Japan	1.3	Venezuela	1.5

Source: World Bank: *World Development Report 2003*.

More specifically, in this chapter we exploit a newly manageable data set from the IMF in order to quantify the extent to which trade patterns have changed over the last two decades. The trade data focus on bilateral trade patterns for 93 countries and are quite robust in cutting across countries of diverse economic, political and cultural traits during a fairly turbulent period of economic history. In Section 2, we describe the data and develop some measures of trade pattern change. We report evidence on the characteristics of countries that hold primary market shares in national import markets and demonstrate that the shares of these countries and other principal suppliers remain relatively constant over the sample period. Then, in Section 3, we present some preliminary thoughts on what is going on and what this might portend for various theories of international trade. Finally, Section 4 offers some conclusions.

2.   EMPIRICS

In this section, we present evidence on the stability of trade patterns for a large number of countries over the past two decades. In developing this evidence, we use data from the International Monetary Fund's *Direction of Trade Statistics* March 2002 CD-ROM. This database provides figures on the values of merchandise exports and imports by trade partners for 186 countries. In our analysis, we focus on bilateral import totals valued in c.i.f. (cost insurance freight) terms. The database reports these values measured in US dollars for all countries. Our study utilizes annual data from 92 countries and one territory (Hong Kong) over the period 1980–2000.[2] The countries chosen for this study cover all geographic regions of the world and employ most economic systems. We chose not to include data from countries such as the states of the former Soviet Union that did not exist at the start of the sample period or countries such as Kuwait and Sierra Leone, where there were breaks in economic data because of wars or other disruptions. A complete list of countries included in our analysis can be found in the Appendix.

Our analysis focuses on the behavior of the nominal market shares of the countries that supply goods to the countries in our sample. We measured these as the ratio of nominal imports to total imports (as reported in the database) times 100. Because of the large number of countries in the database, we present details for only those countries that enjoyed at least 2 percent of a given country's market in 1980. Even with this limitation, we ended up with 926 bilateral trade patterns to analyze, or roughly ten trading partners for each country in the sample.

2.1 Bilateral Trade: Primary Trade Partners

Using these market share data, we focus on a variety of questions related to bilateral trade patterns. The first issue we consider is related to primary trade partners. To clarify the points we would like to make, consider Figure 6.1. This provides a graph of the import market shares for Tunisia over the sample period. The behavior in this graph typifies most of the patterns we found in our sample.

In particular, throughout the sample period, one country (here France) held the largest share of the market. Its market share averaged about 25 percent. For more than two-thirds (66 of 93) of the 93 countries in our sample, the same country had the greatest market share at both the start and the end of the sample period. In addition, the average market share of the primary trade partner was 27 percent in 1980 and 26 percent in 2000.

The fact that France held the largest share of Tunisia's import market is readily explained. France is a high-income, industrialized country located near Tunisia. Perhaps most important, it governed a colonial protectorate in the country for more than 60 years, and, as a result, French is an official language of the country. As it turns out, attributes such as proximity, former colonial relationships, and being the geographically nearest high-income industrialized country appear to be extremely important in explaining market share dominance.[3] This

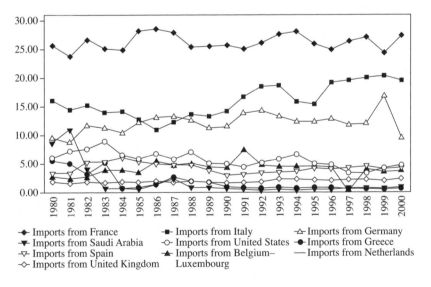

Figure 6.1   Tunisia: major import suppliers

Table 6.3   Characteristics of leading import suppliers

	1980	2000
Neighbor	24	31
Colony	21	16
Nearest HIC	16	15
Oil	7	4
Rest	25	27

Notes: nearest HIC = geographically nearest high-income country; oil = oil exporter; colony = importing country is a former colony of exporter.

is confirmed in Table 6.3, where we show that these characteristics are found in more than two-thirds of the primary market share-holders in our sample.

Table 6.4 summarizes how often various countries held leading market shares at the start and end of the sample period.[4] As the table demonstrates, a small number of high-income countries, including the United States, France, Germany, Japan and the United Kingdom, were most likely to hold the dominant share of a country's market at both the start and end of the period. Moreover, as is exemplified in Figure 6.1, high-income countries tend to maintain market shares in every country in our sample. This, of course, is consistent with the fact that these countries consistently lead world rankings as major exporters in value terms. What may be surprising is the global universality of their market penetration, and the relative stability of this penetration over time.[5] We turn now to the question of market share stability.

2.2   Bilateral Trade: Market Share Stability

Figures 6.2–6.5 provide graphs of the evolution of these market shares for Austria, France, Pakistan and Uruguay. As the figures indicate, there are remarkable differences in these patterns from one country to the next. None the less, it is clear that the shares in Figures 6.2 and 6.3 exhibit considerably more stability than those in Figures 6.4 and 6.5.

To our knowledge, no previous work has compared the behavior of market shares over time for a large set of countries.[6] We do not have strong priors as to what patterns one should expect to find in these shares. None the less, as we noted in the introduction, given all of the changes experienced in the world economy over the past two decades we would not have found it unusual to observe considerable instability in trade patterns and partners. In the remainder of this section, we will try to make the case that stability, rather than variation, in trade shares is a strong and recurring phenomenon.

Table 6.4 Leading import supplier count

	1980		2000
Australia	4	Argentina	1
Brazil	2	Australia	4
Cameroon	1	Brazil	3
Canada	1	Canada	1
Côte d'Ivoire	1	Côte d'Ivoire	1
France	14	France	17
Germany	10	Germany	11
India	1	India	2
Iran	1	Italy	1
Iraq	1	Japan	1
Japan	12	Kenya	1
Kenya	1	Kuwait	1
Netherlands	1	Nigeria	1
Portugal	1	Portugal	2
South Africa	2	People's Republic of China	3
Saudi Arabia	4	South Africa	4
Sweden	1	Singapore	1
Trinidad &Tobago	1	Spain	1
United Arab Emirates	1	Sweden	1
United Kingdom	6	United Arab Emirates	2
United States	26	United Kingdom	3
USSR	1	United States	21

There is no good metric to quantify the behavior we are trying to study. Consequently, we have chosen a simple procedure to make our first pass at the data. In particular, we regressed each series of trade shares on a constant and a time trend. As the plots in Figures 6.2–6.5 indicate, simple linear models should approximate well the behavior of many share patterns, and we found that to be the case throughout. Our purpose in this exercise was to determine how often we would find that the shares were trendless. Our first thought in approaching this question was to see how often we could reject the null hypothesis that the coefficient on the time trend was zero. We also considered testing the joint hypothesis that all of the time trend coefficients were zero. In examining the output from our statistical work, however, it became clear that this would not work well in our context. In particular, if shares were virtually constant, the *t*-statistic on the estimated trend would approach infinity, even as the estimated slope is near zero. Indeed, we found numerous examples of trend

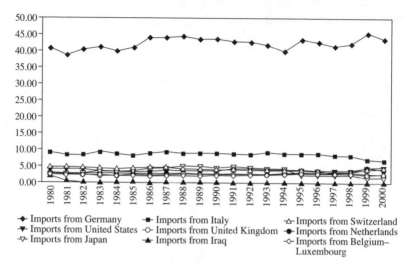

Figure 6.2   Austria: major import suppliers

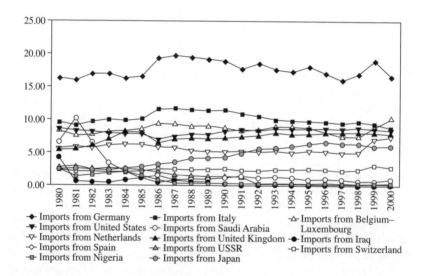

Figure 6.3   France: major import suppliers

coefficient estimates with values almost identically zero, but with *t*-statistics much larger than two.[7] This same problem also confounded our ability to test the joint hypothesis that all of the slopes for a given country were zero.[8] Given these problems with standard hypothesis test procedures, the remainder of this section is devoted to distributions of point estimates.

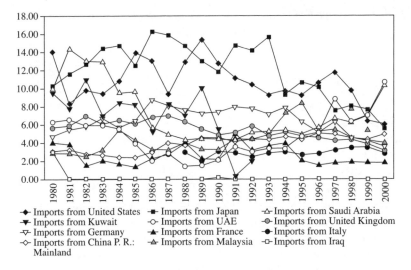

Figure 6.4   Pakistan: major import suppliers

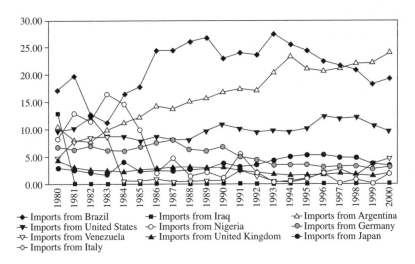

Figure 6.5   Uruguay: major import suppliers

Table 6.5 provides detail on the point estimates from the regression exercise. In order to better interpret the results, we multiplied each of the estimates by 21 in order to determine the estimated change over the sample period in each of the trade shares. As the table shows, the predicted change did not exceed 2 percent in absolute value for almost half (449 of 927) of the possible

Table 6.5   Empirical results: distribution of estimated share growth
              (coefficients on time trend × 21)

	No.	% of total
5% or more	60	6.5
Between 2% and 5%	82	8.9
Between 0 and 2%	162	17.5
Between –2% and 0%	288	31.1
Between –2% and –5%	191	20.6
–5% or less	143	15.4

trade patterns. As the table also shows, falls in shares were estimated for well over half the cases. The median projected decline in market share over the sample period was 1.69 percent. In more than 15 percent of the cases, estimates of trade share falls exceeded 5 percent over the sample period. Many, if not all, of the largest declines were associated with trade shares for petroleum-exporting countries. This pattern is easy to explain and points to a problem with the fact that data availability required us to begin our analysis in 1980. That year coincided with the second world oil shock. In subsequent years, oil prices fell dramatically, leading to significant falls in market shares. These declines are apparent in Figures 6.2–6.5.

As was the case with primary trade partners, a small number of high-income countries held market shares of at least 2 percent for virtually all countries in the sample over the sample period. And, as with the case of all shares, the shares of these countries were relatively stable. These points are illustrated by the information in Table 6.6.

Table 6.6   Market share trend patterns for selected countries

	No.	Median	Mean
United States	88	–0.81381	–0.26414
Germany	84	–1.45281	–1.48571
United Kingdom	83	–1.59655	–2.74939
Japan	80	–2.53008	–3.32239
France	64	–0.64854	–2.3053
Italy	56	–0.08782	0.71017
Netherlands	54	–0.3731	–0.30761
Belgium–Luxembourg	34	0.318948	0.241521
Saudi Arabia	31	–5.67525	–6.95684

As the table shows, the United States held at least 2 percent of the market in 88 of 92 possible cases. Both the median and the mean of the projected market share change over the sample period were between zero and a fall of 1 percent. Germany, the United Kingdom and Japan also held at least 2 percent of the markets in 80 countries or more. Only the mean and median projected change in market shares for Japan exceeded 2 percent in absolute value. France, Italy and the Netherlands all held significant market shares in more than half of the sample countries, and the average expected market share changes for all were less than 1 per cent. Only Saudi Arabia, which held at least 2 percent of the market in 30 countries in 1980 had large (greater than 5 percent) average projected changes in market share. As noted already, this pattern held true for virtually all oil exporters in virtually all countries.

The major point of this section is that trade shares have remained quite stable for most countries over the past two decades, despite significant changes in the economic and political structure of the world trading relationships. There is clearly more work to be done in this analysis and we are beginning these efforts. Our first goal is to derive a metric that allows us to compute and then try to explain how much and why trade patterns have changed on a country-by-country basis. Our plan is to try to develop a test to see if the pattern of annual trade shares we observe for a country look to be a sample drawing from a common distribution. It is possible to develop a statistic that represents the average distance between each of the draws and to use this statistic in subsequent tests of possible models that predict relative stability in trade patterns. Since we are not ready at this time to present these tests, in what follows we discuss several conjectures from trade theory that might explain the stability that we have found in the data.

3. THEORY AND SPECULATION

Three themes seem to recur in our data. First, country size seems to matter and, in particular, trade shares of most nations with the United States and most other high-income countries are especially stable. Second, distance matters. Countries have very stable trade shares with their immediate neighbors. Finally, historical ties seem to matter in the sense that trade shares between former colonies and the mother country are quite stable.

A curiosity of the data is that while trade shares remain fairly stable, the composition of trade changes quite a bit. For example, in 1979, office machines, computers, parts (SITC 751, 753, 759) constituted only 1.4 percent of the share of trade and was ranked 16th by category. In 1999, this group was 6 percent of trade and ranked number one as the most traded commodity group.[9] Yet nations do not appear to be acquiring market share at the expense of other nations. This change in the pattern of trade seems to generalize. That is, the commodity composition of trade changes, but the trade shares between countries do not. This raises some questions that we address here, but we offer only speculation as answers.

Specifically, there seems to be a sort of 'hysteresis' in the pattern of trade. The world changes a lot in terms of prices, technology and so on, but trading partners and trade shares remain constant. This 'evidence' speaks in favor of some trade theories as being more or less important.

3.1 Standard Static Trade Theories

The constancy of bilateral trade shares over time can inform us about the robustness of various trade theories. For example, the standard, variable-proportions – Heckscher–Ohlin (HO) – model predicts that, if tastes are identical and homothetic, then differential (balanced) growth rates among trading partners will lead to changing trade shares. Yet, while growth rates do vary quite a lot between countries (recall Table 6.2), trade shares are relatively constant. While this hardly constitutes a test of the HO model, it is suggestive that one of the model's predictions is questionable. Since technological progress is analytically similar to growth, differential rates of technical progress across countries should similarly lead to changing bilateral trade shares.

Such results, we think, would apply equally to a specific factors model and, in light of the Jones–McKenzie Theorem, to a Ricardian model with many goods and countries. (Specifically, in the multi-good Ricardian model, the conditions for country j to specialize in good j – 'j–j-specialization' depend upon a comparison of a multiplicative string of one set of labor–output coefficients with another such string. But, differential technical progress – some lower labor–output coefficients for some countries – will change the pattern of specialization and so necessarily the share patterns in trade.) Yet economic change in the world does not appear to lead to changes in bilateral trade shares.

Finally, the wave of new preferential trade agreements (PTAs) and new accessions to old PTAs since 1979 should entail trade creation and trade diversion. Thus bilateral trade shares may be affected. On one hand, PTAs are often geographically based. This could strengthen the stability of trade partner relationships. On the other hand, bilateral preferences, if significant, could alter long-standing trade patterns. Here we find mixed experience regarding trade shares in our data. For instance, Mexico's share of North American trade has grown rapidly since the formation of NAFTA, but trade shares of EU countries in Austria have remained virtually constant since Austria's entry into the EU in 1995.

3.2 Geography and Trade

One recently advanced view of the world that is consistent with our findings is the 'economic geography' paradigm, made most familiar to trade economists through Paul Krugman's Gaston Eyskens lectures at the Catholic University of Leuven in Belgium. That paradigm renders country size, proximity and cultural ties – which do not change so rapidly – crucial to the bilateral shares of trade, but not to the commodity composition of bilateral trade. This seems consistent with our findings.

First, the economic geography model focuses on transport networks and scale economies. Firms and industries cluster geographically, and this creates persistent production nodes even as the product lines shift. Transport networks get put into place and, once the costs are sunk, can determine which countries trade with which other countries. For example, if there are three countries in the world – A, B and C – and there are railroads between A and B and B and C, but not A and C, then trade shares might remain fairly constant to the extent that transport costs are important.

This implication of economic geography models is consistent with our finding that distance is an important determinant of why trade shares remain constant between trading partners of the world. Also, if 'distance' is taken to include cultural distance, our findings corroborate a stability in the trade between former colonies and their colonial mother countries.

Finally, the trade shares of large countries, including France, Germany, Japan, the United Kingdom and the United States, seem to remain particularly constant. This is consistent with Krugman (1991). Large countries (regions) exploit scale economies and transport systems in order to maintain an industrial base even as the products themselves change. Thus, for example, the industrial belt of the Midwest in the United States continued to prosper even as the product line changed over time. Consequently, the region was the stable exporter of industrial products for a very long time, even though the products themselves were changing. This is roughly consistent with our findings of constant bilateral trade flows.

4. CONCLUSIONS

The world would appear to have changed in most dimensions quite significantly since 1979. Certainly the economic and political landscapes are wildly different. Yet, when we measure which countries trade with which other countries, the world looks remarkably constant. We cannot find much change in bilateral trade shares among countries. This finding is all the more striking because the commodity composition of trade does appear to change.

While our approach has been simply to report the stability of bilateral trade, we also conjecture that the data support the 'economic geography' paradigm wherein distance, history and country size are important determinants of international trade patterns.

Clearly, the findings in this study are very preliminary and much more work needs to be done. We have already described a possible strategy for testing more rigorously our findings of trade pattern stability, and we plan to pursue that line of research in the near future. In addition, we also plan to study the trade patterns of subsamples of our countries using longer samples of bilateral trade shares.

NOTES

1. Figures on the number of regional trade agreements created over this period are taken from the WTO web page, *Regionalism: Facts and Figures*, http://www.wto.org/english/tratop_e/region_e/regfac_e.htm.
2. Data prior to 1980 are not available on CD–ROM.
3. Note that, in cases such as Mexico, where the United States is the primary trade partner, we classified it as a neighbor rather than the nearest high-income country.
4. More complete detail on the characteristics of dominant trade partners for the countries in our sample can be found in the Appendix, Table 6A.2.
5. As will be discussed below, an exception is Japan, which has lost market share in a number of markets, especially in the 1990s.
6. Wall (2002) examines trade share behavior for Japanese exports to various markets between 1986 and 1997.
7. Only 272 of 926 estimated slope coefficients had t-values small enough to not reject the null that the slope equaled zero.
8. We rejected the null that all slopes equaled zero in every case.
9. See Table 1.3 in Steven Husted and Michael Melvin, *International Economics*, 6th edn, Boston, MA: Addison Wesley Longman, 2003.

REFERENCES

Krugman, Paul (1991), *Geography and Trade*, Cambridge, MA: MIT Press.
Wall, Howard J. (2002), 'Has Japan Been Left Out in the Cold by Regional Integration?' *Review*, Federal Reserve Bank of St Louis, September/October, 25–36.
Warner, Dennis and Mordechai E. Kreinin (1983), 'Determinants of International Trade Flows,' *The Review of Economics and Statistics*, **65** (1), 96–104.
Yarbrough, Beth and Robert M. Yarbrough (2000), *The World Economy: Trade and Finance*, 5th edn, Chicago: Harcourt College Publishers.

APPENDIX

Table 6A.1   Sample countries

Algeria	Ghana	Nigeria
Argentina	Greece	Norway
Australia	Guatemala	Oman
Austria	Guinea	Pakistan
Bangladesh	Guinea–Bissau	Papua New Guinea
Belize	Guyana	Paraguay
Benin	Haiti	Peru
Bolivia	Honduras	The Philippines
Brazil	Iceland	Portugal
Brunei	India	Qatar
Burkina Faso	Indonesia	Saudi Arabia
Burundi	Ireland	Senegal
Cameroon	Israel	Singapore
Canada	Italy	Spain
Central African Rep.	Jamaica	Sri Lanka
Chad	Japan	Suriname
Chile	Jordan	Sweden
Hong Kong	Kenya	Switzerland
People's Rep. of China	Korea	Tanzania
Colombia	Malawi	Thailand
Costa Rica	Malaysia	Tunisia
Côte d'Ivoire	Mali	Turkey
Cyprus	Mauritania	Uganda
Denmark	Mauritius	United Arab Emirates
Djibouti	Mexico	United Kingdom
Fiji	Morocco	United States
Finland	Mozambique	Uruguay
France	Nepal	Vanuatu
Gabon	The Netherlands	Venezuela
Gambia	New Zealand	Zambia
Germany	Niger	Zimbabwe

Table 6A.2 Characteristics of leading market share-holders

Country	1980			2000		
	Leader	Relation	%	Leader	Relation	%
Algeria	France	colony	23	France	colony	31
Argentina	US	nearest HIC	23	Brazil	neighbor	20
Australia	US		22	US		20
Austria	Germany	neighbor	41	Germany	neighbor	44
Bangladesh	US		14	India	neighbor	11
Belize	US	nearest HIC	36	US	nearest HIC	50
Benin	France	colony	23	PRC		28
Bolivia	US	nearest HIC	28	Brazil	neighbor	24
Brazil	US	nearest HIC	19	US	nearest HIC	23
Brunei	Japan		24	Singapore	neighbor	33
Burkina Faso	France	colony	39	France	colony	27
Burundi	Iran	oil	20	France	colony	13
Cameroon	France	colony	38	France	colony	33
Canada	US	neighbor	68	US	neighbor	64
Cent. Afr. Rep	France	colony	62	France	colony	31
Chad	Cameroon	neighbor	40	France	colony	33
Chile	US	nearest HIC	29	US	nearest HIC	20
China–HK	Japan	nearest HIC	23	PRC	neighbor	43
China–PRC	Japan	nearest HIC	27	Japan	nearest HIC	18
Colombia	US	nearest HIC	39	US	nearest HIC	34
Costa Rica	US	nearest HIC	34	US	nearest HIC	41

Country	Source 1	Type 1	No. 1	Source 2	Type 2	No. 2
Côte d'Ivoire	France	colony	40	France	colony	19
Cyprus	UK	colony	15	UK	colony	11
Denmark	Germany	neighbor	18	Germany	neighbor	21
Djibouti	France	colony	25	Saudi Arabia	oil	18
Fiji	Australia		31	Australia		49
Finland	Germany		13	Germany		15
France	Germany	neighbor	16	Germany	neighbor	17
Gabon	France	colony	58	France	colony	65
Gambia	UK	colony	27	PRC		21
Germany	Netherlands	neighbor	11	France	neighbor	10
Ghana	UK	colony	22	Nigeria	oil	19
Greece	Germany		14	Italy		13
Guatemala	US	nearest HIC	35	US	nearest HIC	34
Guinea	France	colony	29	France	colony	19
Guinea-Bissau	Portugal	colony	31	Portugal	colony	31
Guyana	Trinidad	neighbor	28	US	nearest HIC	33
Haiti	US	nearest HIC	53	US	nearest HIC	54
Honduras	US	nearest HIC	42	US	nearest HIC	57
Iceland	USSR		10	Germany		12
India	US		13	US		8
Indonesia	Japan		31	Japan		16
Ireland	UK	neighbor	51	UK	neighbor	33
Israel	US		16	US		18
Italy	Germany	neighbor	17	Germany	neighbor	18
Jamaica	US	nearest HIC	32	US	nearest HIC	45
Japan	US		17	US		19
Jordan	Saudi Arabia	oil	17	Germany		12

Table 6A.2 continued

Country	1980 Leader	1980 Relation	1980 %	2000 Leader	2000 Relation	2000 %
Kenya	Saudi Arabia	oil	18	UAE	oil	11
Korea	Japan	neighbor	27	Japan	neighbor	20
Malawi	S. Africa		37	S. Africa		43
Malaysia	Japan		23	Japan		21
Mali	Côte d'Ivoire	neighbor	29	Côte d'Ivoire	neighbor	17
Mauritania	France	colony	34	France	colony	26
Mauritius	S. Africa	oil	13	S. Africa		15
Mexico	US	neighbor	62	US	neighbor	73
Morocco	France	colony	25	France	colony	25
Mozambique	France	oil	13	S. Africa	neighbor	37
Nepal	India	neighbor	41	India	neighbor	33
Netherlands	Germany	neighbor	22	Germany	neighbor	16
New Zealand	Australia	neighbor	18	Australia	neighbor	22
Niger	France	colony	38	France	colony	20
Nigeria	UK	colony	20	UK	colony	10
Norway	Sweden	neighbor	17	Sweden	neighbor	16
Oman	Japan		20	UAE	neighbor	32
Pakistan	US		14	Kuwait	oil	12
Papua–NG	Australia	neighbor	41	Australia	neighbor	50
Paraguay	Brazil	neighbor	27	Brazil	neighbor	30
Peru	US	nearest HIC	30	US	nearest HIC	30

Philippines	US	colony	24	Japan	nearest HIC	19
Portugal	Germany		12	Spain	neighbor	25
Qatar	Japan		18	Japan		11
Saudi Arabia	US		20	US		21
Senegal	France	colony	34	France	colony	27
Singapore	Japan		18	Japan		18
Spain	US		13	France	neighbor	18
Sri Lanka	Japan		13	Japan		10
Suriname	US	nearest HIC	32	US	nearest HIC	31
Sweden	Germany		18	Germany		17
Switzerland	Germany	neighbor	28	Germany	neighbor	29
Tanzania	UK	colony	16	Japan		9
Thailand	Japan		21	Japan		24
Tunisia	France	colony	25	France	colony	27
Turkey	Iraq	oil	15	Germany		14
UAE	Japan		17	Japan		7
Uganda	Kenya	neighbor	29	Kenya	neighbor	43
UK	US		12	US		13
Uruguay	Brazil	neighbor	17	Argentina	neighbor	24
US	Canada	neighbor	16	Canada	neighbor	19
Vanuatu	Australia	neighbor	25	Australia	neighbor	26
Venezuela	US	nearest HIC	48	US	nearest HIC	36
Zambia	Saudi Arabia	oil	19	S. Africa		57
Zimbabwe	S. Africa	neighbor	25	S. Africa	neighbor	42
Average Share			27			26

Notes: nearest HIC = geographically nearest high-income country; oil = oil exporter; colony = importing country is a former colony of exporter.

7. The role of intra-industry trade in the service sector

Robert C. Shelburne* and Jorge G. Gonzalez

1. INTRODUCTION

International trade in services has become a very important component of overall international trade. Over the past two decades trade in services has grown faster than trade in goods. In 2001 the world traded $1.5 trillion worth of services; this represented over 19 percent of total international trade. Furthermore, the trade of most developed economies tends to be even more concentrated in the service sector. For instance, service exports represented 27 percent of total US exports during 2001.[1] These statistics are likely to underestimate the true volume of services trade, since much of this type of trade is done through subsidiaries and these transactions are often not included in the balance of payments statistics from which the services trade data are usually derived. The growing importance of services in international trade should not come as a big surprise since the service sector has been the largest and most dynamic sector for most developed and leading developing economies for many years. Consequently trade in services is likely to continue to grow at a rapid pace.

Over the previous decades, trade in the service sector has grown in spite of arbitrary and capricious unilateral barriers imposed by national governments. Given the importance of international trade in services, it is puzzling that it was not until the mid-1980s that trade in services was the subject of multilateral trade negotiations. Under pressure from developed nations, services were brought under WTO (GATT) rule during the Uruguay Round. The General Agreement on Trade in Services (GATS), which came into force in January of 1995, is the first legally enforceable multilateral agreement covering services. Although it represents a very preliminary attempt at trade liberalization, it is an important first step. As a result of the GATS, a new round of service negotiations started in 2000.

Despite this beginning, trade in services remains highly restricted. The 'typical' WTO member has undertaken commitments in only 25 of the 160 possible services subsectors; generally, the higher the level of per capita income, the more sectors committed (WTO, 2001). Under the GATS each country chooses which services to open to foreign suppliers. The country may limit the activities of foreign suppliers significantly with six types of limitations, which include such things as quantitative limits on the number of suppliers or the value of transactions, limitations on the share of foreign ownership, restrictions on the types of legal entities allowed, as well as local employment and technology transfer requirements. Thus, if a country wishes, the foreign service providers need not be entitled to national treatment. However, all commitments are available to all WTO members on a non-discriminatory basis, but even this requirement is subject to a ten-year phase-in. The GATS does not cover government-provided services or air transport and traffic services. According to estimates by Brown, Deardorff and Stern (2001), the complete elimination of services barriers would increase the world's GDP by 3 percent; this compares to only a 2 per cent gain from the complete elimination of remaining trade barriers. Services are often classified by their mode of supply. These include: (1) cross-border supply, (2) commercial presence, (3) consumption abroad, and (4) movement of natural persons. The different modes of supply may have different implications for domestic residents. In general, governments have been more open to liberalize the rules covering the establishment of subsidiaries by foreign service providers (i.e., commercial presence) in their territory since it is easier to regulate these operations as opposed to regulating service providers operating from another nation and it may also encourage inward foreign investment. Generally, only cross-border trade and consumption abroad (travel) are recorded in the services trade data. There are ongoing attempts to better integrate the Foreign Affiliates Trade in Services Statistics (FATS) (which cover commercial presence) with the trade in service statistics.

Data on trade in services are generally not provided in the same product or country detail as are data on trade in goods. To some degree this is due to a lag in the recognition of the importance of services trade; however, the most significant factor would appear to be that trade data are collected at the border while services data must be collected through surveys. In order to insure the cooperation of business firms, they are provided protection from disclosure of proprietary information. As a result, trade in services is covered by a 'right to privacy' that does not exist for goods trade. However, the negotiations involving services at the WTO has provided the impetus for improving the statistics on trade in services.

In spite of its growing importance, the international trade literature has neglected the study of the service sector. Most of the previous studies of services trade have focused on conceptual and methodological issues of measuring trade in services; Cuadrado-Roura and Rubalcaba-Bermejo (2002) and Hoekman and Stern (1991) provide good overviews of these issues. In addition, several papers have attempted to investigate the determinants of comparative advantage in services; these include Sapir and Lutz (1981), Sazanami and Urata (1990), and Urata and Kiyota (2000). These papers have generally concluded that a factor endowment explanation as provided by the Heckscher–Ohlin model can partially explain services trade with countries abundant in physical and human capital having a comparative advantage in services. Urata and Kiyota find that the factor intensities of service sectors differ. The communications, insurance, financial, computer and information, royalties and license fees, and government services are found to be both physical and human-capital intensive. Physical capital-intensive services include transportation and construction services while travel, other business services, and personal, cultural and recreational services are labor and human-capital intensive. [2]

Porter (1990) documents how unique domestic conditions often have shaped international competitiveness in niche service markets. Porter's analysis is important for the study of intra-industry service trade because he demonstrates that competitiveness in niche markets is not the result of some fundamental factor that would translate into competitiveness throughout a whole sector but is due to idiosyncratic factors particular to a small segment of a given industry. For example, in construction, the firms that dominate niche markets, such as earthquake-proof buildings, mountainous road projects, hydroelectric plants, subways and so on, were firms that had developed expertise from dealing with unusually severe conditions in their domestic markets.[3] When competitiveness is based upon this type of pattern, the resulting trade pattern is likely to be characterized by significant levels of intra-industry trade. Porter also describes how institutional factors affect competitiveness in the service sector. For example, the Italian government's Byzantine regulations gave Italian firms an advantage in many developing countries where a similar regulatory environment existed.

As nations begin to discuss services trade liberalization, fears about the dislocation and adjustment costs have begun to emerge. In the case of trade in goods, the literature has postulated that intra-industry trade (i.e., two-way trade within a single industry) tends to have relatively lower adjustment costs than inter-industry trade (i.e., trade across different industries). Therefore, one way to judge the likelihood of trade dislocation from trade liberalization in the service sector is to evaluate the importance of intra-industry trade in this sector. However, it must be recognized that trade in services may have significantly different employment implications than trade in goods. For example, a significant portion of trade in services is the result of foreign establishment and many of the employees hired are foreign nationals. Thus exports of these services, unlike exports of goods, are unlikely to produce many jobs for domestic residents. In addition to having lower adjustment costs, when intra-industry trade is present, calls for trade liberalization within an industry come from exporters in both nations. This added impetus normally makes trade liberalization easier to achieve. Finally, intra-industry trade will also improve the X-efficiency and allocative efficiency of the economy.

The organization of the rest of the chapter is as follows. The next section discusses the data available for services trade, and more specifically the OECD data set used in the first part of the chapter. This data set contains overall service trade data for 27 members of the OECD. Also, the measures of intra-industry trade (IIT) employed in the empirical analysis are explained along with a discussion of a number of methodological issues. The third section of the chapter presents results of an empirical analysis of bilateral service trade between the US and 40 other nations or regions. Finally, in the last section some conclusions are presented and avenues for future research are explored.

2.   OECD SERVICES DATA AND THE MEASUREMENT OF IIT

For the calculation of IIT indexes for the service sector, two data sets are used.[4] These are the OECD Statistics on International Trade in Services[5] and the US bilateral service data compiled by the Bureau of Economic Analysis.[6] Unfortunately these two sources of data are not comparable in a transparent manner. Not only do their totals differ by about 10 percent, but they do not present the data in a similar hierarchical structure and it is not clear how data in one category are related to data in another similar category in the other data set. This lack of a consistent hierarchical structure turns out to be a major problem in the empirical estimation of IIT indices. Unlike the trade statistics, where there are uniform standards and classification systems in reporting trade data, the services data are reported using several different structures and methodologies.

There has been some recent progress in increasing and standardizing the data on trade in services. The United Nations Statistical Division, along with five other organizations, has produced a *Manual on Statistics of International Trade in Services*.[7] Despite the progress in producing an internationally comparable data set on services trade represented by the recommendations in the *Manual*, there remains disagreement concerning a number of issues such as the taxonomy to be used in a number of service sectors.

The basic structure of the OECD data is presented in Figure 7.1.[8] The basic data are aggregated into 12 large groupings (the top row of Figure 7.1) and then these are broken down into various subgroups. At the most disaggregated level, there are 36 groups; these 36 disaggregated groups are those boxes in

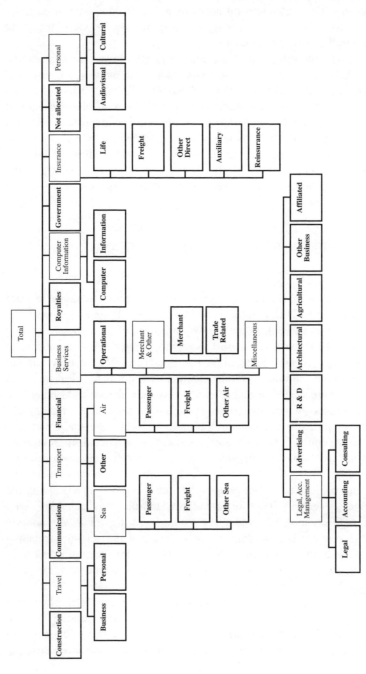

Note: Boxes in heavy type indicate 36 disaggregated groups.

Figure 7.1   OECD services groupings

Figure 7.1 whose borders are in heavy type. Note that some of the aggregated groups, especially business services, are broken down into a large number of subgroups while half (six) of the aggregated sectors are not broken down into any further level of detail. Given this uneven structure, it is not clear what level of detail should be used to calculate the IIT indexes. Two calculations are made, one using the most aggregated level of 12 sectors and the other using the most disaggregated level of 36 sectors.

The OECD data set provided data for 27 members of the OECD (and an EU aggregate). The data apply to overall trade (trade with all partners). Although data were available for some countries starting as early as 1970, this chapter only uses yearly data for 1992 through 1998. During this period, data were available for most countries for 11 of the 12 aggregated groups; the aggregated group 'Not Allocated' appears to be for data that could not be allocated to one of the other 11 groups, probably due simply to lack of specific information. This group does not appear to be a grouping for additional services not covered by the other groups; in other words, services data that are precisely recorded would fall into one of the 11 basic groups. This aggregated level of groupings has the desirable feature that the data are generally available for all countries for all years at this level of detail (apart from a few exceptions). Thus IIT indexes using this grouping are generally comparable from year to year and from country to country.

There was one additional anomaly in the services data that had to be addressed before IIT indexes could be calculated. As noted above, unlike merchandise trade data, which are collected at the border, services data are generally derived from surveys and financial records. The services data have generally been derived from balance of payments statistics, which attempt to measure the claims on, and supply of, foreign exchange; this objective does not always coincide with the purpose of this study, which is to measure trade intensity and/or competitiveness in a sector. In the insurance sector, the payment of claims is recorded as a negative number, as are sales of reinsurance. Therefore it is possible to have negative numbers in either the export (credit) or import (debit) columns. The traditional Grubel–Lloyd (1971, 1975) IIT index,[9] which has become standard in the empirical IIT literature, was designed to deal with trade flows which are always positive.[10] Therefore this index is unable to deal with negative numbers. There are several possible ways of dealing with this, such as making a negative number in a credit simply a positive number in the debit column, and vice versa. However, after careful consideration of the objective of our analysis, it was concluded that a modified index that took the absolute value of the reported data was better able to capture the 'flow of services' which we wanted our index to measure. Thus we propose to use the following generalized IIT index:

$$IIT_j = 1 - \frac{\sum_i | X_{ij} - M_{ij} |}{\sum_i | X_{ij} | + | M_{ij} |}, \tag{7.1}$$

where IIT_j is the IIT index for country j and X_{ij} are exports in sector i from country j, and M_{ij} are imports in sector i by country j. This index also has the desirable property that when the data are all 'well behaved' (i.e., positive), the calculated index is similar to the established Grubel–Lloyd index. Thus the Grubel–Lloyd index, which can only be used when all the data are positive, becomes a special case of this more general index being proposed here. This proposed index also has the desirable property that it is similar in form to the Shelburne (1993) marginal intra-industry index (MIIT), which deals with trade changes through time (as opposed to trade levels at a given point in time); the MIIT index is needed to handle negative numbers since trade changes are often negative (this index is discussed in more detail later in this section). Thus this MIIT index also becomes a special case of the more general index being proposed here except that the changes in trade are substituted for the levels of trade. It should be noted that instances of a reported negative number in an insurance category are relatively rare, so the values of the indexes reported here would not be significantly different if this problem were dealt with in a different manner.

The calculated IIT indexes for the 27 OECD countries (plus an EU aggregate) for the years 1992–98 using the aggregated sectors (top row of Figure 7.1) are presented in Table 7.1.[11] The average level of IIT is about 0.75, a figure that remains essentially unchanged throughout the 1992–98 period. Although an IIT level of 0.75 is generally higher than that reported for goods trade, the number of divisions used for these services IIT indexes is much smaller than the number generally used for trade in goods. In fact, if an IIT index is calculated for total US merchandise trade using the nine sectors of the 1-digit SITC, the index is equal to 0.76; therefore the level of IIT in services appears to be comparable to the level in commodity trade for a similar level of aggregation. The ninth column entitled '% used in 1998' provides information about the percentage of a country's reported total trade in services used in making these calculations. For most countries, this percentage is equal to or close to 100 percent. The 95 percent figure for Greece means that the sum of the trade reported in the aggregated group of 12 summed to only 95 percent of their reported total trade in services.

One of the major factors that have been shown empirically to explain the cross-country variation in IIT for goods has been the level of economic development. Theoretically it has been argued that at low levels of income, consumers demand primarily standardized products while at high levels of

Table 7.1 IIT Indexes for (OECD aggregated) services, 1992–98

Country	IIT 1992	IIT 1993	IIT 1994	IIT 1995	IIT 1996	IIT 1997	IIT 1998	% in 1998	MIT 1992–98
Australia	0.823	0.815	0.798	0.793	0.810	0.833	0.838	100.0	0.628
Austria	0.756	0.809	0.815	0.897	0.905	0.890	0.871	100.0	0.706
Belgium–Lux.	0.859	0.863	0.865	0.841	0.834	0.833	0.851	100.0	0.660
Canada	0.793	0.786	0.825	0.851	0.882	0.880	0.902	100.0	0.685
Czech Rep.	–	0.731	0.818	0.778	0.844	0.824	0.739	100.0	0.760
EU	0.947	0.955	0.959	0.958	0.946	0.943	0.948	99.9	0.836
Finland	0.774	0.787	0.854	0.855	0.862	0.858	0.858	100.0	0.600
France	0.838	0.846	0.854	0.852	0.860	0.852	0.854	100.0	0.687
Germany	0.702	0.704	0.695	0.719	0.733	0.748	0.748	99.9	0.678
Greece	0.456	0.401	0.396	0.426	0.424	0.404	0.485	94.9	0.311
Hungary	0.835	0.877	0.862	0.790	0.708	0.663	0.650	100.0	0.374
Iceland	0.707	0.728	0.727	0.774	0.759	0.754	0.755	99.9	0.776
Ireland	0.654	0.622	0.632	0.578	0.560	0.540	0.484	99.2	0.352
Italy	0.835	0.810	0.762	0.727	0.763	0.786	0.788	100.0	0.528
Japan	0.644	0.665	0.669	0.657	0.673	0.695	0.691	100.0	0.572
Korea	0.829	0.870	0.882	0.888	0.865	0.879	0.823	100.0	0.627
Mexico	0.797	0.739	0.723	0.642	0.631	0.586	0.620	99.5	0.055
Netherlands	0.879	0.877	0.872	0.836	0.827	0.836	0.840	99.9	0.679
New Zealand	0.807	0.816	0.813	0.744	0.751	0.763	0.797	100.0	0.708
Norway	0.745	0.732	0.756	0.733	0.758	0.745	0.717	100.0	0.506
Poland	0.918	0.862	0.636	0.746	0.696	0.714	0.638	100.0	0.479
Portugal	0.573	0.730	0.667	0.722	0.723	0.711	0.711	100.0	0.684
Spain	0.595	0.613	0.599	0.591	0.603	0.594	0.598	100.0	0.502
Sweden	0.846	0.879	0.883	0.904	0.881	0.866	0.828	100.0	0.845
Switzerland	0.739	0.737	0.759	0.770	0.803	0.761	0.663	100.0	0.565
Turkey	0.500	0.483	0.453	0.470	0.529	0.540	0.577	100.0	0.538
UK	0.817	0.833	0.811	0.824	0.792	0.749	0.731	100.0	0.648
USA	0.775	0.763	0.760	0.745	0.744	0.749	0.757	100.0	0.675

income, consumers demand more differentiated products. It may also be the case that the products produced by richer nations are more capital and techno-logically intensive and that these products are, by their nature, more likely to be differentiated. In order to see if this same pattern existed for trade in services, a simple regression is performed with the 1998 IIT index in services (column eight in Table 7.1) as the dependent variable and the log of per capita income (at purchasing power parities) as the independent variable.[12] The log of per capita income is found to be significantly positive at the 95 percent level (*t*-statistic of 2.68); the R^2 of this regression is 22 percent, suggesting that this is only one of several factors likely to determine the level of services IIT.[13] A similar but alternative variable that can proxy the development of a sophisti-cated services sector is the percentage share of services employment in total employment. This variable is found to be positive and significant at almost the 99 percent level (*t*-statistic of 2.69) with an R^2 of 0.24.

Hamilton and Kniest (1991), among others, have concluded that for any issues focusing on changing trading patterns, such as the possible role of changing trading patterns in creating adjustment problems for employment, these trade changes should be analyzed using the MIIT instead of focusing solely on how the IIT index changes through time. For the analysis of MIIT in this chapter, the Shelburne (1993) index[14] is used, where

$$MIIT_j = 1 - \frac{\sum_i |\Delta X_{ij} - \Delta M_{ij}|}{\sum_i |\Delta X_{ij}| + |\Delta M_{ij}|}. \tag{7.2}$$

$MIIT_j$ is the marginal intra-industry index for country j, and ΔX_{ij} is the change in exports in sector i between two points in time, and ΔM_{ij} is the change in imports in sector i between the same two points in time. As stated, this MIIT index is a special case of the more generalized index proposed earlier in this chapter, where each trade flow is replaced by the change in the trade flow. The MIIT indexes for trade changes between 1992 and 1998 are presented in the final column of Table 7.1 (the MIIT for the Czech Republic used 1993–98). Unlike the case for trade in goods, there appears to be a strong (at the 99 per cent level) and positive correlation between the MIIT and both the IIT index in 1998 and the change in the IIT index between 1992 and 1998. The average MIIT is found to be 0.60.

Next, IIT indexes are calculated using the most disaggregated divisions possible – being the grouping of 36 divisions (those with the darkened borders in Figure 7.1). These IIT and MIIT indexes are presented in Table 7.2. As is obvious from looking at the '% used in 1998' column, missing values are a major problem in using these more disaggregated data. These indexes are only

Table 7.2 IIT indexes using the 36 OECD disaggregated groupings, 1992–98

Country	IIT 1992	IIT 1993	IIT 1994	IIT 1995	IIT 1996	IIT 1997	IIT 1998	% in 1998	MIIT 1992–98
Australia	0.722	0.685	0.670	0.666	0.660	0.689	0.729	68.9	0.545
Austria	0.765	0.801	0.751	0.891	0.878	0.842	0.845	46.3	0.868
Belgium–Lux.	0.860	0.849	0.857	0.822	0.823	0.823	0.839	75.0	0.711
Canada	0.758	0.742	0.764	0.786	0.792	0.798	0.818	100.0	0.556
Czech Rep.	–	0.792	0.808	0.773	0.817	0.787	0.755	52.8	0.708
EU	0.873	0.883	0.889	0.885	0.874	0.872	0.878	63.4	0.727
Finland	0.692	0.696	0.641	0.689	0.647	0.631	0.712	70.1	0.570
France	0.816	0.838	0.829	0.822	0.826	0.840	0.842	62.2	0.615
Germany	0.706	0.708	0.702	0.723	0.719	0.718	0.706	61.3	0.304
Greece	0.349	0.411	0.413	0.424	0.449	0.445	0.544	47.0	0.395
Hungary	0.768	0.890	0.785	0.576	0.472	0.476	0.519	70.7	0.317
Iceland	0.374	0.476	0.442	0.437	0.529	0.545	0.438	10.0	0.104
Ireland	0.539	0.514	0.501	0.429	0.418	0.402	0.361	76.9	0.236
Italy	0.779	0.808	0.796	0.775	0.797	0.812	0.822	61.7	0.757
Japan	0.484	0.511	0.524	0.523	0.595	0.620	0.643	70.0	0.572
Korea	0.421	0.534	0.555	0.533	0.524	0.481	0.467	13.2	0.370
Mexico	0.402	0.356	0.622	0.570	0.650	0.555	0.592	91.7	0.000
Netherlands	0.790	0.786	0.797	0.792	0.791	0.798	0.806	74.9	0.618
New Zealand	0.519	0.590	0.610	0.598	0.577	0.561	0.585	26.4	0.507
Norway	0.612	0.635	0.659	0.629	0.606	0.587	0.566	94.0	0.339
Poland	–	–	0.491	0.627	0.550	0.533	0.494	84.8	–
Portugal	0.493	0.669	0.662	0.662	0.628	0.626	0.614	47.6	0.543
Spain	0.713	0.736	0.737	0.775	0.731	0.736	0.757	50.8	0.660
Sweden	0.834	0.825	0.816	0.827	0.796	0.772	0.778	65.4	0.701
Switzerland	0.611	0.602	0.623	0.560	0.580	0.578	0.257	24.4	0.618
Turkey	0.388	0.353	0.377	0.417	0.413	0.516	0.582	61.6	0.576
UK	0.820	0.836	0.821	0.772	0.731	0.709	0.704	61.5	0.717
USA	0.715	0.690	0.675	0.675	0.680	0.683	0.690	68.1	0.551

presented as raw information, and are not comparable from year to year or country to country because different sectors are used in the calculations due to data availability. The exception is the IIT indexes for Canada, which have no unaccounted-for data. By going from 12 to 36 divisions, the Canadian IIT index (for 1998) falls from 0.90 to 0.82, while the marginal IIT index falls from 0.69 to 0.56.

Next the sectoral differences in IIT are examined. The average levels (for all the countries) of the IIT index in each of the 12 aggregated sectors are calculated and presented in Table 7.3.

The transportation, communications and other business services have the highest calculated levels of IIT, while royalties and license fees and insurance have the lowest IIT indexes. Although there may be some small trends for a number of these industries, these indexes remain rather similar from year to year.[15]

3.   US BILATERAL SERVICES DATA

The US Bureau of Economic Analysis (BEA) collects and publishes data on US trade in services, and unlike the OECD data, these data include a bilateral breakdown for each of the major trading nations.[16] In 1999, the US exported $254.7 billion and imported $174.8 billion in services. Data on US trade in services are organized by BEA using a different hierarchical structure than the OECD data. This structure is presented in Figure 7.2; the first level (top row) is composed of five divisions, three of which are further broken down into additional detail. At the lowest level of detail, there are 32 categories; these are shown in Figure 7.2 as the boxes with the dark borders.

Unlike in the case of the OECD data, insurance losses (which appear as negative numbers) are represented as a separate category. Since the objective of this chapter is to measure trade intensity – and not the payment and receipt of foreign exchange – the insurance losses category (which has negative numbers) is dropped from the final group of 32 sectors under the assumption that the insurance premiums category is fully able to capture the trade in insurance services (the remaining 31 categories are shown in Figure 7.2 as the boxes with the dark borders).[17] Therefore the adjustment to the Grubel–Lloyd index proposed in the previous section is not required for this data set. Each box in Figure 7.2 contains US exports and imports of services in that category. The IIT index for US services trade to 43 geographical areas (33 countries and 10 region groupings) using the 31 disaggregated divisions and the five aggregated divisions are presented in Table 7.4. Also, for each area, the percentages of trade, using the five service divisions (which are either a net export or a net import) are given. Thus, for any commodity division, net exports, net imports

Table 7.3 Average IIT by OECD aggregated service sector

SERVICE SECTOR	IIT 1992	IIT 1993	IIT 1994	IIT 1995	IIT 1996	IIT 1997	IIT 1998
Communications services	0.800	0.800	0.813	0.837	0.842	0.838	0.819
Computer and information services	0.647	0.657	0.652	0.687	0.652	0.643	0.629
Construction services	0.681	0.643	0.577	0.641	0.661	0.665	0.612
Financial services	0.724	0.744	0.784	0.771	0.781	0.778	0.743
Government services, n.i.e.	0.601	0.592	0.584	0.631	0.646	0.630	0.648
Insurance services	0.551	0.569	0.589	0.557	0.616	0.593	0.581
Other business services	0.792	0.782	0.794	0.807	0.826	0.806	0.780
Personal, cultural and recreation	0.544	0.571	0.629	0.598	0.622	0.626	0.649
Royalties and license fees	0.511	0.509	0.479	0.499	0.512	0.530	0.531
Services not allocated	0.786	0.751	0.783	0.675	0.693	0.776	0.547
Transportation	0.824	0.843	0.833	0.855	0.872	0.857	0.863
Travel	0.713	0.720	0.702	0.685	0.688	0.696	0.692

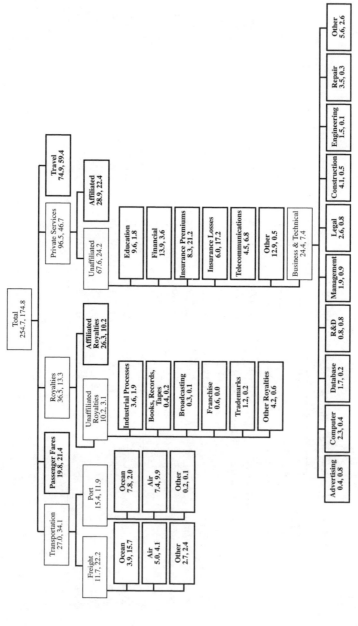

Total
254.7, 174.8

Transportation
27.0, 34.1

Royalties
36.5, 13.3

Private Services
96.5, 46.7

**Travel
74.9, 59.4**

**Passenger Fares
19.8, 21.4**

Port
15.4, 11.9

Freight
11.7, 22.2

Ocean
7.8, 2.0

Air
7.4, 9.9

Other
0.2, 0.1

Ocean
3.9, 15.7

Air
5.0, 4.1

Other
2.7, 2.4

Unaffiliated
Royalties
10.2, 3.1

**Affiliated
Royalties
26.3, 10.2**

Industrial Processes
3.6, 1.9

Books, Records,
Tapes
0.4, 0.2

Broadcasting
0.3, 0.1

Franchise
0.6, 0.0

Trademarks
1.2, 0.2

Other Royalties
4.2, 0.6

Unaffiliated
67.6, 24.2

**Affiliated
28.9, 22.4**

Education
9.6, 1.8

Financial
13.9, 3.6

Insurance Premiums
8.3, 21.2

Insurance Losses
6.0, 17.2

Telecommunications
4.5, 6.8

Other
12.9, 0.5

Business & Technical
24.4, 7.4

Advertising
0.4, 0.8

Computer
2.3, 0.4

Database
1.7, 0.2

R&D
0.8, 0.8

Management
1.9, 0.9

Legal
2.6, 0.8

Construction
4.1, 0.5

Engineering
1.5, 0.1

Repair
3.5, 0.3

Other
5.6, 2.6

Note: Boxes in heavy type indicate group of 31.

Figure 7.2   US service trade data by sectors (in millions: exports, imports)

122

Table 7.4   US bilateral IIT in services, 1999

Country	IIT 1999 Group of 31	IIT 1999 Group of 5	Net exports Group of 5	Net imports Group of 5
All countries	0.716	0.773	0.206	0.020
Argentina	0.394	0.411	0.589	0.000
Australia	0.740	0.790	0.196	0.014
Belgium–Luxembourg	0.701	0.730	0.240	0.031
Bermuda	0.247	0.376	0.001	0.622
Brazil	0.511	0.486	0.514	0.000
Canada	0.787	0.796	0.183	0.020
Chile	0.628	0.702	0.298	0.000
China	0.476	0.610	0.291	0.099
Eastern Europe	0.606	0.690	0.247	0.063
European Union	0.734	0.780	0.185	0.034
France	0.767	0.811	0.145	0.044
Germany	0.596	0.708	0.247	0.045
Hong Kong	0.611	0.761	0.083	0.156
India	0.569	0.795	0.183	0.022
Indonesia	0.296	0.367	0.633	0.000
International organizations	0.180	0.349	0.577	0.074
Israel	0.657	0.819	0.158	0.023
Italy	0.635	0.679	0.188	0.133
Japan	0.543	0.597	0.362	0.041
Korea	0.490	0.658	0.216	0.126
Malaysia	0.407	0.419	0.540	0.041
Mexico	0.593	0.684	0.206	0.110
Netherlands	0.589	0.572	0.392	0.036
New Zealand	0.596	0.703	0.162	0.135
Norway	0.444	0.593	0.326	0.081
Other Africa	0.641	0.645	0.329	0.027
Other Asia	0.265	0.610	0.132	0.258
Other Europe	0.559	0.587	0.255	0.158
Other Middle East	0.474	0.618	0.382	0.000
Other South Central America	0.623	0.670	0.330	0.000
Other West Hemisphere	0.687	0.696	0.232	0.072
Philippines	0.724	0.825	0.121	0.055
Saudi Arabia	0.570	0.569	0.392	0.040
Singapore	0.552	0.530	0.391	0.080
South Africa	0.530	0.531	0.323	0.146
Spain	0.655	0.666	0.304	0.030
Sweden	0.471	0.589	0.411	0.000
Switzerland	0.602	0.624	0.250	0.126
Taiwan	0.482	0.616	0.272	0.111
Thailand	0.509	0.575	0.260	0.165
United Kingdom	0.716	0.851	0.109	0.041
Venezuela	0.332	0.361	0.639	0.000

and the IIT (i.e., the last three columns) must sum to one. For example, when the value for net imports equals 0, as with Argentina, this means that the US exported more than it imported to Argentina in every division. The IIT index is lower when using the more disaggregated group of 31 service divisions. The group of 31 IIT index is presented but because there were numerous missing values in this data set, the indexes have limited comparability with different areas. For the group of five, however, all of the areas except Bermuda, International organizations, Mexico, and Other South Central America had all of their services trade allocated fully to these five divisions. Thus the group of five IIT indexes is comparable across areas and varies considerably from a low of 0.36 for Venezuela to a high of 0.85 for the United Kingdom. The US has a consistent surplus in services trade, not only through time but also across regions; the net import percentage was greater than net export percentage for only Bermuda, Hong Kong and Other Asia.

Given that the OECD data revealed that on a cross-section the level of IIT is positively related to the per capita income of a nation, a regression is performed to see if the US bilateral IIT is related to the per capita income of the other country. A sample of 29 countries is used after dropping the regional groups and a few countries for which there are no per capita income data (such as Bermuda).[18] The log of per capita income is significant at the 98 percent level (*t*-statistic of 2.57, R^2 of 0.20) in explaining the IIT bilateral index. In explaining the bilateral pattern of IIT in goods trade, both the level of per capita income and the similarity in per capita incomes of the two nations have been found to be explanatory variables. Since the US has the highest level of per capita income (PPP – purchasing power parity), these results are also consistent with the proposition that bilateral IIT in services is positively related to similarity in per capita income. Without bilateral data from additional countries, it is not possible to determine if the determining factor is the level of per capita income or similarity in per capita income.

4. CONCLUSIONS

The study of intra-industry trade in the service sector poses several difficulties compared to previous studies of IIT in goods. Data availability is a significant limitation, especially for comparisons across countries and through time. Even when data are available, countries use different hierarchical structures to classify their service trade, and this further complicates cross-country comparisons. The presence of negative numbers in the insurance categories of the balance of payments also presents a conceptual challenge for the computation and interpretations of traditional intra-industry trade indexes.

In spite of the limitations inherent in this type of analysis, the empirical analysis conducted here produced some interesting conclusions. There is no doubt that intra-industry trade is an important characteristic of international trade in services. It appears that nations tend to be both exporters and importers in most of their service sectors. The level of IIT in services is comparable to the level in merchandise trade at a similar level of aggregation. The preliminary analysis presented here indicates that GDP per capita and the relative size of the domestic service sector are significant determinants of a nation's level of intra-industry trade. These findings coincide with results obtained in the analysis of international trade in goods. This is likely to be the result of both consumers in richer countries demanding more differentiated services and richer nations producing more differentiated services. This result helps to explain the relative importance that richer nations have placed on trade liberalization for the service sector. Since they already have relatively high levels of service IIT, they are unlikely to face high adjustment costs as trade in services grows. The comparison of the IIT indexes with the marginal IIT indexes shows that they tend to be highly correlated. This means that the increases in services trade have been of the intra-industry variety for those nations that already have relatively high levels of intra-industry services trade. The study of the IIT indexes by disaggregated service sector shows that these indexes are the lowest in the 'royalties and license fees.' This suggests that technology gaps and legal barriers to entry also affect the level of services IIT.

NOTES

* The views are those of the authors and do not represent the official position of the US Department of Labor. A preliminary version of this paper was presented at the Annual Conference of the Internationla Trade and Finance Association in Washington, DC in May 2001. We thank Peter Gray for useful comments.
1. The source of these statistics is *International Trade Statistics 2002*, World Trade Organization, 2002 (Table I.8, p. 28).
2. After this chapter was completed, Lee and Lloyd (2002) published a paper that studies intra-industry trade in the service sector, but their data and methodology differ from the analysis in this study.
3. This explanation coincides with Linder's 1961 hypothesis that has been used to explain comparative advantage in merchandise trade.
4. The International Monetary Fund also provides data on services trade but those data were not used.
5. *OECD Statistics on International Trade in Services: 1985/1998* 2000 edition, CD-ROM, Paris: OECD.
6. 'US International Services,' *Survey of Current Business*, October 2000, pp. 119–61.
7. The other participating institutions are the European Commission, International Monetary Fund, Organization for Economic Co-operation and Development, United Nations Conference on Trade and Development, and the World Trade Organization.
8. With the publication of services trade through 1998 (OECD, 2000), the OECD has expanded slightly the sector breakdown for services trade; this is shown in Figure 7A.1 in the Appendix. However, since most nations did not provide trade for many of these new divisions, the analysis here used the structure in the 1999 edition.

9. The Grubel–Lloyd index for country j and i sectors is

$$IIT_j = 1 - \frac{\sum_i |X_{ij} - M_{ij}|}{\sum_i (X_{ij} + M_{ij})},$$

10. Vona (1991) presents strong arguments in favor of using the Grubel and Lloyd (1971, 1975) index instead of other indexes suggested in the literature.
11. The results presented here for 1992–96 differ slightly from the results in Gonzalez and Shelburne (2001) covering 1992–96 because the earlier results used the 1999 edition of the OECD statistics while the results here use the 2000 edition, which incorporated minor revisions.
12. Data for per capita income as well as the service sector's share of total employment are from Table 3.8 (p. 99) of the *OECD Employment Outlook*, June 2000.
13. Since this is a regression with only one independent variable, the correlation coefficient between the variables is the square root of the R^2, which in this case equals 0.40.
14. This index has also been referred to as the A-Index or the Brulhart A-Index; however, Shelburne (1993) was the first to propose and use this index.
15. Note that if a country was missing data in a sector for any year, that country was deleted for all years in that sector so as to make the yearly indexes comparable.
16. 'US International Services,' *Survey of Current Business*, October 2000, pp. 119–61.
17. The insurance losses category is dropped from the disaggregated grouping, but those numbers remain incorporated into the other private services aggregated category. In theory, insurance losses could have been subtracted out of this aggregated category, but we chose not to do so to keep the data used more consistent with published values.
18. Purchasing power parity per capita income data for 1999 were obtained from *World Development Report 2000/2001*, Table 1, pp. 274–5.

REFERENCES

Brown, Drusilla, Alan Deardorff and Robert Stern (2001), 'CGE Modeling and Analysis of Multilateral and Regional Negotiating Options,' University of Michigan School of Public Policy Research Seminar in International Economics, Discussion Paper No. 468.
Cuadrado-Roura, Juan R. and Luis Rubalcaba-Bermejo (2002), *Trading Services in the Global Economy*, Cheltenham, UK and Northampton, MA, USA: Edward Elgar.
Gonzalez, Jorge G. and Robert C. Shelburne (2001), 'Intra-Industry Trade in the Service Sector: Measurement and Implications,' in Khosrow Fatemi and Susan E.W. Nichols, *Europe and the New Global Economy*, Volume 2, Calexico, CA: International Trade and Finance Association, May, Chapter 27, pp. 479–500.
Grubel, H. and P. Lloyd (1971), 'The Empirical Measurement of Intra-Industry Trade,' *The Economic Record*, **47**, 494–517.
————— (1975), *Intra-Industry Trade: The Theory and Measurement of International Trade in Differentiated Products*, New York: John Wiley & Sons.
Hamilton, C. and P. Kniest (1991), 'Trade Liberalization, Structural Adjustment and Intra-industry Trade: A Note,' *Weltwirtschaftliches Archiv*, **127** (2), 356–67.
Hoekman, Bernard M. and Robert M. Stern (1991), 'Evolving Patterns of Trade and Investment in Services,' in Peter Hooper and J. David Richardson (eds), *International Economic Transactions: Issues in Measurement and Empirical Research*, Chicago: University of Chicago Press, pp. 237–84.

Lee, Hyun-Hoon and Peter J. Lloyd (2002), 'Intra-Industry Trade in Services,' in Peter J. Lloyd and Hyun-Hoon Lee (eds), *Frontiers of Research in Intra-Industry Trade*, New York: Palgrave Macmillan, pp. 159–79.

OECD (2000), *OECD Statistics on International Trade in Services: 1985/1998* (CD-ROM, 2000 edition), Paris: OECD.

Porter, Michael E. (1990), *The Competitive Advantage of Nations*, New York: Free Press.

Sapir, Andre and Ernst Lutz (1981), 'Trade in Services: Economic Determinants and Development Related Issues,' World Bank Staff Working Paper No. 480.

Sazanami, Yoko and Shujiro Urata (1990), *Service Trade: Theory, Present and Future Topics*, Tokyo: Toyokeizai Shinpo-sha.

Shelburne, Robert C. (1993), 'Changing Trade Patterns and the Intra-Industry Trade Index: A Note,' *Weltwirtschaftliches Archiv*, **129** (4), 829–33.

United Nations (2001), *Manual on Statistics of International Trade in Services*, United Nations Statistics Division.

Urata, Shujiro and Kozo Kiyota (2000), 'Service Trade in East Asia,' presented at the Eleventh Annual NBER East Asian Seminar on Economics, Seoul, Korea, 22–24 June.

Vona, S. (1991), 'On the Measurement of Intra-Industry Trade: Some Further Thoughts,' *Weltwirtschaftliches Archiv*, **127** (4), 678–700.

World Trade Organization (2001), *Market Access: Unfinished Business*, Geneva: WTO.

APPENDIX

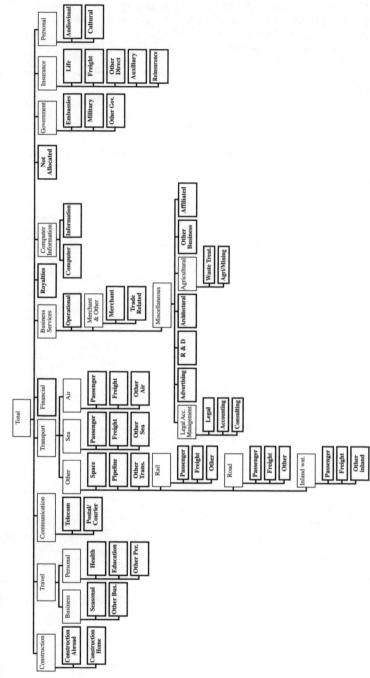

Figure 7A.1   OECD enhanced service sector categories

128

8. Global production networks and regional integration

Sven W. Arndt

1. INTRODUCTION

Cross-border production sharing is probably one of the more important new elements in trade relations among countries. It occurs with or without the overlay of preferential trade liberalization. An example of the latter is the production networks of Japanese firms in Asia.[1] An example of the former is production sharing between Canada, the US, and Mexico in the North American Free Trade Area (NAFTA).

Production sharing based on intra-product specialization has been shown to be welfare-enhancing under conditions of free trade, while its effects are ambiguous in the context of a most-favored-nation (MFN) tariff regime.[2] This chapter examines the implications of production sharing in the context of preferential trade liberalization. Of particular interest is the case in which a free-trade area which is clearly trade-diverting under traditional circumstances becomes trade-creating with joint production.

Trade in components has important implications for the interaction between exchange rates and the trade balance. Trade tends to become less sensitive to exchange-rate changes and trade-balance accounting needs to distinguish between the value of total trade and trade in value-added.

When production sharing takes place between advanced and emerging economies, foreign investment flows occur and capacity accumulation typically precedes the onset of joint production. This introduces cycles into the behavior of the real-exchange rate and the current account. The real rate appreciates and the current balance deteriorates during the investment phase of the process, followed by real depreciation and current account improvement.

The rest of the chapter is organized as follows. Section 2 lays out the basic argument in a standard general equilibrium framework, while Section 3 examines key welfare effects of joint production in a partial equilibrium framework. Section 4 studies the effect of production sharing on the exchange-rate sensitivity of trade and discusses alternative measurements of the balance of trade. Section 5 deals with the real-exchange-rate effects of an investment cycle associated with the implementation of joint production. Section 6 considers exchange-rate regime choice. Section 7 concludes.

2. TRADE LIBERALIZATION VERSUS ECONOMIC COOPERATION

While production sharing may take place across a broad range of trade regimes, it is not welfare-enhancing in every regime. It is unambiguously welfare-improving under conditions of free trade. It increases welfare by allowing specialization to be extended beyond finished products to the level of constituent production activities. In a standard Heckscher–Ohlin framework, variations in factor intensity across the components of a product imply potential gains from intra-product specialization, the magnitude of those gains depending on transport and coordination costs. Modern innovations in communication and transportation technologies have sharply reduced those costs and have thereby created new opportunities for profitable production sharing.[3]

In a tariff-ridden world, on the other hand, production sharing may reduce rather than improve welfare. A tariff on imports of the final product reduces the efficiency of resource allocation in the economy. While production sharing in that industry tends to mitigate the degree of comparative disadvantage of that industry and thus improves the efficiency of resource reallocation, it may not be able to fully offset the initial inefficiencies. Both the tariff and production sharing shift specialization toward the sector in which the country has comparative disadvantage, and the end result can be overall specialization in the wrong direction.

In Figure 8.1, points Q_0 and C_0 represent production and consumption in the presence of a tariff, t, on imports of finished product X. The size of the tariff is given by the wedge between the world price, P_w, and the tariff-inclusive domestic price, P_d. As shown in the literature cited above, production sharing in a sector has an effect similar to technical progress in that sector and shifts the production possibility curve out along the axis representing that sector. This shift is indicated by the move from point T to T' along the X axis.

When the country is small, these changes do not affect prices; the new production and consumption equilibria are located at points Q_1 and C_1, respectively, where the domestic price ratio is tangent to the new production possibility curve and an appropriate indifference curve. Output of the good subject to production sharing (X) thus increases at the expense of the second good (Y). Consumption falls to a lower indifference curve. The trade triangle shrinks.

It is apparent from the figure that welfare need not fall. Whether it rises or falls depends on the slope of the Rybczynski line (RR) relative to the slope of

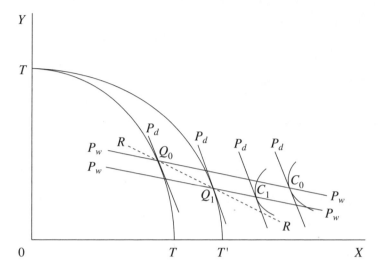

Figure 8.1   Production sharing and protectionism

the world price ratio.[4] When the line is steeper than the world price, welfare falls; it rises when the Rybczynski line is flatter than the world price.

When production sharing is introduced together with preferential tariff liberalization, welfare may rise or fall relative to the MFN level. While this is consistent with the well-known possibility that preferential trade arrangements may be net trade-creating or trade-diverting, production sharing mutes the trade-diverting tendencies of preferential trade liberalization.

In Figure 8.2, the analysis starts with an MFN tariff, domestic price P_d and production and consumption at points Q_0 and C_0, respectively. Introduction of a preferential trade agreement without production sharing generates intra-area price P_{pta} and moves production to Q_1 and consumption to C_1. Welfare declines, making this a trade-diverting free-trade area. Whether welfare declines or not depends on the intra-area price relative to the tariff-inclusive domestic price and the world price. As the intra-area price ratio becomes flatter and thus approaches the world price ratio, elements of trade creation expand, while the importance of trade-diverting elements declines. At a sufficiently flat price ratio, welfare improves relative to the MFN equilibrium.

This is a well-known feature of preferential trade liberalization. Suppose, however, that the partner countries engage in deeper economic integration, creating an economic area (EA) in which traditional preferential trade liberalization is combined with production sharing. The latter shifts the production possibility curve outward along the X axis from T to T', causing output to move to Q_2 and consumption to C_2. While this is still a trade-diverting

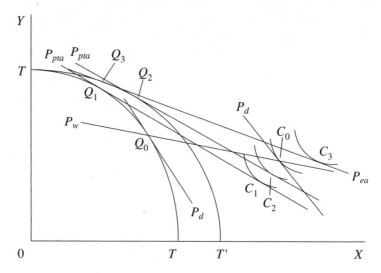

Figure 8.2   Production sharing and trade liberalization

arrangement, welfare falls by less than before. Thus deeper integration, which includes production sharing, mitigates the negative welfare effects of narrow preferential trade liberalization.[5]

Production sharing may, however, reduce the relative price of X and thus flatten the price ratio relative to its slope under the traditional PTA. By specializing in the components of product X in which each has comparative advantage, the two countries can improve productivity. We assume that this rise in efficiency is passed through to a lower intra-area price ratio, which is represented in Figure 8.2 by the flatter line P_{ea}. Production and consumption move to points Q_3 and C_3, respectively. This improvement in the country's terms of trade raises welfare.[6]

3.   TRADE CREATION AND DIVERSION UNDER PRODUCTION SHARING

Implementation of NAFTA led to what were at times substantial shifts in trade patterns away from non-members to Canada and especially Mexico. In the automobile sector, for example, Mexico's share rose significantly, as Figure 8.3 suggests.[7] It would be tempting to interpret these shifts as evidence of trade diversion and hence of a welfare decline. Such a conclusion may appear warranted by the reasonable assumption that Mexico is the high-cost producer of automobiles.

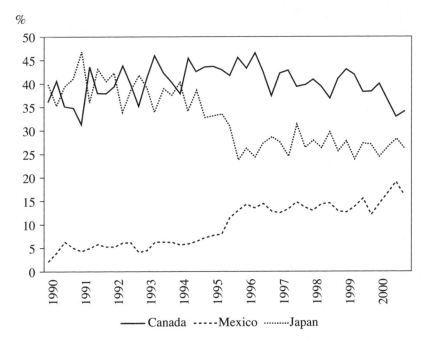

Figure 8.3   US motor vehicle import proportions

While trade diversion is certainly a possible outcome in the standard model of preferential trade liberalization, such an outcome is less likely in the context of the deeper integration associated with an economic area in which preferential trade liberalization is accompanied by production sharing. In that case, automobiles made entirely in Japan are replaced by imports from Mexico which contain parts and components made in the United States, with Mexico specializing in labor-intensive assembly. With both the US and Mexico specializing in activities in which they are respectively the low-cost producers, production sharing enables them to capture significant cost savings, so that trade diversion is now limited to activities in which Japan holds the edge.

Consider the situation depicted in Figure 8.4. In order to simplify the set-up, we assume linear supply curves for Japan, and for conventional production methods in Mexico and the United States. The term 'conventional' is used to denote that the good is produced in its entirety in each country, without resort to cross-border sourcing. We assume that Japan is the low-cost producer and Mexico the high-cost producer under these conventional conditions. Curves S_j and S_{mx} in Figure 8.4 represent supply conditions in Japan and Mexico, respectively.

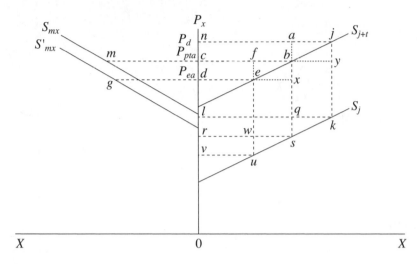

Figure 8.4   Trade creation and trade diversion

The starting situation is characterized by a specific non-discriminatory (MFN) tariff, *t*, imposed by the United States on all imports of product *X*. The full general equilibrium set-up was discussed above; here we focus on certain features of adjustment in a partial equilibrium context. The tariff-inclusive Japanese supply curve is given by curve S_{j+t}. The tariff-inclusive Mexican supply curve is not drawn, because the assumed magnitude of the tariff is such as to knock Mexico out of the US market. The rest of the picture, which would include US supply and demand curves, is not drawn in order to keep the figure simple and readable.

The initial price of *X* in the United States, P_d, is determined by the intersection between US demand (not drawn) and the sum of US and tariff-inclusive Japanese supply. At price P_d, Japanese exports to the US amount to *nj* in Figure 8.4. Tariff revenue collected by US authorities is given by rectangle *jkln*.

Implementation of a conventional free-trade area (that is, without production sharing) between the US and Mexico generates a lower price, such as P_{pta}, determined by the intersection between the aforementioned US demand curve and a new supply curve (not drawn) composed of $S_{us} + S_{mx} + S_{j+t}$. US imports rise to *mb*, with *mc* units coming from Mexico and *cb* units from Japan. Imports from Mexico partly replace imports from Japan, as well as US production. It is well known that the changes in price and output in conventional US production generate a transfer from producers to consumers and a net efficiency gain, which is a key element of trade creation.

The changes involving imports from Japan are the source of trade diversion. Trade diversion results from the inefficiencies associated with the switch of imports from Japan, which supplies the product along the low-cost supply curve, S_j, to Mexico's conventional producers, who supply the product along the relatively high-cost curve S_{mx}. As noted, before the PTA, US customs authorities collect tariff revenues equal to the area *njkl*. After implementation of the PTA, tariff revenues amount to *cbsr*. The lost revenue encompassed by rectangle *nabc* is compensated by the terms-of-trade gain given by *lqsr*. Area *nabc* is thus a pure gain in consumer surplus. The revenue loss contained in rectangle *bykq*, on the other hand, is a pure efficiency loss and thus represents the degree of trade diversion. The revenue loss represented by area *ajyb* is an internal transfer to consumer surplus. It is well known that the area of trade diversion may be larger or smaller than the sum of the areas representing trade creation, which makes the welfare effect of conventional preferential trade liberalization ambiguous.

Suppose that good X is made up of two components, x_1 and x_2, and that Japan possesses comparative advantage over the US not only in the final product, but in the production of each of the two components. Mexico is assumed to be at a competitive disadvantage *vis-à-vis* both countries in overall terms and in producing the first component, but to have comparative advantage with respect to the second component. In an endowment-based model, therefore, this information, together with Mexico's relative labor abundance, would imply that the second component is the labor-intensive component (of which automobile assembly is an example).

Introduction of production sharing represents a deepening of economic integration. We refer to this, more complex, type of integration as an economic area (EA). Under the stated assumptions, production sharing in such an area would have the US specializing in producing the first component and Mexico the second. Improvements in efficiency from production sharing may come in two forms. The ability to obtain certain components at reduced cost lowers production costs of the final product, which would be represented by downward shifts in both the US and Mexican supply curves. In this case, each country continues to produce the final product, but each unit of the final product contains imported components.

Cost reductions of the type discussed serve to lower the price of X relative to its level in the conventional PTA and hence generate improvements in welfare. In Figure 8.4, curve S'_{mx} represents such a cost-improving change in supply conditions in Mexico. This is a welfare gain, which helps offset elements of trade diversion.

The decline in price to P_{ea} reduces Japanese exports to the US to *de*, on which the US authorities collect *deuv* in tariff revenues. The revenue loss contained in area *cfed* is offset by the welfare gain associated with the terms-of-trade improvement of *rwuv*, so that *cfed* represents a net gain in consumer surplus, rather than an internal transfer from revenues to consumer surplus.

Area *fbxe*, on the other hand, is an internal transfer from revenues to consumer surplus and thus does not change overall welfare. Area *exsw* measures the extent of trade diversion in the move from the conventional preferential trade area to the economic area. The welfare gains appear to exceed the welfare losses, particularly since the lower price at which the US obtains imports from Mexico represents a pure consumer surplus gain.[8] The decline in the price of US-produced units breaks down into the usual internal transfer from producer to consumer surplus and a pure efficiency gain.

An alternative approach to exploiting the advantages of production sharing is to establish joint production facilities, which shifts some or all production of the product to new entities.[9] In that event, the supply curves representing conventional production remain unchanged, but there appears a new supply curve for joint production (not shown). This supply curve would be expected to lie below the two countries' respective conventional supply curves, but may lie above or below Japan's supply curve, depending on the degree of productivity improvement embodied in joint production. The extent of improvement depends on the initial gap between the US and Japan in x_1 production and on Mexico's edge in x_2 production.

The market now clears at the intersection (not shown) between the US demand curve and the sum of the joint supply curve, the conventional supply curves for the United States and Mexico, and the tariff-inclusive Japanese supply curve. It is clear that the market-clearing price, P_{ea}, will lie above relevant segments of the Japanese tariff-free supply curve, as shown, which implies that elements of trade diversion will persist even at this deeper degree of economic integration. As noted, imports from Japan decline to *de*, and this reduction causes the Japanese supply price to drop to the level indicated by *v*.

The welfare analysis then follows the discussion of production sharing which reduces costs relative to conventional production. There is an efficiency loss as low-cost Japanese imports are replaced by joint production, which supplies the product at the equilibrium price. That price lies above the tariff-free Japanese supply price, typically even if the joint production supply curve itself lies below that Japanese supply curve. The efficiency losses are given by the area *exsw*. It is important to note that, under conditions of increasing costs, conventional producers will lose market share, but they need not disappear altogether.[10]

4. THE EXCHANGE RATE AND THE TRADE BALANCE

Whether it occurs with or without preferential trade liberalization, production sharing affects the sensitivity of the trade balance to exchange-rate movements and requires additional care in interpreting changes in the trade balance.

In the standard model, currency depreciation reduces imports and raises exports, as the domestic-currency price of imports rises and the foreign-currency price of exports falls. The net effect on the trade balance is subject to a variety of influences and conditions, including the degree of pass-through. Production sharing changes the role of pass-through, to the extent that a country's exports enter into its imports and its imports become part of its exports. That is because the exchange-rate effect on the price of imports denominated in one currency is offset by the exchange-rate effect on the price of exports expressed in the other currency.

There are several layers of pass-through at work here, but suppose that the depreciation of the peso is passed through completely to an increase in the peso price of component imports into Mexico, which in turn is fully passed through to the peso price of the assembled vehicle. When the vehicle is priced in dollars, again assuming full pass-through, the dollar price will fall only to the extent that the vehicle contains Mexican value-added.

This is the important difference between trade involving goods of joint production and traditional trade in products made entirely at home. The smaller the share of Mexican value-added in a commodity imported into the United States, the smaller the effect of the peso depreciation on Mexican exports of the finished product and US exports of the components that go into it.

These considerations have implications for the behavior of the trade balance. Conventionally, a country's demand for imports is modeled as a function of home GDP, relative prices and the exchange rate. An increase in GDP and in relative inflation at home, and a nominal appreciation all raise the demand for imports and thus worsen the trade balance. A rise in foreign GDP, foreign inflation and domestic currency depreciation tend to improve the trade balance. Suppose, however, that Mexican imports from the US consist mainly of components for use in exports to the United States. Then, changes in Mexican GDP should have little influence on imports. Instead, it would be changes in US demand for imports from Mexico which would be expected to determine the rise and fall of Mexican imports. Thus US end-product imports become an important determinant of US parts exports and the importance of Mexican GDP declines.

Production sharing also affects the interpretation of changes in the trade balance, particularly with respect to the distinction between the value of trade flows across borders and the movement of value-added. When an imported automobile from Japan, valued at $20 000, is replaced by a vehicle of equal value from Mexico, which contains US-made components worth $15 000, combined with $5000 consisting of Mexican components and assembly, the value of US car imports does not change. Imports of foreign value-added, however, fall from $20 000 (on the assumption that the Japanese automobile was made entirely in Japan) to $5000. This suggests an 'improvement' in the US value-added trade balance of $15 000.[11]

Over time, as motor vehicle imports from Mexico expand, exports rise by $15 000 for every $20 000 increase in imports, for a worsening of the conventional trade balance of $5000 per vehicle. If the $15 000 of US-made components is netted out of the imported motor vehicle, on the other hand, the value-added trade balance 'improves' by $10 000 for each vehicle included in joint production.

5.   PRODUCTION SHARING AND FOREIGN DIRECT INVESTMENT

Implementation of cross-border production sharing is often preceded by flows of foreign direct investment (FDI) from the advanced to the emerging economy, accompanied by shipments of capital goods and other goods and services needed for the creation of productive capacity in the emerging economy. These initial flows affect the balance of payments and the exchange rate. In the FDI-receiving country, the investment boom increases demand for both tradables such as capital goods, and non-tradables such as construction services. There is upward pressure on prices in both sectors.

But while non-tradables prices may adjust freely to such pressures, the movement of tradables prices in a small, open economy is limited by competition in the world market. With given world prices of tradables, changes in tradables prices expressed in the domestic currency are brought about by fluctuations in the nominal exchange rate.

A rise in the demand for tradables, such as capital goods, is readily satisfied through increased imports, but the rise in the demand for non-tradables, such as construction services, can only be satisfied by moving productive resources into the non-tradables sector. If there are unutilized resources in the economy, they represent an important source. When full employment prevails, the additional resources must come from the tradables sector and this shift is brought about by an increase in the relative price of non-tradables. This represents a real appreciation of the domestic currency.

In Figure 8.5, the real exchange rate, expressed as the ratio of tradables to non-tradables prices, is measured on the vertical axis, and quantities of tradables and non-tradables are measured horizontally in the right and left panels, respectively. Starting at an initial equilibrium in which both markets are assumed to clear, an investment boom shifts out demand for both tradables (D_t) and non-tradables (D_n). As noted, the rise in tradables demand can be met at the initial exchange rate by an increase in imports, which is financed by the inflow of FDI. The rise in non-tradables demand, however, creates an excess

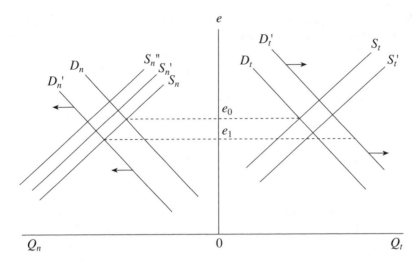

Figure 8.5   Real exchange rate patterns

demand at the initial exchange rate which can be resolved only by appreciation of the currency in real terms from e_0 to e_1. This change allows domestic
production of non-tradables to increase. The real appreciation contributes to
the deterioration of the trade balance.

Thus an investment boom created by production sharing causes the capital-
receiving country's currency to appreciate in real terms, while its current
account deteriorates. As new productive capacity comes on stream, the real-
exchange rate and the current account adjust once more. An increase in non-
tradables capacity shifts that sector's supply curve out, thereby causing
non-tradables prices to fall and the currency to depreciate in real terms. An
increase in tradables capacity has no direct effect on the real-exchange rate,
but the outward shift of the supply curve in the right-hand panel tends to
reduce the current account deficit. The supply-side effect of the investment
boom thus runs in the opposite direction to the earlier demand-side effect: it
reduces the real exchange rate and improves the current account.

The extent of the exchange-rate adjustment depends on the magnitude of
the capacity build-up in the non-tradables sector. If the bulk of investment
goes into tradables, there will be a sustained real appreciation. The currency
will remain 'strong,' perhaps even 'overvalued' in the view of some.

The expansion of capacity amounts to an increase in national income and
wealth, which tends to raise the demand for both tradables and non-tradables.
Demand in both sectors shifts out, as indicated by the arrows emanating from
the outermost demand curves in the two panels. The rise in non-tradables

demand tends to sustain the real appreciation and trade balance deterioration, while the rise in tradables demand leads to trade balance deterioration, but has no direct effect on the real exchange rate. How the real exchange rate and the current account evolve over time thus depends on the distribution of supply and demand changes between the two sectors. As noted, an investment boom that is heavily biased in favor of tradables will be accompanied by sustained currency appreciation and current-account improvement over the long run.

6.   FIXED VERSUS FLOATING RATES

The aforementioned movements in the real exchange rate take place under both fixed and floating rates, but the burden of adjustment is distributed differently in the two regimes. In a floating exchange-rate regime, adjustments in the real rate may be brought about by changes in nominal rates, in non-tradables prices, or in both, assuming that world tradables prices are given. When the nominal rate is fixed, the entire burden of adjustment falls on non-tradables prices, which rise to bring about real appreciation and fall to induce real depreciation. These price movements may create political difficulties for incumbent governments. Rising non-tradables prices not only risk inflaming inflationary expectations, but may reduce real incomes, especially among tradables workers whose wages are held down by foreign competitive pressures.[12] The political difficulties are probably even more severe when the real rate needs to depreciate, because then prices and wages in non-tradables industries must fall.

When the country is large, changes in tradables demand and supply affect tradables prices in the world or in the free-trade area. Foreign tradables prices will tend to rise when the large country's demand for tradables rises during the early phase of the investment boom; they will tend to fall when productive capacity comes on stream in the large country and the world supply of tradables rises.

7.   CONCLUDING REMARKS

Creation of an economic area, in which trade liberalization is combined with investment liberalization and cross-border production sharing, thus has both micro- and macroeconomic implications. Production sharing among members is capable of converting a trade-diverting free-trade area into a trade-creating one. Observed shifts of imports from low-cost non-members to higher-cost members do not necessarily imply trade diversion. By pushing specialization to the level of components, joint production among members may generate costs that undercut the low-cost outsider, if that country's cost advantage in the end product does not carry through to *all* of the component activities.

Production sharing tends to reduce the sensitivity of the trade balance to exchange-rate movements, because a country's exports are now linked to its imports, so that exchange-rate effects on one side of the trade balance are offset by changes on the other.

When production sharing takes place between advanced and emerging economies, foreign direct investment flows often precede joint production. These flows and the subsequent movement of components and products have important implications for the real exchange rate. In the FDI-receiving country, an investment boom tends to cause the real rate to appreciate initially and the current account to worsen, followed by real depreciation and current account improvement.

NOTES

1. See Kimura and Ando (2003) for new evidence on the extent of production sharing by Japanese firms in Asia and Latin America.
2. See note 3.
3. For a detailed analysis in the Heckscher–Ohlin framework, see Arndt (1997, 1998). For an assessment of cross-border 'fragmentation' in a Ricardian framework, see Jones and Kierzkowski (2001). See Deardorff (2001a, b) for an examination of fragmentation in a multi-cone context. See also Kohler (2001). For the role of service links in international production networks, see Jones and Kierzkowski (1990). Recent empirical studies include Egger and Egger (2001), Egger and Falkinger (2003) and Kimura and Ando (2003).
4. For details, see Arndt (2001).
5. It is clear that the first-best solution with and without production sharing is non-discriminatory trade liberalization.
6. While the overall welfare change depends on several factors, the main point is that deeper integration is welfare-improving relative to the base-line free-trade area.
7. This figure is taken from Arndt and Huemer (2001).
8. From Mexico's point of view, of course, it is a loss of producer surplus and thus a transfer of welfare to the trading partner.
9. When joint production is located in the emerging economy, direct investment inflows (FDI) may precede the onset of joint production. See Arndt (2002) for a discussion.
10. See Egger and Falkinger (2003) for a related treatment.
11. An important caveat, here, pertains to transfer-pricing practices by the multinationals involved in production sharing. These can affect the nature of pass-through and the value of trade. Where accounting practices distinguish between in-bond and regular exports, the distinction will be more readily apparent.
12. See Robertson (2003) for a study of Mexico.

REFERENCES

Arndt, S.W. (1997), 'Globalization and the Open Economy,' *North American Journal of Economics and Finance*, **8** (1), 71–9.
——— (1998), 'Super-Specialization and the Gains from Trade,' *Contemporary*

Economic Policy, **XVI** (October), 480–85.

Arndt, S.W. (2001), 'Production Networks in an Economically Integrated Region,' *ASEAN Economic Bulletin*, **18** (1), 24–34.

—— (2002), 'Production Sharing and Regional Integration,' in T. Georgakopoulos, C.C. Paraskevopoulos and J. Smithin (eds), *Globalization and Economic Growth*, Toronto: APF Press, pp. 97–107.

Arndt, S.W. and A. Huemer (2001), 'North American Trade After NAFTA: Part I,' *Claremont Policy Briefs*, Claremont, CA, Lowe Institute of Political Economy, Claremont McKenna College.

Deardorff, A.V. (2001a), 'Fragmentation Across Cones,' in S.W. Arndt and H. Kierzkowski (eds), *Fragmentation: New Production Patterns in the World Economy*, New York: Oxford University Press, pp. 35–51.

—— (2001b), 'Fragmentation in Simple Trade Models,' *North American Journal of Economics and Finance*, **12** (2), 121–37.

Egger, H. and P. Egger (2001), 'Cross-border Sourcing and Outward Processing in EU Manufacturing,' *North American Journal of Economics and Finance*, **12** (3), 243–56.

Egger, H. and J. Falkinger (2003), 'The distributional effects of international outsourcing in a 2 × 2 production model,' *North American Journal of Economics and Finance*, **14** (2), 189–206.

Feenstra, R.C. (1998), 'Integration of Trade and Disintegration of Production in the Global Economy,' *Journal of Economic Perspectives*, **12** (Fall), pp. 31–50.

Jones, R.W. and H. Kierzkowski (1990), 'The Role of Services in Production and International Trade: A Theoretical Framework,' in R.W. Jones and A.O. Krueger (eds), *The Political Economy of International Trade*, Oxford: Blackwell, pp. 31–48.

—— (2001), 'A Framework for Fragmentation,' in S.W. Arndt and H. Hierzkowski (eds), *Fragmentation: New Production Patterns in the World Economy*, New York: Oxford University Press, pp. 17–34.

Kimura, F. and M. Ando (2003), 'Fragmentation and agglomeration matter: Japanese multinationals in Latin America and East Asia,' *North American Journal of Economics and Finance* **14** (3), pp. 287–317.

Kohler, W. (2001), 'A Specific-factors View on Outsourcing,' *North American Journal of Economics and Finance*, **12** (1), 31–53.

Robertson, R. (2003), 'Exchange rates and relative wages: evidence from Mexico,' *North American Journal of Economics and Finance*, **14** (1), 25–48.

PART III

Empirical Approaches to Economic Integration

9. The WTO Agreement on Safeguards: an empirical analysis of discriminatory impact

Chad P. Bown and Rachel McCulloch

1. INTRODUCTION

The Uruguay Round Agreement on Safeguards (AS) represents an effort to improve the safeguards process and thereby encourage countries to choose this option over anti-dumping and 'gray-area' measures such as bilaterally negotiated export restraints. In contrast to anti-dumping, which is designed to protect domestic firms from injury due to 'unfair' trade, safeguards provide temporary relief to domestic industries that suffer 'serious injury' due to fairly traded imports. In contrast to anti-dumping and gray-area measures, safeguards are intended to limit imports across the board rather than from particular exporters, and the AS explicitly reaffirms the principle of most-favored-nation (MFN) treatment in application of safeguards. However, the AS also authorizes explicit discrimination among exporters in specified circumstances. Moreover, implementation of safeguards (SG) according to the procedures laid out in the AS may entail implicit discrimination among exporters to the SG-protected market. This chapter offers a first empirical analysis of the way safeguards initiated under the AS have been implemented in practice.

The non-discriminatory treatment of trading partners, known as most-favored-nation treatment, was a fundamental principle of the original GATT system (Article I) and has been carried over into the World Trade Organization. Its continuing appeal reflects both political and economic-efficiency considerations. Yet exceptions to treatment profoundly affect trade among members of the WTO. GATT Article XXIV permits the formation of preferential, that is, discriminatory, trading arrangements among groups of countries, and such arrangements now constitute an important feature of national trade policy. 'Special and differential' treatment of developing countries, including the Generalized System of Preferences, became an element of the GATT system in 1971, as membership expanded beyond the original 'rich man's club' of the early postwar period to include many newly independent nations. The Tokyo Round negotiations enlarged the scope of this 'differential and more favorable' treatment, and the Uruguay Round agreements likewise incorporated special terms for developing countries.

GATT/WTO-sanctioned relief from import competition is likewise subject to rules that entail discrimination among trading partners. With regard to injurious unfair trade, permitted remedies (anti-dumping duties or other arrangements, countervailing duties) are applied only to those import suppliers found to sell below fair value or to benefit from government subsidies.[1] Action on unfair trade is thus inherently selective, that is, discriminatory. GATT rules on safeguards allow temporary protection of sectors experiencing serious injury due to fairly traded imports.[2] Because affected exporters are not alleged to have violated any norm, GATT/WTO safeguard rules impose a more stringent injury test than in the case of unfair trade (serious versus material injury) and also require compensation of exporting countries in some cases. Moreover, because there is less focus on the source of the imports, safeguard measures are generally assumed to apply equally to all import sources and thus to be consistent with the MFN principle of the GATT/WTO system.[3]

In practice, however, the distinction between cases of injury due to unfair versus fair trade is not sharply drawn. The various GATT/WTO provisions allowing new restrictions on troublesome imports have proven to be 'quite fungible' over time (Finger, 1998).[4] During the early years of the GATT, the preferred instrument was renegotiation of tariff concessions with principal exporters. This approach gave way first to negotiation of quantitative restraints with specific suppliers, and later on to anti-dumping actions. Now safeguards may be emerging as the newest preferred mode of dealing with troublesome imports.[5] Moreover, despite the view that safeguards represent a more MFN-consistent approach to import relief than action on unfair trade, the application of safeguard protection may incorporate discriminatory elements, either because of the rules laid out in Article XIX and the Agreement on Safeguards, or because of the way in which these rules are implemented.[6] The purpose of this chapter is to identify the discriminatory elements of safeguard protection, as measured by the differential impact of safeguard policies across trading partners.

The empirical literature assessing use of safeguards is limited, largely due to safeguards' historically infrequent use. Moreover, researchers have tended to focus on either the industry (or government) decision to use safeguard protection as opposed to some other measure, or the government response to petitions and the decision whether to grant protection at all.[7] Examples include Baldwin and Steagall (1994), who use data on US safeguard cases between 1975 and 1988 to assess what economic factors best explain the International Trade Commission's injury determinations. Hansen and Prusa (1995) investigate US industry use of unfair (anti-dumping and countervailing duty) versus fair (safeguard) trade laws and also the differential impact of these laws on imports. Finally, Bown (2004) investigates countries' choice between GATT-legal safeguard measures that avoid the risk of potential retaliation by affected trading partners and other policies that may lead to a formal trade dispute. However, none of these papers addresses whether safeguard application has a discriminatory impact on foreign suppliers, which is the issue under investigation here.[8]

We examine the actual trade effects of 14 safeguard actions covering 85 different 6-digit Harmonized System (HS) product categories that were carried out by WTO signatories from 1995 through 2000. Our main focus is the extent to which the trade *effects* of safeguards deviate from the principle of non-discrimination among trading partners. Specifically, we identify systematic ways that implementation method and trading-partner characteristics influence exporter shares in the SG-protected market. We identify two types of discrimination that may arise in the application of safeguards: explicit departures from MFN treatment through formal exclusion of some exporters, and implicit departures from MFN treatment as indicated by trade impacts that differ systematically across supplying countries. Using data on WTO safeguard actions initiated between 1995 and 2000, we test empirically for evidence of a discriminatory impact of the safeguard measure on import shares in the SG-protected market. To preview some of the results, we find that the impact of a SG action on a given exporter depends on the specific form of the safeguard policy: quotas tend to preserve historical market shares more than tariffs. We also find evidence that the non-discrimination 'loopholes' favoring small developing-country suppliers and PTA partners do allow these countries to gain market share on average.

The rest of this chapter proceeds as follows. Section 2 summarizes the GATT/WTO rules on safeguards and highlights potential sources of discriminatory impact. Section 3 presents data from 14 cases of safeguard action from 1995 until 2000 and our econometric approach to estimating the impact of the form of safeguard protection on market shares. Section 4 presents our empirical results, and Section 5 concludes with a discussion of potential future research.

2. ARTICLE XIX AND THE AGREEMENT ON SAFEGUARDS

International commitments to limit import protection in specific industries typically include the conditions under which countries may restore protection for the same industries. Under Article XIX of the GATT (Emergency Action on Imports of Particular Products), a country is allowed to take safeguard actions when imports seriously injure or threaten serious injury to the competing domestic sector. Article XIX also specifies that affected exporters may request compensation for loss of market access. Hoekman and Kostecki (2001) suggest two distinct motives for including an escape clause in the GATT/WTO system: as insurance and as a safety valve. The insurance motive reflects that without such provisions, governments may be reluctant to sign trade agreements leading to substantial liberalization. Including an escape clause may thus facilitate liberalization of trade by encouraging negotiators to be bolder in their offers of concessions. The safety valve motive reflects that governments may later feel pressure to renege on certain negotiated liberalization commitments. By legalizing some backsliding under carefully specified circumstances, an escape clause can protect the integrity of the remainder of the agreement and therefore improve the overall durability of a liberal trade regime.

However, few countries actually appealed to Article XIX in coping with fairly traded but injurious imports. During the GATT period, the United States and other countries opted instead to negotiate bilateral trade restrictions outside the framework of the GATT or, especially more recently, to apply GATT-sanctioned anti-dumping measures.[9] These preferred remedies could be applied selectively to a few trading partners, thus obviating any need for even the appearance of MFN treatment of exporters. Moreover, use of dumping action rather than safeguards eliminated any requirement of compensation for affected exporters[10] and had the political appeal of attributing the domestic industry's problems to unfair foreign competition.

The Uruguay Round Agreement on Safeguards added specificity to the ambiguous language of Article XIX in a number of key areas.[11] Some elements of the agreement are largely procedural, including clarification of the injury requirement and of the timing and duration of safeguard protection, and establishment of a monitoring body (the WTO Committee on Safeguards) to which members must report safeguard actions. An important substantive change in rules is that bilateral arrangements such as voluntary export restraints (VERs) and orderly marketing agreements (OMAs) are explicitly prohibited (Article 11.1(b)).

Under the AS, countries may implement safeguard protection through tariffs, quotas, or tariff-rate quotas (TRQs). The empirical analysis below suggests that inclusion of quotas and TRQs along with tariffs as allowable instruments has important implications for the distribution of the economic impact of safeguard protection across affected exporters. A second important change in rules concerns compensation for exporters affected by safeguard actions. Specifically, a country facing an absolute import surge is no longer required to offer compensation for the first three years that a safeguard is in effect. *Ceteris paribus*, this change should make safeguards relatively more attractive in comparison with alternative means of obtaining relief from injurious imports, especially anti-dumping.[12]

A final set of provisions in the AS deals with the impact of safeguards across exporters. Article 2.2 states the general principle that '[s]afeguards measures shall be applied to a product being imported irrespective of its source,' that is, on a non-discriminatory basis. If quantitative restrictions are used, quota allocations should be based on market shares in a prior representative period unless all affected suppliers can agree to a different allocation scheme (Article 5.2(a)). However, allocation on the basis of market shares in a prior period implicitly favors established suppliers over recent entrants. Two other provisions open the door to explicit discrimination among suppliers. Article 5.2(b) allows countries to depart from MFN treatment when imports from certain members have increased 'disproportionately.' As with quotas based on market shares in a prior period, this provision shifts the burden of safeguards toward recent entrants into the market.[13] However, a second departure from MFN treatment exempts developing-country members from safeguard action, provided that a given member accounts for no more than 3 percent of total imports, and that exempted developing countries collectively account for no more than 9 percent (Article 9.1).[14] This exception introduces a bias in favor of developing countries that are new entrants or at least small producers of goods whose market is still dominated by suppliers in developed countries.

3. ECONOMETRIC MODEL AND DATA

3.1 Estimation Equations

To approach these issues empirically, we use a set of safeguard actions that WTO members have taken under the Agreement on Safeguards between 1995 and 2000. The data are compiled from country notifications made to the Committee on Safeguards and published on the WTO's website (WTO, 2000, 2001, 2002). As our primary interest relates to the market shares of exporters affected by the safeguard action, our sample consists of those cases for which we are able to match the products identified in the notifications with the most disaggregated trade data that are available systematically, that is, the TRAINS 6-digit Harmonized System (HS) import data provided in UNCTAD (1995, 2001, 2002).[15]

For each case, define year t as the year the SG was imposed and country j as an exporter of the product i that the SG-imposing country has chosen to protect. Then our first estimation equation is given by

$$M_{i,j,t+1} = \alpha_0 + \alpha_1 \bar{M}_{i,j} + \sum_{k=1}^{2} \alpha_{2k} \tau_k \bar{M}_{i,j} + \alpha_3 \Delta M_{i,j,t-1}$$

$$+ \sum_{k=1}^{2} \alpha_{4k} \tau_k \Delta M_{i,j,t-1} + \alpha_5 R_j + \alpha_6 X_{i,j,t+1} + \varepsilon_{t+1}. \qquad (9.1)$$

Our dependent variable, $M_{i,j,t+1}$, is exporting country j's share in the SG-imposing country's total imports of product i in year $t + 1$. We focus on $t + 1$ because the SG may have been imposed at any time during year t; thus, trade data for year $t + 1$ are more likely to show the full effect of the safeguard action.

In terms of our explanatory variables, $\bar{M}_{i,j}$ is country j's average share of the SG-imposing country's import market for the three calendar years prior to imposition of the SG. We include this regressor both independently and then interacted with two of the three possible forms that a safeguard action can take, that is, policy $\tau_k \in \{TRQ, \ tariff\}$. The omitted policy, and thus benchmark category in the estimation, is for a safeguard implemented as a quota. Next consider $\Delta M_{i,j,t-1}$, which is the percentage change in exporting country j's share of the SG-imposing country's import market for product i between year $t - 3$ and year $t - 1$. A positive value of $\Delta M_{i,j,t-1}$ indicates that country j was gaining market share in the period prior to imposition of the safeguard. R_j is a measure of exporter j's capacity to retaliate. Furthermore, $X_{i,j,t+1}$ is the share of country j's exports of the same product in world markets, which is included to capture country j's revealed comparative advantage as a supplier of product i. Finally, ε_{t+1} is the additive error term and the αs are the vectors of parameters to be estimated.

In addition to equation (9.1), we also estimate the following:

$$\Delta M_{i,j,t+1} = \beta_0 + \beta_1 \bar{M}_{i,j} + \sum_{k=1}^{2} \beta_{2k} \tau_k \bar{M}_{i,j} + \beta_3 \Delta M_{i,j,t-1}$$

$$+ \sum_{k=1}^{2} \beta_{4k} \tau_k \Delta M_{i,j,t-1} + \beta_5 E_j + \beta_6 R_j + \beta_7 \Delta X_{i,j,t+1} + v_{t+1}. \qquad (9.2)$$

In this second equation, our dependent variable, $\Delta M_{i,j,t+1}$, is the *percentage change* in exporting country j's share of the SG-imposing country's import market for product i between year $t - 1$ and year $t + 1$. The explanatory variables τ_k, $\bar{M}_{i,j}$, $\Delta M_{i,j,t-1}$ and R_j are defined as in equation (9.1). Another explanatory variable in equation (9.2) is E_j, a dummy variable that indicates whether the exporting country j has been formally exempted from the SG action by the imposing country. Furthermore, instead of $X_{i,j,t+1}$, in this equation we include an explanatory variable $\Delta X_{i,j,t+1}$, which is designed to capture the *change* over the base period in country j's revealed comparative advantage as a supplier of product i; $\Delta X_{i,j,t+1}$ is defined as the percentage change in country j's share of total exports of product i to the rest of the world, over the period $t - 1$ to $t + 1$. Finally, v_{t+1} is the additive error term and the βs are the parameters to be estimated.

We estimate equations (9.1) and (9.2) separately by ordinary least squares (OLS) and correct for heteroskedasticity by clustering according to the SG cases.

3.2 Variable Construction and Data

3.2.1 Dependent variables
The dependent variable in equation (9.1), $M_{i,j,t+1}$, is the share of country j's exporters in the SG-imposing country's total imports of product i in year $t + 1$, the year after the SG was first imposed. For the most part, we use data on the value of trade to construct this share measure because the value import series for the 6-digit HS products is more systematically available from the TRAINS data set than the corresponding volume series. We do, however, use the volume series where possible for a robustness check on our results.

In equation (9.2), rather than the share level, we use $\Delta M_{i,j,t+1}$, which is the percentage change in exporting country j's share of the SG-imposing country's total imports of product i between years $t - 1$ and $t + 1$. One concern in our data set is the non-trivial number of observations in which the 6-digit HS imports from a particular country j were zero in either $t - 1$ or $t + 1$. This generates problems for calculating percentage changes in market shares. To deal with this issue, we use the approach suggested by Davis and Haltiwanger (1992) and define the percentage change of import share as

$$\Delta M_{i,j,t+1} = \frac{M_{i,j,t+1} - M_{i,j,t-1}}{1/2(M_{i,j,t+1} + M_{i,j,t-1})},$$

where $M_{i,j,t+1}$ $(M_{i,j,t-1})$ is country j's share of the SG-imposing country's total imports of product i in year $t + 1$ $(t - 1)$. This measure of percentage change is symmetric around zero; it lies in the closed interval $[-2, 2]$, with trade flows that end (start) at zero corresponding to the left (right) endpoint.[16]

3.2.2 Historical market share and policy choice
The explanatory variable representing exporting country j's historical market share is defined as

$$\bar{M}_{i,j} = \frac{M_{i,j,t-1} + M_{i,j,t-2} + M_{i,j,t-3}}{3}.$$

We would expect $\bar{M}_{i,j}$ to have a strong positive impact on $M_{i,j,t+1}$ in equation (9.1) when SG policy is implemented as an import quota because the Agreement on Safeguards specifies that, unless all affected exporters agree on an alternative scheme, allocation of import licenses should reflect the proportions supplied during a previous representative period. This, therefore, is one way that implementation of a safeguard may implicitly discriminate among exporters. We would likewise expect the parameter estimate on $\bar{M}_{i,j}$ to be positive in the case of a TRQ and a tariff, but with a progressively smaller size.

On the other hand, in equation (9.2) we expect $\bar{M}_{i,j}$ to have no impact on $\Delta M_{i,j,t+1}$ if the SG policy is a quota, since market shares for $t + 1$ would then be expected to reflect historical averages. In equation (9.2), we also expect any impact of the historical average variable to be largest when the policy is implemented as a tariff, with the impact of the TRQ policy somewhere in between. However, the expected sign in the case of a tariff or TRQ is unclear *a priori*. A positive coefficient estimate, that is, a high historical average leading to an increased import share after the SG, would suggest that tariffs somehow favor larger suppliers at the expense of smaller ones, perhaps due to fixed costs of serving a particular export market,[17] whereas a negative result would indicate an outcome more favorable to smaller suppliers.

3.2.3   Trend in market share and policy choice

The explanatory variable representing exporting country j's percentage change in market share over the prior three-year period is defined as

$$\Delta M_{i,j,t-1} = \frac{M_{i,j,t-1} - M_{i,j,t-3}}{1/2(M_{i,j,t-1} + M_{i,j,t-3})},$$

where we again use the Davis and Haltiwanger measure to deal with exporters entering and exiting at the 6-digit HS level over the historical period.

In equation (9.1), we expect $\Delta M_{i,j,t-1}$ to have a positive impact on $M_{i,j,t+1}$, regardless of the trade measure (tariff, TRQ, quota) used to implement the SG. An exporting country that increased its market share over the prior period would tend to have a larger market share in $t + 1$, *ceteris paribus*.

In equation (9.2), consider first the case of a SG implemented through a quota. We expect $\Delta M_{i,j,t-1}$ to have a negative impact on $\Delta M_{i,j,t+1}$, because the SG-imposing country is permitted to discriminate against exports that have experienced a recent 'disproportionate' percentage increase under Article 5.2(b). Furthermore, the allocation of market shares under the SG quota should be determined by the historical average, according to the statute. If the exporter's market share was greatest in year $t - 1$, immediately prior to imposition of the SG (i.e., if the country's market share had been trending upward), then its market share would be expected to fall following imposition of the SG. Conversely, if the exporter's market share was smallest in the year immediately prior to imposition of the SG (i.e., if the country's market share had been trending downward), then market share after imposition of the SG would be expected to rise.

On the other hand, in the observations in which the SG takes the form of a tariff, we would expect the historical trend variable to have a less pronounced impact on the post-SG percentage change in market share. While we expect a negative relationship due to mean-reversion, a safeguard against a fast-growing exporter should be less punishing in the case of a tariff (where changes in market shares are more likely to be determined by market forces) than in quota cases (where changes in market shares are determined by the SG-imposing country's allocation decision). Nevertheless, a positive impact of historical growth on import share after the SG would suggest that tariffs favor newer entrants at the expense of established suppliers, whereas a negative result would indicate an outcome more favorable to established suppliers that may have suffered a loss in market share in the three-year period prior to imposition of the SG.

3.2.4   Retaliation

The variable R_j is country j's share of the SG-imposing country's total exports, where we derive the export data from Feenstra (2000). We use R_j as a measure of exporting country j's capacity to retaliate against the SG-imposing country, as this has been shown in other contexts to affect policy decisions.[18] In equation (9.1) we expect $M_{i,j,t+1}$ to be positively affected by a greater retaliatory capacity: the more reliant is the SG-imposing country on country j's market as an outlet for its own exports, the greater the resulting import share in the SG-protected market. An alternative interpretation is that the SG-imposing country rewards with higher import market shares those exporting countries with which it has exchanged concessions, that is, countries accounting for a substantial share of the SG-imposing country's own exports.

In equation (9.2) we would also expect $\Delta M_{i,j,t+1}$ to be positively affected by a greater retaliatory capacity – that is, if the SG-imposing country is particularly reliant on exporter j as a market for its own exports, country j might be rewarded with an increase in its market share after the imposition of the safeguard.[19]

3.2.5   Revealed comparative advantage

We also control for other factors that might affect import market shares of the SG-protected product i. In particular, country j may have a revealed comparative advantage in good i, which would lead us to expect that it would have a greater share of the SG-imposing country's import market. To control for this, we include a variable $X_{i,j,t+1}$, defined as country j's share of total exports of the 6-digit HS product i to the rest of the world. We would expect a positive relationship – if country j has a large share of the world market for good i, we would expect it to have a large share of the SG-imposing country's market as well, *ceteris paribus*.

When we seek to estimate the impact on the change in market shares in equation (9.2), we must also take into account that exporter j may experience some sort of country-specific shock that changes its comparative advantage in producing good i relative to the other exporters. Therefore we include an explanatory variable $\Delta X_{i,j,t+1}$ designed to capture such changes in comparative advantage.[20] The variable $\Delta X_{i,j,t+1}$ is defined as the percentage change in country j's share of total exports of product i to the rest of the world between year $t-1$ and year $t+1$. We would expect a positive relationship: if country j enjoys a change in comparative advantage that gives it a larger share of the rest of the world's import market for product i, then country j's share in the SG-imposing country's import market should also increase.

3.2.6   Exempted countries

The SG-imposing countries in our sample typically exempted exporting countries from the measure for two reasons: (1) developing countries that satisfied certain *de minimus* requirements (each country supplying less than 3 percent of total imports, and in the aggregate less than 9 percent), and (2) partners in a preferential trading arrangement (PTA).[21] The explicit exemptions were notified to the WTO and were provided in the country's report submitted to the Committee on Safeguards. We would expect those exporters exempted from the safeguard to enjoy an increase in market share after imposition of the SG.[22] To control for the effect of such exemptions, in equation (9.2) we include a dummy variable that takes on a value of one if the exporting country was formally exempted from the SG by the imposing country.[23]

3.3   Descriptive Analysis

To estimate equations (9.1) and (9.2), we require five years of trade data around the year of the SG's implementation – the three years before the SG was enacted, in addition to the year of and the year after the SG application. After matching the products and generating the required time series for the trade data, we are left with 14 different safeguard actions initiated between 1995 and 2000, which are presented in Table 9.1.[24] These 14 SG actions cover a total of 85 different 6-digit HS product categories. The mean number of 6-digit HS products per case is 6.0, while half of all safeguards in the sample

Table 9.1 WTO safeguard actions in the sample

No.	Country	Product (number of 6-digit HS Codes in sample)	Year	Measure	Exempted countries
1.	Argentina	Footwear (21)	1997	tariff	Brazil, Paraguay, Uruguay, 19 other countries
2.	Argentina	Footwear[a] (4)	2000	TRQ	Brazil, Paraguay, Uruguay, 4 other countries
3.	Brazil	Toys (15)	1997	tariff	Paraguay, Uruguay, 18 other countries
4.	Chile	Wheat, wheat flour, cane/beet sugar, edible vegetable oils (27)	2000	tariff	None listed
5.	Chile	Socks of synthetic fibres (1)	2000	tariff	Canada, Mexico, Peru, developing countries satisfying the small-supplier criterion
6.	India	Acetylene/Carbon black[b] (1)	1998	tariff	Developing countries satisfying the small-supplier criterion except China, Philippines, Singapore and South Africa
7.	India	Slabstock polyol (1)	1998	tariff	Developing countries satisfying the small-supplier criterion except Singapore
8.	India	Propylene glycol (1)	1998	tariff	Developing countries satisfying the small-supplier criterion except Singapore
9.	Korea	Dairy products (3)	1997	quota	Developing countries satisfying the small-supplier criterion
10.	US	Broom corn brooms (1)	1996	tariff	Canada, Israel, 147 other countries
11.	US	Wheat gluten (1)	1998	quota	Canada, Mexico, Israel, countries named in the Caribbean Basin Economic Recovery Act and Andean Trade Preference Act, 140 other countries
12.	US	Lamb meat (6)	1999	TRQ	Canada, Mexico, Israel, countries named in the Caribbean Basin Economic Recovery Act and Andean Trade Preference Act, 142 other countries
13.	US	Steel wire rod (2)	2000	TRQ	Canada, Mexico
14.	US	Circular welded pipe (1)	2000	tariff	Canada, Mexico

Notes:
[a] A subset of the footwear in the tariff SG of case 1 was restructured into a TRQ SG for case 2.
[b] The carbon black tariff SG was actually initiated in February 1999, but it has the same 6-digit HS code as acetylene black (imposed December 1998) so we have combined the two SGs into one.

155

Table 9.2 Summary statistics*

Explanatory variables	Predicted sign for equation (9.1)	Predicted sign for equation (9.2)	Mean	Standard deviation	Minimum	Maximum
Exporter's historical share over $t-3$, $t-2$, and $t-1$ × (i.e. interacted with) . . .	Positive (=1)	Zero	0.0955	0.1779	0	1
. . . SG policy was a TRQ	Positive	Ambiguous	0.0174	0.0852	0	0.9729
. . . SG policy was a tariff	Positive	Ambiguous	0.0737	0.1596	0	1
Percent change in exporter's share between $t-3$ and $t-1$ × (i.e. interacted with) . . .	Positive	Negative	−0.0323	1.2891	−2	2
. . . SG policy was a TRQ	Positive	Ambiguous	−0.0134	0.5591	−2	2
. . . SG policy was a tariff	Positive	Ambiguous	−0.0171	1.1308	−2	2
Dummy if the exporting country was formally exempted × (i.e. interacted with) . . .	N/A	Positive	0.3704	0.4832	0	1
. . . Exporter is not a PTA partner	N/A	Positive	0.2859	0.4521	0	1
SG-imposing country's share of exports sent to affected exporting country	Positive	Positive	0.0524	0.0784	0	0.2874
Exporter's share of the ROW's 6-digit HS import market in $t+1$	Positive	N/A	0.0940	0.2066	0	1
Percentage change in exporter's share of the ROW's 6-digit HS import market between $t-1$ and $t+1$	N/A	Positive	−0.0495	0.7896	−2	2

Note: *   All statistics are based on the value of trade share variables. The analogous summary statistics for the volume of trade share variables used in the estimation of specifications (4) and (8) presented in Tables 9.3 and 9.4 are omitted from the table but are available from the authors upon request.

affect just one 6-digit product. Within each SG action, for each product we use the 6-digit HS import data to reveal the affected exporting countries. This leaves us with 899 country–product pairs affected by a SG action. Table 9.1 also presents a list of some of the exporting countries that the SG-imposing country exempted from the particular policy action.

In terms of the specific form of the safeguard policies, nine were implemented as tariffs, three were implemented as tariff rate quotas (TRQs) and two were implemented as quotas. There was also some variation in the way the TRQs were administered, though in most cases the quota element appeared to be binding, with a defined allocation of market shares among foreign exporters.

Table 9.2 presents summary statistics on the data used in the estimation and the expected sign of the impact of each explanatory variable in equations (9.1) and (9.2).

4.   EMPIRICAL RESULTS

4.1   Raw Data Analysis

Consider first a graphical representation of some of the key data in the analysis. Figure 9.1 plots the average share of country j in the SG-imposing country's imports of product i for the three years prior to imposition of the SG against country j's import share in the year after the SG was imposed. Each of the three panels shows data for a specific SG-policy choice: tariff (a), TRQ (b), and quota (c). The graphs look much as we would expect. The data fit most tightly around the 45-degree line in panel (c), cases in which the safeguard is implemented as a quota. At the other extreme, for the case of a tariff (a), the data are much more dispersed. As we expected, the TRQ policy leads to an outcome that is between the other two.

4.2   Formal Estimation Results

4.2.1   Import market share in $t + 1$
The results of estimating equation (9.1) are presented in Table 9.3. The first column presents estimates for the baseline specification of the determinants of exporters' shares in the SG-imposing country's imports in year $t + 1$. The historical share variable (mean share for the three years before the year the SG was implemented) is entered first independently and then interacted with two of the three potential SG policies (TRQ and tariff), so the quota policy is the omitted category. In specification (1), the estimate of 0.799 for the coefficient of the historical share variable in the case of a SG quota is positive and statistically

(a) Safeguard implemented as a tariff

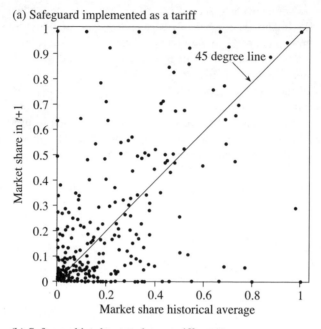

(b) Safeguard implemented as a tariff rate quota

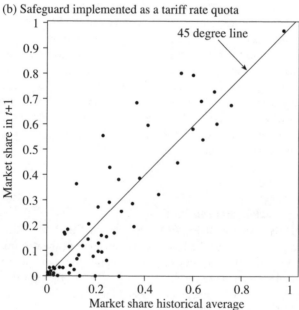

Figure 9.1   Historical market shares versus market share after the SG application

(c) Safeguard implemented as a quota

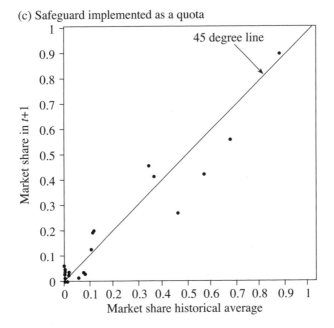

Figure 9.1   (continued)

different from zero, as we expected, though the estimated coefficient is also statistically different from 1. Furthermore, while the impact of the quota is larger (closer to 1) than the impact of the SG in the case of a tariff (which is –0.104 less), the impact for the TRQ case is still larger than in the quota case, rather than smaller as we would have anticipated. However, this result is not robust to all specifications, as we see below.

Specification (1) includes SG case dummy variables among the explanatory variables. With this specification, the historical trend variable, that is, the percentage change in exporter j's market share between $t - 3$ and $t - 1$, has no impact on market share in year $t + 1$, when the policy is implemented as a quota. This result does not change when the policy is a TRQ, though the trend does have a positive and significant impact for a SG action implemented as a tariff. The other control variables in estimation equation (9.1) are also positive, as suggested by the theory, but only the retaliation variable is statistically significant in specification (1).

In specification (2) we substitute 6-digit HS product dummies for the SG case dummies included in specification (1). The pattern of results is largely unchanged, except that the coefficient of the historical trend variable for a SG

Table 9.3 Estimation results: import market share in t + 1

	Dependent variable: exporter's share of the SG-imposing country's 6-digit HS import market in $t + 1$			
Explanatory variables	Baseline specification (1)	Add product dummies (2)	Add exporter dummies (3)	Volume share (4)
Exporter's historical share over $t-3$, $t-2$ and $t-1$	0.799***	0.803***	0.876***	0.848***
	(0.058)	(0.062)	(0.088)	(0.121)
× (i.e. interacted with) SG policy was a TRQ	0.126**	0.132**	−0.042	–
	(0.059)	(0.059)	(0.102)	
× (i.e. interacted with) SG policy was a tariff	−0.104*	−0.083	−0.176*	−0.228
	(0.056)	(0.063)	(0.091)	(0.169)
Percentage change in exporter's share between $t-3$ and $t-1$	−0.001	−0.001	0.003	0.008
	(0.001)	(0.001)	(0.007)	(0.008)
× (i.e. interacted with) SG policy was a TRQ	0.002	0.010***	−0.002	–
	(0.003)	(0.003)	(0.008)	
× (i.e. interacted with) SG policy was a tariff	0.009***	0.010***	0.003	−0.001
	(0.003)	(0.003)	(0.008)	(0.008)
Share of SG-imposing country's exports sent to affected exporting country	0.350**	0.300	0.541***	0.485**
	(0.169)	(0.187)	(0.123)	(0.219)
Exporter's share of the ROW's 6-digit HS import market in $t+1$	0.077	0.084	0.135**	0.240***
	(0.087)	(0.097)	(0.059)	(0.076)
SG case dummy variables	Yes	No	No	No
Product dummy variables	No	Yes	Yes	Yes
Exporting-country dummy variables	No	No	Yes	Yes
Number of observations	899	899	899	503
Adjusted R^2	0.57	0.60	0.61	0.48

Notes: White's standard errors correcting for heteroskedasticity and clustering on the SG case are in parentheses, with ***, **, and * denoting variables statistically different from zero at the 1, 5 and 10% levels, respectively. Time t is the year of the application of the SG. Each specification estimated with a suppressed constant term.

implemented as a TRQ is now positive, as anticipated, while the retaliation variable is insignificant. Neither of the latter changes is robust to all alternative specifications, however.

In specification (3) we add exporting-country dummies to the estimation equation. This addition gives us the anticipated ranking (based on type of policy) of the size of the parameter estimates relating to the historical share variables, an estimated coefficient on the historical average in the quota SG case that is not statistically different from 1, and also an improvement in the statistical significance of the retaliation and revealed-comparative-advantage variables.

In specification (4) we perform a final robustness check by replacing dependent and explanatory variables based on trade *values* with counterparts based on trade *volumes*.[25] This cuts the number of observations available for the estimation nearly in half. By coincidence, all observations in which a SG policy was implemented as a TRQ had to be dropped from the estimation due to insufficient data on trade volumes. Nevertheless, the estimation results are comparable to the otherwise analogous specification (2) in terms of the sign and size of parameter estimates.

To summarize Table 9.3, our results document the implicit discriminatory impact of a safeguard arising from the choice of trade-protecting policy instrument. Since post-SG market shares are more tightly linked to historical market shares under a quantitative restriction than under a tariff, the implication is that quantitative measures implicitly discriminate in favor of exporting countries whose share of the import market has been falling in recent years, to the detriment of exporting countries whose share of the import market has been increasing.

4.2.2 Growth in import market share

The results from estimation of equation (9.1) suggest that past import shares are an important determinant of import shares following imposition of a safeguard, but they are not the only determinant. What other variables determine post-SG *changes* in market shares? Table 9.4 presents results from estimation of equation (9.2) using specifications similar to those of Table 9.3, but now also adding the variables that allow for the explicit exceptions to the MFN rule through exporting-country-specific exemptions. Specification (5) is again the baseline specification and includes SG case dummies. With respect to the estimated coefficient on the historical average market share variable, the impact of a SG implemented as a quota is not statistically different from zero, as we expected. On the other hand, where the policy was implemented as a tariff, the impact of the historical average is strongly negative, suggesting that historically smaller exporters (perhaps new entrants) experience a greater increase in market share than do larger suppliers. For a SG implemented as a TRQ, the

Table 9.4   Estimation results: percentage change in import market share

Explanatory variables	Dependent variable: percentage change in exporter's share of the SG-imposing country's 6-digit HS import market between $t-1$ and $t+1$			
	Baseline specification (5)	Add product dummies (6)	Add exporter dummies (7)	Volume share (8)
Exporter's historical share over $t-3$, $t-2$ and $t-1$	-0.265 (0.295)	-0.289 (0.309)	-0.239 (0.432)	0.053 (0.267)
× (i.e. interacted with) SG policy was a TRQ	-0.653 (0.444)	-0.576 (0.436)	-0.726 (0.753)	—
× (i.e. interacted with) SG policy was a tariff	-0.937*** (0.326)	-0.910** (0.362)	-1.076** (0.447)	1.381*** (0.428)
Percentage change in exporter's share between $t-3$ and $t-1$	-0.382*** (0.131)	-0.370** (0.146)	-0.290** (0.114)	-0.155 (0.138)
× (i.e. interacted with) SG policy was a TRQ	0.051 (0.138)	0.062 (0.157)	-0.029 (0.123)	—
× (i.e. interacted with) SG policy was a tariff	0.073 (0.140)	0.060 (0.158)	-0.040 (0.115)	-0.069 (0.112)
Dummy if the exporting country was formally exempted	0.315*** (0.108)	0.317*** (0.118)	0.149 (0.410)	1.205** (0.611)
× (i.e. interacted with) . . . . . . Exporter is not a PTA member	-0.165 (0.175)	-0.182 (0.191)	0.115 (0.434)	-0.622 (0.566)
Share of SG-imposing country's exports sent to affected exporting country	0.368 (0.562)	0.191 (0.442)	0.953 (1.348)	3.606* (1.863)
Percentage change in exporter's share of the ROW's 6-digit HS import market between $t-1$ and $t+1$	0.138*** (0.037)	0.146*** (0.048)	0.091** (0.038)	0.060 (0.041)
SG case dummy	Yes	No	No	No
Product dummy variables	No	Yes	Yes	Yes
Exporting-country dummy variables	No	No	Yes	Yes
Number of observations	899	899	899	503
Adjusted R^2	0.13	0.11	0.17	0.14

Notes: White's standard errors correcting for heteroskedasticity and clustering on the SG case are in parentheses, with ***, ** and * denoting variables statistically different from zero at the 1, 5 and 10 percent levels, respectively. Time t is the year of the application of the SG. Each specification estimated with a suppressed constant term.

estimate is also negative and lies between the estimates for the quota and tariff, as we would expect.

How do past changes in market share influence post-SG changes? In specification (5), the impact of the trend variable is negative for the cases in which the SG took the form of a quota. This is consistent with the application of safeguards in these cases being biased against exporters who have recently experienced a 'disproportionate' percentage increase in market share. However, the impact of the historical trend variable is also negative and statistically significant in the instances in which the SG was applied as a tariff, suggesting that this outcome may not be due to an explicit discrimination against exporters whose trade has recently surged, but instead may simply be due to random shocks causing country j's exports in any given year to deviate from the 'normal' value, or mean-reversion.

Next consider the impact of the exempted-country dummy variables, which control for instances in which the SG-imposing country has formally excluded a particular exporting country from the SG policy and thus explicitly discriminated in favor of certain trading partners. Note that we also interact this variable with a dummy for instances in which the exempted country was not a member of a common PTA with the SG-imposing country, to check for whether there is a significantly differential effect on the outcomes experienced by exempted countries that are PTA members versus those exporters that are exempted because of the small-supplier, developing-country exception. Does the explicit discrimination of an exemption lead to a discriminatory effect on market shares? In Table 9.4, the estimation results do suggest that a formal exemption leads to a statistically significant increase in market share. While the estimated impact is smaller for the case of non-PTA members than for PTA members (the negative estimates on the dummy interacted with the non-PTA member), the difference across PTA and non-PTA members is not statistically different from zero.[26] The exception to this result is specification (7), which includes exporting-country-specific effects. In this specification, the statistical significance of the exempted-country parameter is eliminated, as the country-specific effects are likely absorbing the effects of the exemptions as well.

Finally, consider the estimated coefficients of the retaliation and percentage change in revealed comparative variables. The estimated coefficients are also positive, as suggested by the theory, but only the latter is statistically significant in specification (5).

Specifications (6) through (8) document analogous robustness checks to those presented in Table 9.4. Adding various sets of dummy control variables [specifications (6) and (7)] and substitution of the volume share for the value share variables [specification (8)] yield an almost identical qualitative pattern of results to those for specification (5).

5.   CONCLUSIONS

Our results indicate that the impact of SG action on a given exporter depends on the specific form of the safeguard policy. A SG implemented through a quota tends to preserve historical market shares more than a SG implemented as a tariff. When a SG is implemented as a tariff, countries that have recently increased market share gain at the expense of other suppliers, while a quota tends to have the opposite effect. Although we are not able to compare these results to the hypothetical case of a purely MFN SG, it seems safe to conclude that SG implementation through a tariff comes closer to achieving non-discriminatory results. We also find evidence that formal exceptions for developing countries and PTA partners do allow these countries to gain market share on average, although the estimated effect is larger for PTA partners than for developing countries. Nonetheless, the departure from MFN treatment intended to shelter new developing-country suppliers from the full effect of SG action appears to have been effective at least in qualitative terms.

While we have not addressed the issue explicitly here, Bown and McCulloch (2003) also document evidence that safeguards have a discriminatory impact on the exit response of new entrants, when compared to the exit response rate of earlier 'new entrants' that were not faced with a safeguard and when compared to other small, but historically present, suppliers that were also faced with the imposition of a safeguard.

Because the form of a SG policy is key to its impact across suppliers, a logical follow-up study would investigate the political-economy determinants of the SG-imposing country's decision to initiate a safeguard and its choice of SG policy. The markets in which the 14 SG actions were taken had experienced recent increases in the *number* of supplying countries, not just in the total value of competing imports. However, such an analysis requires a comparison set of otherwise similar markets in which no SG was subsequently imposed in order to determine whether the increased number of suppliers played a significant role in the decision to apply safeguards. Data from our cases also suggest that the timing of new supplier entry may play a role in the choice of SG instrument. When the new entry occurs in the year immediately prior to initiation of the SG, use of a non-tariff measure with market shares based on historical averages favors established suppliers over new entrants. However, if the new entry occurred two or three years before initiation of the SG, non-tariff measures would no longer be expected to differ significantly from tariffs in their relative impact on established versus new suppliers.

NOTES

1. Economists believe these remedies often target exporting nations that have recently increased competitiveness in the relevant industry, and especially countries lacking the capacity to retaliate in kind. Blonigen and Bown (2003) find evidence that threat of retaliation affects US anti-dumping activity.
2. Originally designed as an 'escape clause' to allow temporary re-protection of an import-competing industry that suffers unforeseen damage due to trade liberalization, safeguard protection has become increasingly available to any industry that can demonstrate serious injury due to competing imports, even when the competing imports have not benefited from a recent improvement in market access. An escape clause in the modern sense was introduced in the US Reciprocal Trade Agreements Act of 1934 (Jackson, 1997, p. 179). Recent US safeguards have been initiated under Section 201 of the Trade Act of 1974.
3. For example, Leidy (1995, p. 29), in a paper critical of the broad use of anti-dumping, cites the GATT safeguards provision (Article XIX) as a preferred means of defusing protectionist opposition to trade liberalization through 'temporary protection on a most-favored-nation basis in sectors experiencing serious injury'.
4. Finger (1998) notes that developing countries may likewise find it administratively convenient to declare as restrictions to protect the balance of payments (Article XVIII.B) trade measures actually applied to protect infant industries (Article XVIII.C).
5. While not included in the empirical investigation undertaken here because of data limitations due to the recent activity, the use of safeguards greatly increased in 2002, largely because of the high-profile US steel safeguard and the associated response of steel safeguards imposed by many other WTO members.
6. Discrimination in the actual application of safeguard protection has been a longstanding concern. Jackson (1993, p. 227) identifies 'the controversy about discriminatory application of safeguards measures' as a key topic in the Uruguay Round discussions on reform of the safeguards provisions.
7. For a more complete review of this literature, see Bown and Crowley (forthcoming).
8. A related paper is Prusa (2001), which investigates the trade-diversionary impact of discriminatory anti-dumping measures on 'non-named' exporters of the product targeted by an anti-dumping measure.
9. Thanks to elastic legal criteria for dumping, most injurious imports can be labeled successfully as unfair. An OECD review of anti-dumping cases in Australia, Canada, the European Union and the United States concluded that in 90 percent of cases where imports were found to be unfairly priced under anti-dumping rules, the goods would be considered fairly priced under domestic antitrust or competition policy (Finger, 1998, p. 13).
10. In contrast, use of VERs encouraged affected exporters to form cartels and also provided compensation in the form of quota rents.
11. Reform of safeguards was also a goal in the Tokyo Round. This effort failed because of disagreement on several issues, notably including discriminatory application of safeguard measures (Jackson, 1997, p. 209). On the concerns that motivated the Uruguay Round negotiation on safeguards and details of the final agreement, see Bown and Crowley (forthcoming) and references cited there.
12. For a discussion of these and other economic incentives affected by Uruguay Round reforms to safeguards, anti-dumping and dispute settlement under the WTO, see also Bown (2002).
13. A possible justification for the discriminatory treatment is that traditional suppliers have 'paid' for their market access with their own earlier concessions, while newer entrants have not. As the empirical analysis below indicates, newer entrants are often also new to the GATT/WTO system. For the 14 cases studied, new entrants to the market often included transition economies in Central Europe.
14. Developing countries are also subject to less stringent limits on their own use of safeguards (Article 9.2).

15. The safeguard notifications are typically made at the 8- or 10-digit HS level, and there may be multiple 8- or 10-digit HS products named in a given SG action. Because we use 6-digit HS trade data, our results will be estimated imprecisely to the extent that variation in a given 6-digit product is driven by variation in 8- or 10-digit products that were not subject to the SG action.
16. Davis and Haltiwanger (1992) note that this measure is monotonically related to the conventional growth rate measure, with the two measures being approximately equal for small rates of growth. This methodology has also been used in empirical international trade research by Bernard, Jensen and Schott (2002), for example, in order to address the issue of US manufacturing plant 'births' and 'deaths.'
17. Haveman et al. (2003) investigate differences in tariffs and four types of non-tariff barriers and find evidence that higher trade barriers tend to shift trade toward large exporters, which the authors interpret as a desire to minimize fixed costs of trading.
18. See, for example, Blonigen and Bown (2003) or Bown (2004).
19. The potential retaliation threats may derive either through negotiations under the Committee on Safeguards, if there has been no 'absolute surge' in imports so that compensation is due, or through a formal trade dispute under the Dispute Settlement Understanding if a country affected by the SG initiates a claim. This is likely due to increased imports from the developing countries that entered the market as a result of exemptions under the first safeguard.
20. This variable also captures the effects on country j's exports of any change in domestic prices and exchange rate relative to competing exporters and actual and potential importers of good i.
21. For example, in its 1998 SG on wheat gluten, the United States formally exempted its PTA partners Canada, Mexico and Israel, as well as all countries named in the Caribbean Basin Economic Recovery Act or the Andean Trade Preference Act and a list of other developing countries.
22. This is conditional on the exempted country being an exporter of the product subject to the SG. A SG-imposing country often exempts from the policy many developing countries that do not export the relevant product. We do not add such non-exporting countries to our data set. In the analysis we include only those exempted countries that have been revealed by the data as exporters to the SG-imposing country. However, an exempted country might subsequently begin exporting to the SG-protected market due to its advantage over established exporters subject to the SG policy.
23. We do not include this dummy variable in estimating equation (9.1) for endogeneity reasons. The Agreement on Safeguards requires that the SG-imposing country use market shares to determine whether a developing country is eligible to be exempted.
24. For the purpose of our empirical exercise, we treat the second Argentine footwear safeguard as distinct from the initial footwear safeguard as its form was changed from a tariff to TRQ, the HS products subject to the safeguard were changed, and the countries exempted from the measure were changed. An additional nine SG actions initiated during the same period are omitted from our analysis because the required import data were not available: Bulgaria (ammonium nitrate), Czech Republic (cane/beet sugar), Ecuador (matches), Egypt (safety matches; common fluorescent lamps), India (phenol; acetone), Korea (garlic), and Latvia (swine meat).
25. For two explanatory variables in Table 9.3, the share of the SG-imposing country's total exports that are sent to the affected exporting country and the exporter's share of the ROW's 6-digit HS import market in $t + 1$, quantity data were not sufficiently available to allow their inclusion.
26. Interestingly, Argentina did not exempt most of the developing countries in its second footwear safeguard in 2000 that were exempted in the first footwear safeguard in 1997. This is likely due to the increased imports resulting from the developing countries that may have entered the market as a result of the first safeguard and its exemptions.

REFERENCES

Baldwin, Robert E. and Jeffrey W. Steagall (1994), 'An Analysis of ITC Decisions in Antidumping, Countervailing Duty and Safeguard Cases,' *Weltwirtschaftliches Archiv* **130**, 290–308.

Bernard, Andrew B., J. Bradford Jensen and Peter K. Schott (2002), 'Survival of the Best Fit: Competition from Low Wage Countries and the (Uneven) Growth of US Manufacturing Plants,' NBER Working Paper No. 9170, September.

Blonigen, Bruce A. and Chad P. Bown (2003), 'Antidumping and Retaliation Threats,' *Journal of International Economics*, **60** (2), 249–73.

Bown, Chad P. (2002), 'Why are Safeguards under the WTO so Unpopular?', *World Trade Review,* **1** (1), 47–62.

——— (2004), 'Trade Disputes and the Implementation of Protection under the GATT: An Empirical Assessment,' *Journal of International Economics*, **62** (2), 263–94.

Bown, Chad P. and Meredith A. Crowley (forthcoming) 'Safeguards in the World Trade Organization,' in A. Appleton, P. Macrory and M. Plummer (eds), *The Comprehensive Guide to the World Trade Organization*, Springer.

Bown, Chad P. and Rachel McCulloch (2003) 'Nondiscrimination and the WTO Agreement on Safeguards,' *World Trade Review*, **2** (3); 327–48.

Feenstra, Robert (2000), 'World Trade Flows, 1980–1997,' UC-Davis, Center for International Development Working Paper 5910 and Accompanying CD-ROM, March.

Finger, J. Michael (ed.) (1993), *Antidumping: How It Works and Who Gets Hurt,* Ann Arbor, MI: University of Michigan Press.

——— (1998), 'GATT Experience with Safeguards: Making Economic and Political Sense out of the Possibilities that the GATT Allows to Restrict Imports,' Policy Research Working Paper 2000. Washington, DC: World Bank, Development Research Group, October.

Hansen, Wendy and Thomas Prusa (1995), 'The Road Most Taken: the Rise of Title VII Protection,' *The World Economy*, **18** (2), 295-313.

Haveman, Jon D., Usha Nair Reichert and Jerry G. Thursby (2003). 'How Effective are Trade Barriers? An Empirical Analysis of Trade Reduction, Diversion and Compression,' *The Review of Economics and Statistics,* **85** (2), 480–85.

Hoekman, Bernard M. and Michael M. Kostecki (2001), *The Political Economy of the World Trading System: The WTO and Beyond*, 2nd edn, New York: Oxford University Press.

Irwin, Douglas A. (2002), 'Causing Problems? The WTO Review of Causation and Injury Attribution in US Section 201 Cases,' *World Trade Review*, **2**, (3), 297–325.

Jackson, John H. (1993), 'Safeguards and Adjustment Policies,' in Robert M. Stern (ed.), *The Multilateral Trading System: Analysis and Options for a Change*, Ann Arbor: University of Michigan Press.

Jackson, John H. (1997), *The World Trading System: Law and Policy of International Economic Relations*, 2nd edn, Cambridge, MA: MIT Press.

Leidy, Michael (1995), 'Antidumping: Unfair Trade or Unfair Remedy?' *Finance and Development*, March, 27–9.

Prusa, Thomas J. (2001), 'On the Spread and Impact of Antidumping,' *Canadian Journal of Economics*, **34** (3), 591–611.

UNCTAD (1995), *Trade Analysis and Information System* (TRAINS), Version 3.0. Geneva: UNCTAD.

UNCTAD (2001), *Trade Analysis and Information System* (TRAINS), Version 8.0. Geneva: UNCTAD.

———— (2002), *Trade Analysis and Information System* (TRAINS), Version 9.0. Geneva: UNCTAD.

WTO (2000), 'Report (2000) of the Committee on Safeguards,' online document at http://www.wto.org/ classified as G/L/409, 23 November.

———— (2001), 'Report (2001) of the Committee on Safeguards to the Council for Trade in Goods,' online document at http://www.wto.org/ classified as G/L/494, 31 October.

———— (2002), 'Report (2002) of the Committee on Safeguards to the Council for Trade in Goods,' online document at http://www.wto.org/ classified as G/L/583, 4 November.

10. Organized labor's campaign contributions after the NAFTA vote: rhetoric or retribution?[1]

Gretchen Anne Phillips and Edward Tower

Labor unions were extremely vocal about their intent to punish all legislators who did not vote against NAFTA. In the words of William Bywater (of the International Union of Electronic, Electrical, Salaried, Machine and Furniture Workers, AFL–CIO), If you support NAFTA, 'we're gonna whip your ass and throw you out of office. And those that are with us, we oughta break our ass to see that they're elected.'

(Quoted in Jennings and Steagall, 1996, p. 71).

According to National Public Radio's Morning Edition, 12 April 2000, George Meany, ex-President of the AFL–CIO, instructed unionists on their lobbying visits to legislators to impress upon them: 'We never threaten, we never beg, and we never forget.'

1. INTRODUCTION

Many scholars have conducted trade policy studies and have come to the conclusion that interest-group donations affect congressional voting (see Tosini and Tower, 1987; Steagall and Jennings, 1996; Baldwin and McGee, 2000). However, few studies have sought to examine the reverse – whether or not a congressional vote is related to contributions received thereafter. More specifically, few studies have asked whether interest groups use campaign contributions as a means of reward or punishment based on specific voting outcomes. In this chapter, we seek to investigate this question as it applies to the North American Free Trade Agreement.

This section describes the political environment in which NAFTA was enacted and why we chose to examine campaign contributions surrounding the NAFTA vote. Section 2 describes how we selected the data and reviews the literature. Section 3 describes our expected results and what we discovered. Section 4 summarizes the chapter in two revealing graphs. Section 5 concludes.

1.1   Introduction to NAFTA

Professor Kreinin (1981) was one of the first to evaluate the idea of North American economic integration. He contributed an article to a special issue of Duke Law School's *Law and Contemporary Problems* edited by Alain Sheer, one of Tower's first Ph.D. students at Duke. Kreinin summarized his findings (p. 31) as follows:

> A North American FTA in manufactured products can yield considerable economic benefits to the three countries involved. It is also likely to be beneficial for world-wide resource allocation. However, all three countries would undergo a painful adjustment process, during which resources would be reallocated both between and within industries to attain greater efficiency and rationalization of industrial production. This dictates a rather lengthy transitional period during which trade liberalization is staged, perhaps longer for Mexico and Canada than for the United States. Large scale government assistance within each country would be required to smooth out the transition. Once completed, however, the benefits would far outweigh the adjustment costs.

The concept of the North American Free Trade Agreement (NAFTA) became politically possible when it was advocated by Mexican president Carlos Salinas de Gotari in 1990. At that time, it was expected that the most formidable obstacle to the treaty would be its acceptance by the Mexican public, which had a history of distancing itself from its northern neighbor. Surprisingly, the first signs of trouble came not in Mexico but in the United States, when a coalition of labor and environmental groups sought to defeat the extension of fast-track authority that President George Bush would need from Congress in order to negotiate a free-trade agreement with Mexico. Although a bitter public debate ensued, by 24 May 1991 both the House of Representatives and the Senate had voted to extend fast-track for two years.

When negotiations began formally in June of 1991, it was expected that an agreement would be reached within a year. This was to limit the opportunity for a powerful opposition to organize in Mexico and to allow the United States to focus on its foremost trade issue – the conclusion of the Uruguay Round of the GATT. As it turned out, the terms of NAFTA were not agreed upon until August of 1992. However, the ultimate passage of the treaty in the US would depend on the negotiation of supplemental agreements initiated in 1993 to mollify the concerns of NAFTA's most formidable opponents: organized labor and environmental groups.

In the United States, labor unions and business associations mounted strong public relations campaigns about NAFTA. Labor unions, fearing competition from open trade with neighboring southern countries with lower costs of production, insisted that they would discontinue financial support of any congressman who supported NAFTA. Further, labor unions asserted that they would defeat all legislators who voted for NAFTA (Steagall and Jennings, 1996, p. 515). Despite these threats from historical allies of the Democratic Party, NAFTA passed in the Senate without incident on 20 November 1993 (with a vote of 61–38), after its more precarious approval by the House three days before (with a vote of 234–200). This outcome required a YES vote from a significant number of Democrats in the House and Senate, in addition to the expected YES votes of the Republicans.

1.2 Why NAFTA?

We chose NAFTA as a case study to investigate interest-group donation behavior for several reasons, but primarily because of the public nature of the debate. Labor unions made defeating NAFTA one of their top priorities and mounted a strong campaign against the treaty. They were also extremely vocal about their intent to punish all legislators who did not vote against NAFTA. In the words of William Bywater (of the International Union of Electronic, Electrical, Salaried, Machine and Furniture Workers, AFL–CIO), 'we're gonna whip your ass and throw you out of office' (quoted in Jennings and Steagall, 1996, p. 71).

NAFTA was also a convenient case study because of its timing and political circumstances. The NAFTA vote occurred in late November 1993, which means that it fell almost exactly at the mid-point of the 1993–94 election cycle. Therefore, in looking at pre- and post-NAFTA contributions, one can examine the change in contribution levels as a function of vote and party affiliation. Finally, NAFTA was introduced into the House of Representatives under fast-track authority. This meant that legislators were forced to cast a YES or NO vote without amendments, thereby sending a clear message to labor unions regarding their position on this trade issue.

2.   LABOR PACS' CAMPAIGN CONTRIBUTIONS

2.1   Data

This study investigates whether labor PACs did in fact punish or reward politicians for their vote on NAFTA. To answer this question, an analysis of labor PAC contributions before and after the NAFTA vote was conducted.

In the analysis of Congress, the relationship between the NAFTA vote and subsequent labor PAC contributions in the Senate was excluded because the treaty was expected to pass in the Senate without any major opposition, and it seemed unlikely that labor PACs would reward or punish on the basis of a vote where individual votes didn't matter. Therefore, only data for the House of Representatives were examined. Until the week before the NAFTA vote was to occur in the House, it was uncertain whether there would be sufficient votes to pass the agreement. This meant that labor PACs had the opportunity to try to influence Representatives with their donations. Moreover, with elections every two years for the members of the House, a loss of contributions over a two-year election cycle could be very important to them.

We also had to decide how to define 'Labor PACs.' The data for this study were extracted from the Federal Election Commission Information page (accessible online at http://www.tray.com). This source breaks down labor PACs into five categories: Building Trades Unions, Industrial Unions, Transportation Unions, Public Service Unions and Miscellaneous Unions. We compiled data from all categories with the exception of Public Service and Miscellaneous. We eliminated Public Service Unions working under the assumption that its jobs were not directly threatened by Mexican labor. Miscellaneous represented a random group of unions organized by default, and therefore it seemed problematic for analysis and interpretation.

Having decided to focus on labor PACs, we generated a list of the contributions for all 434 members of the House of Representatives during the 1993–94 election cycle. Period 1 (pre-NAFTA) contributions were defined as those from 1 January 1993 through 16 November 1993, and Period 2 (post-NAFTA) contributions were defined as those from 17 November 1993 through 31 December 1994. After data had been compiled for each individual congressman, summary statistics were generated and the pattern of the relationship between labor PAC contributions in Period 1 before the vote and Period 2 after the vote was analyzed.

2.2   Literature

As Engel and Jackson (1998, p. 815) note, Jennings and Steagall (1996) claim that labor did not punish pro-NAFTA Democrats, because they did not lose more frequently than anti-NAFTA Democrats in the 1994 election. But as Engel and Jackson (EJ) note, this doesn't mean that labor did not use campaign contributions to reward and punish. EJ conducted the only previous study of the use of punishment strategies relating to the NAFTA vote. Their study examined both short- and long-term punishment strategies. Using a linear regression, EJ determined that labor PACs did indeed punish or reward congressmen in the short term. They concluded (p. 821) that during the post-NAFTA portion of the 1993–94 election cycle, on average each Democrat who voted for NAFTA received $25 024 less from labor PACs than did their anti-NAFTA democratic colleagues, holding everything else constant.

EJ also found that there was no statistically significant reduction in contributions to pro-NAFTA House Democrats over the 1995–96 contribution cycle relative to contributions received by their anti-NAFTA democratic colleagues (the *t*-value being slightly less than 1). These results lead to their conclusion that 'the stick strategy begun after the NAFTA vote was a short-term rather than a long-term punishment strategy. The reduction in funding for pro-NAFTA Democrats appears to have been a one-time occurrence' (p. 822). Thus, EJ tested the George Meany hypothesis: 'We never forget,' and found it lacking.

McCloskey and Ziliak (1996) argues that economic significance and statistical significance are two different issues, and that the former may be more important than the latter. Their point is particularly relevant with regard to EJ's interpretation of non-significant long-term effects of labor PAC contributions. Their point estimate is that a YES vote reduced campaign contributions in the 1995–96 election cycle by $0.000733 * $16 490 443 = $12 087, which is 12 078/110 674 = 10.9 percent of the mean labor PAC contribution received by Democrats. Thus the magnitude of this dollar amount loss from a pro-NAFTA vote would seem to be an economically significant impact on contributions in the long term. As George Meany might have said: 'We never forget – at least over a three-year horizon.'

This study differs from that of Engel and Jackson in several respects:

1. Only the 1993–94 election cycle was examined, breaking all the campaign contributions into pre- and post-NAFTA vote. Whereas EJ also considered the short-term post-NAFTA vote contributions to be the second half of the 1993–94 election cycle, their pre-NAFTA vote contributions were 1991–92 contributions. Using data from the 1991–92 cycle could be problematic because several other labor issues were voted on during this period, all of which might have affected the level of campaign contributions. Examples include amendments of the National Labor Relations Act (1991), the Railway Labor Act (1991), the Civil Rights Act (1991), the Job Training Partnership Act (1991), and passage of the Trade Expansion Act (1992), the Unemployment Insurance Reform Act (1992), and the Emergency Unemployment Compensation Act (1992). Perhaps most significantly, fast track was voted on in 1991. Therefore the key distinction between these studies is that in looking at pre-NAFTA contributions, we considered the first half of the 1993–94 election cycle and compared it to the second half of the same cycle, whereas EJ compared the entire 1991–92 election cycle to the second half of 1993–94.

2. EJ modeled a YES vote on NAFTA as shifting labor PAC contributions downward by a fixed amount, whereas this study explored both proportional and parallel downward shifts in the labor PAC contribution function, where the contribution function is defined as the relationship between the post-NAFTA contributions on the vertical axis and pre-NAFTA contributions on the horizontal axis.
3. Whereas EJ only investigated incumbent Democrats, all Republicans and Democrats receiving contributions were included in this study.

There have been several studies conducted on the subject of pre-NAFTA PAC contributions and their effect on the NAFTA vote. Kahane (1996) and Steagall and Jennings (1996) addressed the NAFTA vote specifically and concluded that interest-group contributions had an effect on congressional voting behavior. Kahane's study used a single-equation logit regression for both the House and the Senate to argue their point, while Steagall and Jennings used a single-equation probit regression in the House only. In a distinguished study, Baldwin and Magee (2000) also examined this relationship, recognizing that campaign contributions are endogenous. Their econometrics is sophisticated and their counterfactual simulations imaginative and informative. Incorporating Tobit analysis into the method of full information maximum likelihood so as to disentangle the endogeneity of both campaign contributions and the vote, they found that:

> In the NAFTA vote, a $1000 increase in a [House] member's contributions from labor groups beyond the mean level reduced the probability of voting for the agreement by 0.52 percentage points, whereas a $1,000 addition to contributions from business PACs increased the probability of voting to approve the agreement by 0.12 percentage points . . . These are rather large impacts on voting probabilities . . . (p. 92).

They also find (p. 97) that to swing one more vote from NAFTA, labor would have had to contribute $825 additional per Representative. These results led them to conclude that in the House of Representatives 'trade policy is for sale or that money buys access, which interest groups are able to use effectively to influence legislative decisions'(p. 96).

Baldwin and Magee also state 'Conventional wisdom suggests that interest groups are buying something when they contribute to a politician's campaign' (p. 79). Using this analogy, shoppers who go to a particular store and find that they can no longer purchase a desired product will take their money elsewhere. This prediction sets the stage for our inquiry, which seeks to investigate whether voting behavior affects post-vote campaign contributions.

3.   THE DATA

3.1   Anticipated Results

The NAFTA vote came at an important time in US history. Bill Clinton had just been elected to the Presidency, and Democrats had a majority in both the House of Representatives and the Senate. Therefore Democrats had the unusual fortune of controlling both the Executive and the Legislative branches of government. This presented an interesting predicament for labor PACs because although they may have wished to make good on their threats to punish those who voted for NAFTA, almost half of those people who fell into that category were Democrats, and it would not be in the best interests of the labor PACs to weaken the position of their historical allies. Therefore one might expect that contributions for Democrats who voted for NAFTA would not decrease by a substantial amount.

If the NAFTA vote did produce a noticeable effect on contributions, one might postulate that it would be more pronounced among Republicans, with labor PACs systematically rewarding anti-NAFTA Republicans in the period following the vote. However, the far right was anti-NAFTA too, and labor might feel that the far right was following its own agenda and was generally insensitive to labor's concerns, so that money donated to the far right would be wasted. Also, in absolute terms pre-NAFTA campaign contributions to Republicans were relatively inconsequential (due to the fact that Republicans are generally allied against the interests of organized labor), so in absolute terms, one might not expect as much punishment among Republicans given that they were already receiving such low levels of contributions.

Finally, it is important to remember that contributions to politicians are endogenous, reflecting votes over a long period on many issues (Chappell, 1982). Taking this into consideration, labor PACs tend to allocate money to politicians – regardless of their party – who are allied with their interests, and may be hesitant to break such alliances over any one particular vote, supporting the view that the threats were empty. In sum, it is expected that labor unions will use a short-term reward and punishment strategy relative to the NAFTA vote.

3.2   Tabulating Campaign Contributions

NAFTA passed in the House of Representatives with a vote of 234 to 200. Of the Ayes, 132 were Republicans and 102 were Democrats. Of the Nays, 43 were Republicans, 156 were Democrats, and one was an Independent. Table 10.1 summarizes this information and indicates the number of congressmen who received contributions from labor PACs. Tables 10.2 and 10.3 show the data separated into pre- and post-NAFTA periods respectively. Table 10.4 shows the differences between the two periods.

Table 10.1 Summary of pre- and post-NAFTA labor PAC contributions

Party/vote	Number of legislators	Number of legislators receiving contributions over the entire period	Legislators receiving contributions over the entire period (%)	Pre-NAFTA total contributions ($)	Post-NAFTA total contributions ($)	Total contributions ($)
Republican / YES	132	48	36.4	82 975	129 950	212 925
Republican / NO	43	37	86.0	83 578	235 169	318 747
Democrat / YES	102	88	86.3	1 014 522	1 827 797	2 842 319
Democrat / NO	156	145	92.9	2 938 776	7 300 040	10 238 816
Independent / NO	1	1	100.0	4 000	92 700	96 700
Total	434	319	73.5	4 123 851	9 585 656	13 709 507

Table 10.2 The pre-NAFTA contribution period

Party/vote	Number of legislators receiving contributions	Percentage receiving contributions (%)	Average contribution to legislators receiving contributions initially ($)	Average contribution per legislator ($)	Maximum contribution to any legislator ($)
Rep. / YES	29	22.0	2 861	629	8 500
Rep. / NO	14	32.6	5 970	1 944	18 200
Dem. / YES	86	84.3	11 797	9 946	124 638
Dem. / NO	136	87.2	21 609	18 838	137 050
Ind. / NO	1	100.0	4 000	4 000	4 000
Total	266	61.3	15 503	9 502	137 050

Table 10.3   The post-NAFTA contribution period

Party/vote	Number of legislators receiving contributions	Percentage receiving contributions (%)	Average contribution to legislators receiving contributions initially ($)	Average contribution to legislators receiving no initial contributions ($)	Average contribution per legislator ($)	Maximum contributor to any legislator ($)
Rep. / YES	39	29.5	3 395	189	984	20 750
Rep. / NO	37	86.0	15 434	659	5 469	32 650
Dem. / YES	79	77.5	25 362	783	17 920	108 000
Dem. / NO	145	92.9	53 171	3 440	46 795	127 400
Ind. / NO	1	100.0	92 700	n. a.	92 700	92 700
Total	301	69.4	36 916	713	22 087	127 400

Table 10.4 Comparison of pre- and post-NAFTA contribution periods

Party/vote	Change in % of legislators receiving contributions (% age points)	Post- to pre-NAFTA ratio of contributions to legislators receiving contributions initially	Post- to pre-NAFTA ratio of contributions to all legislators	Post- minus pre-NAFTA average contribution to legislators receiving contributions initially ($)	Post- minus pre-NAFTA average contribution to all legislators ($)
Rep./YES	7.5	1.19	1.57	534	356
Rep./NO	53.4	2.58	2.81	9 464	3 525
Dem./YES	–6.8	2.15	1.80	13 566	7 973
Dem./NO	5.8	2.46	2.48	31 562	27 957
Ind./NO	0	23.18	23.18	88 700	88 700
Total	8.0	2.38	2.32	21 413	12 585

The most important conclusions from the tables follow.

1. Of Republicans who voted YES, only 36 percent received contributions, while 86 percent of those voting NO got money. Of the Democrats, 86 percent who voted YES received donations in contrast to 93 percent of those who voted NO.
2. Republicans who received no initial contributions and voted YES saw their contributions rise to $189 post-NAFTA, while corresponding Republican NO voters received a larger $659. The corresponding figures for Democrats are $783 and $3440.
3. Republican YES voters saw the fraction of legislators receiving contributions rise by 7.5 percentage points, while Republican NO voters saw their fraction rise by a gigantic 53.4 percentage points. Corresponding Democratic figures are –6.8 percentage points and 5.8 percentage points.
4. Republicans who received initial contributions and voted YES saw their contributions multiply by 1.2, while corresponding Republican NO voters saw theirs multiply by a larger 2.6. The corresponding Democratic multipliers are 2.2 and 2.5.
5. Republican YES voters saw their campaign contributions rise to a multiple of 1.6 times their initial contributions, while Republican NO voters had a larger multiple of 2.8. The corresponding Democratic multipliers are 1.8 and 2.5. The gap is greater for Republicans (1.2) than for Democrats (0.7). Thus in proportional terms retribution was greater for Republicans.
6. Republicans who received initial contributions and voted YES saw their contributions rise by $534, while corresponding Republican NO voters saw a much larger rise of $9464. The corresponding figures for Democratic voters are $14 000 and $32 000.
7. Republican YES voters saw their contributions rise by $356, while Republican NO voters saw a corresponding rise of $3525. The corresponding figures for Democrats are $8000 and $28 000. The gap is greater for Democrats ($20 000) than for Republicans ($3000). Thus, in absolute terms retribution was greater for Democrats.

The only evidence of punishment comes from the fact that a smaller fraction of Democratic YES voters received contributions in the second period. There are no anomalous results. The YES voters from each party saw their contributions climb by a larger dollar amount. They also saw their initial contributions multiplied by a larger fraction in the second period. These last two observations also hold when we restrict the sample to those who received contributions initially, and the last one also holds when we restrict the sample to those who did not receive contributions initially.

3.3 Regressions

A complete set of the data is given in Phillips (2000). Three regressions were run for both Republicans (Rep1, Rep2 and Rep3) and Democrats (Dem1, Dem2 and Dem3), and a fourth for just the Republicans (Rep4):

1. Post-NAFTA contributions = α YES + β Pre-NAFTA contributions + γ (YES * Pre-NAFTA contributions) + constant
2. Post-NAFTA contributions = α YES + β Pre-NAFTA contributions + γ (YES * Pre-NAFTA contributions) + δ (Pre-NAFTA contributions)^2 + constant
3. Post-NAFTA contributions = α YES + β Pre-NAFTA contributions + constant
4. Post-NAFTA contributions = β Pre-NAFTA contributions + γ (YES * Pre-NAFTA contributions) + δ (Pre-NAFTA contributions)^2 + constant

In the regression equations listed above and in Table 10.5:

- The dependent variable is post-NAFTA labor PAC contributions to individual House members in thousands of dollars.

The independent variables are:

- YES, a dummy variable, where YES = 1 for a Yes vote on NAFTA and YES = 0 for a NO vote;
- pre-NAFTA labor PAC contributions, in thousands of dollars;
- YES * Pre-NAFTA contributions, which has a value of zero for members who vote NO, and a value of the pre-NAFTA contribution for members who vote YES; and
- [Pre-NAFTA contributions]^2. A negative coefficient on this variable reflects the tendency for members who received very large contributions in the pre-NAFTA period to receive smaller contributions in the second period.

Table 10.5 summarizes the results of the seven regression models. All models fit the data reasonably well, accounting for between 40 percent and 70 percent of the variance of the dependent variable. The best equations are Dem2 for the Democrats and Rep2 for the Republicans, using the adjusted R^2 as the criterion.

The second-period contributions to Democrats are best explained by Dem2, which contains all the independent variables above. Predicted post-NAFTA contributions for a Democrat who voted NO are [(2.2 * first period contributions)

Table 10.5 OLS regressions explaining post-NAFTA vote labor PAC contributions to legislators

Equation Independent variable	Dem1	Dem2	Dem3	Rep1	Rep2	Rep3	Rep4
YES	-18.3***	-12.1***	-21.6***	-1.51*	-1.07	-2.22***	—
	(-4.54)	(-3.37)	(-6.66)	(-2.44)	(-1.76)	(-3.75)	
Pre-NAFTA contributions	0.907***	2.20***	0.831***	1.95***	3.02***	1.72***	3.19***
	(8.77)	(12.9)	(9.49)	(15.9)	(9.87)	(17.0)	(11.0)
YES * Pre-NAFTA contributions	-0.264	-0.283	—	-0.656**	-1.22***	—	-1.38***
	(-1.37)	(-1.68)		(-3.14)	(-4.86)		(-6.04)
Pre-NAFTA contributions^2	—	-0.0140***	—	—	-0.0789***	—	-0.0859***
		(-8.99)			(-3.78)		(-4.17)
Constant	29.7***	15.3***	31.1***	1.68**	1.16*	2.12***	0.324
	(10.7)	(5.28)	(12.1)	(3.10)	(2.15)	(3.94)	(1.26)
R^2	0.411	0.553	0.407	0.687	0.712	0.669	0.706
Adjusted R^2	0.404	0.546	0.402	0.682	0.705	0.665	0.701
Observations	259	259	259	175	175	175	175

Notes: Significance of the coefficients is denoted by: *** $p<.001$ (two-tailed test), ** $p<.01$ (two-tailed test), * $p<.05$ (two-tailed test). In each row, the top figure is the coefficient, in thousands of dollars. The bottom figure is the *t*-statistic.

– (0.0140 * first period contributions^2) + \$15 300]. A Democratic YES voter's predicted post-NAFTA contributions are the same as above, except that they are *reduced* by [\$12 100 + 0.283 * first-period contributions]. For a Democrat who receives the mean first-period contribution for NO voters, the cost of a YES vote measured as a reduction in post-NAFTA contributions is \$12 100 plus an additional 0.283 * 18.838 = \$5371 for a total of \$17 431. For a member who receives the maximum contribution of \$137 050 in the first period, the cost of a YES vote is a total of \$50 885.

Second-period contributions to Republicans are best explained by Rep2. YES voters predicted post-NAFTA contributions are reduced by [\$1070 + 1.216 * first-period contributions] relative to those of a NO voter. Given that the maximum pre-NAFTA contribution to any Republican legislator who voted YES on NAFTA was \$8500, the maximum loss suffered by a YES-voting Republican legislator is \$1070 + \$10 385 = \$11 355.

Thus the expected cost of voting YES is higher for every Democrat than for any Republicans who voted YES. For members of both parties, the cost of a YES vote increases with the contributions they received from labor PACs in the pre-NAFTA period. Assuming that members anticipated this pattern of contributions, it is not surprising that Democratic YES voters tended to receive smaller first-period contributions than did Democratic NO voters.

Conceptually, we can think of the regression equation as defining a second-period contribution function, with second-period contributions measured on the Y axis and first-period contributions measured on the X axis. A Democratic YES vote causes a downward parallel shift of the contribution function by 12.1 thousand dollars plus a further downward shift of 28.3 percent times first-period contributions – a proportional downward shift – where the proportion is expressed as a fraction of the X variable. A Republican YES vote causes a smaller parallel downward shift and a larger proportional downward shift (121 percent) than for Democrats.

Thus we can think of first-period contributions not as buying votes, but rather as providing the basis of a threat to YES voters. While George Meany's lobbyists did not threaten legislators verbally, perhaps their contributions spoke so loudly that there was no need for threatening words.

For the Democrats, four of the variables are significantly different from zero on a two-tailed *t* test at the 0.001 level. The proportional shift variable is not significant on a two-tailed test even at the 0.05 level. We explored alternative parameter specifications in Dem1 and Dem3. These alternatives leave out some of the independent variables, but neither of them generates such high adjusted R^2, so Dem2 remains our preferred model.

Similar results apply to the equations for Republicans, Rep1 through Rep4. As we found for the Democrats, Rep2 is our preferred equation. For the Republicans, all terms achieved statistical significance with the exception of the YES variable in the second regression model and the constant in Rep4. Although seven regression models were run, it is important to recognize that they are all fundamentally quite similar. The fact that all produce comparable results indicates that our conclusions are robust with respect to alternative specifications.

4.　GRAPHICAL SUMMARY

Our two favorite regressions are Dem2 and Rep2. Figure 10.1 shows the contribution schedules for Democrats who voted each way on NAFTA according to Dem2. Figure 10.2 shows the corresponding schedules for Republicans. The figures illustrate the conclusions discussed in the text. The schedules for Democrats reach a peak in the range of pre-NAFTA contributions actually observed. This peak occurs at over three times the mean first-period contributions for both YES and NO voters. Looking at the scatter of data points confirms that the regression is replicating the observations. This finding was initially counter-intuitive to us. We explain it by suggesting that labor PACs who gave generously in the pre-NAFTA period felt they had done enough to last them through the post-NAFTA period. In other words very large contributions in the first period may substitute for contributions in the second period.

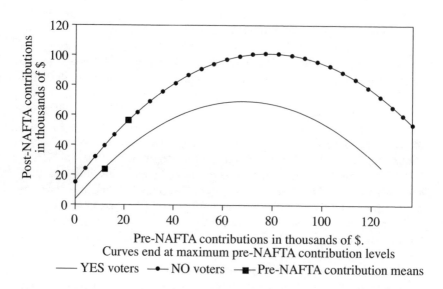

Figure 10.1　Contribution schedules for Democrats

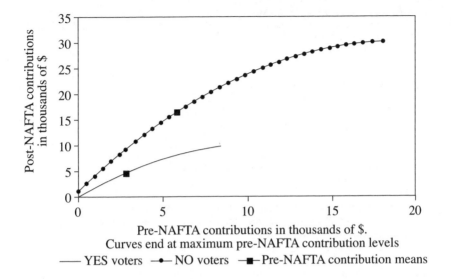

Figure 10.2   Contribution schedules for Republicans

5.   CONCLUSION

In an article in the *Wall Street Journal*, columnist Albert R. Hunt (2000) points out some of the inconsistencies that exist between members of the Democratic Party and the voting records of those legislators who represent them. What is the wedge that can account for this gap? Evidence points to labor PAC contributions. Because of the financial importance that labor contributions play – particularly in Democratic campaigns – many scholars have made the connection between donations and roll-call voting. This chapter further investigates the relationship between labor PACs and congressmen, and answers the question of whether PACs use their dollars as part of a punishment/reward strategy. As the data clearly indicate, the answer is a resounding yes. In this study, punishment manifests itself as both a parallel shift and proportional shift downward. Therefore, with reference to George Meany's quote, it seems that labor unions do threaten, and at least in the short term, 'they never forget.'

NOTE

1.   This chapter is a modestly revised version of Phillips's senior thesis (2000), which was advised by Tower.
    We would also like to thank the following for their comments and suggestions: Jesus Araiza, Nick Cabiati, Ruth Carlitz, Stephan Kretzschmar, Merlise Clyde, Omer Gokcekus,

Mia Mikic, Ryan Millner, Dmitri Mirovitski, Edward Phillips, Karen Phillips, Mike Plummer and Jennifer Socey. Tower did part of his work on this chapter while being hosted at the University of Zagreb on a Fulbright grant.

REFERENCES

Baldwin, Robert E. and Christopher S. Magee (2000), 'Is Trade Policy for Sale? Congressional Voting on Recent Trade Bills,' *Public Choice*, **105**, 79–101.

Chappell, H. (1982), 'Campaign Contributions and Congressional Voting: A Simultaneous Probit–Tobit Model,' *Review of Economics and Statistics*, **64**, 77–83.

Engel, Steven and David J. Jackson (1998), 'Wielding the Stick Instead of the Carrot: Labor PAC Punishment of Pro-NAFTA Democrats,' *Political Research Quarterly*, **51**, 813–28.

Hunt, Albert (2000), 'A Paper Tiger on Trade,' *Wall Street Journal*, 23 March, A23.

Jennings, K. and J.W. Steagall (1996), 'Unions and NAFTA's Legislative Passage: Confrontation and Cover,' *Labor Studies Journal*, **21**, 61–79.

Kahane, L. (1996), 'Congressional Voting Patterns on NAFTA: An Empirical Analysis,'*American Journal of Economics and Sociology*, **55**, 395–409.

Kreinin, Mordechai E. (1981), 'North American Economic Integration,' in Economic Integration of North America, a symposium edited by Alain Sheer, *Law and Contemporary Problems*, **44**, Durham, NC: Duke University, Summer, pp. 7–31.

McCloskey, Diedre and Stephen T. Ziliak (1996), 'The Standard Error of Regressions,' *Journal of Economic Literature*, **34**, 97–114.

Phillips, G.A. (2000), *Labor PACs and NAFTA Legislators: An Examination of Reward, Punishment, and the NAFTA Vote*, honors thesis, Duke University.

Steagall, J.W. and K. Jennings (1996), 'Unions, PAC Contributions, and the NAFTA Vote,' *Journal of Labor Research*, **17**, 515–21.

Tosini, S. and E. Tower (1987), 'The Textile Bill of 1985: The Determinants of Congressional Voting Patterns,' *Public Choice*, **54**, 19–25.

11. Korea's direct investment in China and its implications for economic integration in Northeast Asia[*]

Joon-Kyung Kim and Chung H. Lee

1. INTRODUCTION

Economic relations between the Republic of Korea (henceforth Korea) and the People's Republic of China (henceforth China) have been expanding ever since China undertook the Four Modernization reforms in the late 1970s. Ever since then, bilateral trade between the two countries has been growing steadily in terms of both volume and variety of goods traded. Capital flows between the two have likewise been increasing although the flows have been mostly from Korea to China and in the form of direct investment. Between 1989 and 2000, for instance, Korea's merchandise exports to China grew from $213 million to $18.4 billion while China's merchandise exports to Korea grew from $3.9 million to $11.3 billion (ICSEAD, 2002). In fact, China has now emerged as Korea's third largest trading partner. Also, by the end of 1999 Korea had invested $4.3 billion in China, where it had virtually no investment before the late 1970s, and in the year 2000 alone Korea invested $307 million in China (China Statistical Press, 1999; Lee, 2001). These increases in both trade and investment are signs of growing economic interdependence and integration of the two economies, which, we expect, will further economic growth in both countries.[1]

China and Korea are two key players in Northeast Asia, a region that stretches from Japan on its eastern edge to the Mongolian People's Republic in the west and the Russian Federation's Far Eastern provinces in the north. It is one of the most dynamic regions in the world, although it has yet to develop into a well-integrated economic entity with formal regional machinery similar to the European Union (EU) and the North American Free Trade Area (NAFTA).

The European experience has clearly demonstrated that the establishment of formal regional institutions such as a free-trade area and supranational or intergovernmental institutions can pave the way to greater regional economic integration. Such institutions are, however, unlikely to emerge unless the region develops its own identity through economic interdependence and creates political support for them (Seliger, 2002). Trade and investment are what brings national economies together into close economic interdependence and will thus contribute to the process of regional economic integration.[2]

In this chapter we investigate Korea's direct investment in China and its implications for economic integration in Northeast Asia by investigating its effect on bilateral trade between Korea and China and other possible effects on economic integration. These two countries are key players in Northeast Asia and increasing interdependence between them through trade and investment will significantly contribute to region-wide economic integration, as their increasing interdependence will lead to a greater division of labor, greater scale economies, and a higher rate of growth in their economies and, thus, create further incentives for other countries to join in.

In the following section we lay out various possible linkages between outward direct investment (ODI) and bilateral trade between home and host countries. In Section 2 we discuss the motives for Korea's ODI in China with the purpose of shedding light on the investment–trade linkages between the two economies, and in Section 3 we investigate the geographical distribution of Korea's ODI within China and its determinants. We offer some concluding remarks in Section 4.

2.   OVERSEAS DIRECT INVESTMENT, TRADE AND ECONOMIC INTEGRATION

ODI makes a direct contribution to economic integration of home and host economies by leading to the establishment of an affiliate or a subsidiary in a foreign country and thus transforming a national enterprise into a transnational one. Within this enterprise, as within any internal organization, there is a hierarchical relationship between home office and affiliates and a vertical flow of information and personnel. Such exchange between home office and affiliates is not readily quantifiable as it bypasses the market, but being an intra-firm relationship it is a closer and more intimate person-to-person relationship than the typical arm's-length relationship between independent agents across the market, and thus has a greater integrative effect on the two economies.

What effect ODI has on the trade relationship between home and host economies is less clear, as it can either increase or reduce bilateral trade, or may even have no effect at all. It will have no effect on bilateral trade if it simply creates in the host country an 'export platform' for third-country markets and replaces the home-country exports to those markets with the exports from the affiliate. This kind of ODI is most likely to occur when a firm is seeking to minimize the labor cost by relocating its production site from home to a low-labor-cost country. Even in that case, however, ODI will have a positive effect on bilateral trade if the affiliate imports intermediate goods from the home country.

ODI will have a positive effect on bilateral trade if it leads to 'reverse importing,' that is, the home country importing the affiliate's output and replacing what has been produced for the home market with the goods from the affiliate. This will happen when the home country is losing its comparative advantage in labor-intensive industries and transfers them, through ODI, to another country that has a latent comparative advantage in the same industries. In this case, seeking to minimize the labor cost is obviously the main motive for ODI. This kind of ODI took place in Japan in the 1970s (Kojima, 1996; Lee, 1994) and also in Korea since the mid-1980s, as will be shown below.

ODI will also have a positive effect on bilateral trade if it is for exploiting natural resources that the home country lacks. Imports of natural resources from the host country may displace its imports of the same from a third country, but this 'trade diversion' is likely to be welfare-improving for both countries since for the home country it is from a more costly to a less costly supplier of natural resources and for the host country it expands the market for its natural resources.

ODI will have a negative effect on bilateral trade if it leads to a partial or full displacement of the home country's exports to the host country with locally produced goods. This will occur if the motive for ODI is to serve the host-country market regardless of whether it is to jump a tariff wall or to reduce the cost of serving the market such as the cost of transportation. But even in this case ODI will not completely displace bilateral trade if the affiliates import intermediate products from their parent companies or home-country suppliers, which appears generally to happen.

It is clear from the above discussion on the relationship between ODI and bilateral trade that we can infer the effect of ODI on bilateral trade from its motive. If the motive for ODI is to take advantage of low-cost labor in the host country or exploit its natural resources, it is likely to have a positive effect on bilateral trade, whereas if the motive is to exploit the host-country market it is likely to have a negative effect (though negligible or even positive if intermediate inputs are supplied from the home country).

The discussion so far of the effect of ODI on bilateral trade is based on the assumption that in the economic relationship between two countries trade precedes ODI. It is quite possible, however, as happened in China after the Four Modernizations, that foreign investment comes in first to manufacture products in the host country, which then are exported. Such investment will have a positive effect on bilateral trade as it generally leads to importing intermediate products from the home country and possibly to exporting final products to the home country.

These investment–trade linkages are a direct effect of ODI on bilateral trade between home and host countries and do not take into account any indirect effect that ODI may have on bilateral trade through its effect on economic growth. As is well documented in the literature (e.g. Bende-Nabende, 2002; Graham and Wada, 2001; Henley, Kirkpatrick and Wilde, 2002; OECD, 2000; Tseng and Zebregs, 2002), ODI generally has a positive effect on the economic growth of the host country, and definitely in the case of China, as it brings in capital, advanced technology and managerial know-how, and expands employment while increasing competitive pressure on local enterprises and, thus, enhancing their efficiency. It is also likely to have a long-run positive effect on the home-country economy by transferring abroad the industries in which it is losing its comparative advantage and thus facilitating structural adjustment in accordance with changing comparative advantage. These changes in both home and host countries will have a positive effect on bilateral trade, provided that it is positively related to economic growth.

If this indirect positive effect of ODI is taken into account, ODI motivated by low-cost labor will have a positive effect on bilateral trade whereas the effect of ODI motivated by host-country market will remain ambiguous, its sign depending on the relative magnitude of direct and indirect effects.[3]

In addition to the ODI–trade linkages there is another reason why ODI will have a positive effect on regional economic integration, and that is the backward linkages created by ODI in the host country. To the extent that the affiliates purchase locally produced intermediate goods the local suppliers participate in the production network that runs across national boundaries and become indirectly linked with the affiliates' parent companies. This inclusion in parent companies' production network will have as strong an effect on regional economic integration as bilateral trade, as demonstrated in the case of Southeast Asia and the coastal areas of China where foreign direct investment has been instrumental in promoting economic growth. As will be shown below, Korea's ODI in China has led to extensive local procurement and, therefore, to the inclusion of local Chinese firms into Korean firms' production networks.

3.   MOTIVES FOR KOREA'S ODI IN CHINA AND ITS EFFECT ON BILATERAL TRADE

In investigating the effect of Korea's ODI in China on the two countries' bilateral trade, we rely on the results of two recent surveys on Korea's ODI, one carried out by the Korea Institute for Industrial Economics and Trade (KIET) and the other by the Korean Export–Import Bank (KEXIM). The KIET survey, conducted by two KIET researchers, Ha and Hong (1998), was based on a sample of 615 Korean companies (216 large firms and 399 small and medium-sized enterprises) and their 952 offshore affiliates. It contains information on the motives for overseas investment, the patterns of sales and procurement, and other activities of offshore affiliates, as reported by their parent companies registered officially as overseas investors in 1996.

The KEXIM survey was based on a smaller sample of 290 large offshore affiliates with an outstanding investment of at least US$10 million at the end of 1998. Of these affiliates, 191 (66 percent) were the affiliates of the top 5 *chaebols* and 29 (10 percent) the affiliates of the next 25 largest *chaebols*. Given that small and medium-sized enterprises (SMEs) are not included in the KEXIM survey, we hope to draw some inferences about ODI by Korea's SMEs and its effect on economic integration by comparing the results of this survey with those of the KIET survey.

3.1   Motives for Investing in China

Table 11.1 reports the results of the KIET survey on the motives for Korea's ODI in general. The survey asked the firms to pick the two most important from a number of motives for investing overseas – natural resource or raw materials, low-cost labor, market access, high technology and 'others.' Out of 305 firms with investment in China, 179 firms (58.7 percent) reported low-cost labor and 66 firms (21.6 percent) market access as the most important motive for investing in China. These motives are quite different from those for investing in North America and Europe, which, according to the survey, are market access, 'others' and high technology in descending order of importance (Table 11.1).[4]

Table 11.2, based on the KEXIM survey on the motives for Korea's ODI, shows that export expansion from Korea was chosen by 34.3 percent of the respondents as the most important reason for investing in China whereas low-cost labor was chosen by only 16.4 percent. This is significantly less than the 58.7 percent of the respondents in the KIET survey that reported low-cost labor as the most important motive for investing in China. Given that the KEXIM survey covers only the affiliates of large firms whereas the KIET survey covers the affiliates of large firms as well as SMEs, we take the difference in the reported percentage as an indication that the motives for investing in China differ between large firms and SMEs. That is, for large firms the access to markets in China is the most important reason for investing in China whereas for SMEs China's low-cost labor is the most important.[5]

The two surveys also report the motives for ODI by industry, which are summarized in Tables 11.3 and 11.4. It is clear that, as expected, low-cost labor was the most important motive for Korea's ODI in labor-intensive industries.[6] According to the KIET survey (Table 11.3), for a majority of firms in

Table 11.1 KIET survey on motives for Korea's ODI by region (as of 1996)(%)

	Natural resource or raw materials	Low-cost labor	Market access	High technology	Others	Total (number of sample)
Asia	10.1	52.5	27.7	0.8	8.9	100 (651)
China	12.8	58.7	21.6	0.0	6.9	100 (305)
North America	6.5	8.7	58.7	9.4	16.7	100 (138)
Europe	3.2	4.8	73.0	7.9	11.1	100 (63)
Latin America	29.5	23.0	34.4	0.0	13.1	100 (61)
All regions	11.3	39.6	36.3	2.5	10.3	100 (938)

Note: The figures indicate the shares of the firms having the most important motive for investing abroad in total number of surveyed firms.

Source: Ha and Hong (1998).

Table 11.2 KEXIM survey on motives for Korea's ODI by region (as of 1998) (%)

	Natural resource or raw materials	Low-cost labor	Export expansion	High technology	Others	Total (number of sample)
Asia	12.4	11.7	37.2	0.7	37.9	100 (145)
China	1.5	16.4	34.3	0.0	47.7	100 (67)
North America	29.8	1.8	42.1	0.0	26.4	100 (57)
Europe	20.0	1.7	51.7	0.0	26.7	100 (60)
Latin America	26.6	0.0	53.3	0.0	20.0	100 (15)
All regions	19.3	6.6	41.7	0.3	32.1	100 (290)

Note: The figures indicate the shares of the firms having the most important motive for investing abroad in total number of surveyed firms.

Source: KEXIM.

Table 11.3 *KIET survey on motives for Korea's ODI in manufacturing (as of 1996) (%)*

	Natural resource or raw materials	Low-cost labor	Market access	High technology	Others	Total (number of sample)
Manufacturing	10.8	55.5	22.8	1.5	9.4	100 (618)
Food and beverages	26.8	31.7	36.6	0.0	4.9	100 (41)
Textiles and apparel	8.6	72.8	11.3	0.0	7.3	100 (151)
Footwear and leather	2.6	66.7	15.4	0.0	15.3	100 (39)
Wood	31.0	48.3	20.7	0.0	0.0	100 (29)
Paper and printing	14.3	57.1	7.1	0.0	21.4	100 (14)
Petroleum and chemicals	14.7	35.3	38.2	4.4	7.4	100 (68)
Non-metallic metals	11.5	73.1	0.0	0.0	15.4	100 (26)
Basic metals	14.7	41.2	41.2	0.0	2.9	100 (34)
Fabricated metals	0.0	55.6	38.9	5.6	0.0	100 (18)
Machinery and equipment	14.8	44.4	18.5	11.1	11.1	100 (27)
Electrical machinery	0.0	69.0	27.6	0.0	3.4	100 (29)
Electronics and telecomm. equipment	5.4	49.5	21.5	2.2	21.4	100 (93)
Motors and freight	6.9	41.3	44.8	0.0	7.0	100 (29)

Note: The figures indicate the shares of the firms having the most important motive for investing abroad in total number of surveyed firms.

Source: Ha and Hong (1998), pp. 124-5.

Table 11.4 KEXIM survey on motives for Korea's ODI in manufacturing by industry and region (as of 1998) (%)

	Natural resource or raw materials	Low-cost labor	Export expansion	High technology	Others	Total (number of sample)
Asia [China]						
Manufacturing	8.9 [0.0]	18.9 [26.2]	46.7 [50.0]	0.0 [0.0]	15.6 [9.5]	100 (90) [42]
Food and beverages	33.3 [0.0]	0.0 [0.0]	16.7 [0.0]	0.0 [0.0]	50.0 [100]	100 (6) [3]
Textiles and apparel	15.4 [0.0]	46.2 [100]	15.4 [0.0]	0.0 [0.0]	15.4 [0.0]	100 (13) [2]
Footwear and leather	0.0 [0.0]	100 [100]	0.0 [0.0]	0.0 [0.0]	0.0 [0.0]	100 (3) [2]
Petroleum and chemicals	33.3 [0.0]	11.1 [25.0]	22.2 [50.0]	0.0 [0.0]	33.3 [25.0]	100 (9) [4]
Basic metals	0.0 [0.0]	0.0 [0.0]	75.0 [80.0]	0.0 [0.0]	0.0 [20.0]	100 (8) [5]
Machinery and equipment	0.0 [0.0]	28.6 [33.3]	57.1 [66.7]	0.0 [0.0]	14.3 [0.0]	100 (7) [6]
Electronics and telecomm. equipment	0.0 [0.0]	12.5 [18.8]	68.8 [62.5]	0.0 [0.0]	6.3 [18.8]	100 (32) [16]
Motors and freight	0.0 [0.0]	16.7 [33.3]	16.7 [66.7]	0.0 [0.0]	33.3 [0.0]	100 (6) [3]
United States						
Manufacturing	9.1	0.0	63.6	0.0	18.2	100 (11)
Machinery and equipment	0.0	0.0	100	0.0	0.0	100 (2)
Electronics and telecomm. equipment	0.0	0.0	80.0	0.0	20.0	100 (5)
Europe						
Manufacturing	15.4	3.8	50.0	0.0	19.2	100 (26)
Electronics and telecomm. equipment	21.4	0.0	57.1	0.0	7.1	100 (14)
Motors and freight	0.0	14.3	57.1	0.0	14.3	100 (7)
Latin America and Africa						
Manufacturing	14.3	0.0	50.0	0.0	7.1	100 (14)
Textiles and Apparel	0.0	0.0	100	0.0	0.0	100 (2)
Basic metals	0.0	0.0	0.0	0.0	0.0	100 (2)
Electronics and Telecomm. equipment	12.5	0.0	62.5	0.0	0.0	100 (8)
All region						
Manufacturing	10.6	12.8	48.9	0.0	15.6	100 (141)

Notes: The figures indicate the shares of the firms having the most important motive for investing abroad in total number of surveyed firms. Figures in brackets indicate the share of the firms having the most important motive for investing in China in total number of surveyed firms.

Source: KEXIM.

the textiles and apparel and in the footwear and leather industries, which are all labor-intensive, low-cost labor was the most important motive for investing overseas (72.8 percent and 66.7 percent of the respondents, respectively). According to the KEXIM survey (Table 11.4), which breaks down the responses by region/country as well, 46.2 percent of the respondents in the textiles and apparel industry and 100 percent of the respondents in the footwear and leather industry that had invested in Asia regard low-cost labor as the most important motive for ODI. The corresponding figures for China are 100 percent for the two groups of industries.

The textiles and apparel and the leather and footwear industries had been two of Korea's major export industries until it began losing its comparative advantage in labor-intensive industries in the mid-1980s, owing in part to rapid wage increases. Korean firms in those industries had already established highly developed international marketing networks and could thus continue to utilize them in marketing the products of their affiliates in China and other low-cost labor countries. In the case of those two industries it is reasonable to conclude that the exports from the Korean affiliates in China were displacing the export of the same goods from Korea. Whether it has led to bilateral trade in intermediate goods and 'reverse imports' will be addressed later in the chapter.

Tables 11.3 and 11.4 also show that low-cost labor in the host country was an important factor in the decision to invest overseas for firms in capital-intensive heavy industries such as machinery and equipment, electronics and telecommunications equipment, and motors and freight. This is particularly evident in the case of Korea's ODI in China (Table 11.4). This apparent contradiction with the theory of comparative advantage (i.e., investment in capital-intensive industries in labor-abundant China) can be easily explained, however, once we recognize the increasingly widespread practice of intra-firm inter-process production arrangements or 'international fragmentation' in production process (Jones, 2001).[7]

Production processes in heavy industries involve, relative to light manufacturing industries, a large number of separable sub-processes with different requirements for technology and factor intensity – some sub-processes requiring high-tech materials and component parts and others requiring an intensive use of low-cost labor. A firm in such an industry can minimize the unit cost of producing the final output by locating some processes in countries well endowed in physical and human capital and others in countries where low-cost labor is in abundant supply. For example, it may produce high-tech components in the home country where there is a high technological capability while the assembling of components is done in China where there is an ample supply of low-cost labor. Indeed, many Korean firms in heavy industries have made such production arrangements since the late 1980s by establishing assembly plants in China. International fragmentation thus makes it possible for a developing country to become a site for producing some parts of a previously wholly integrated process and to acquire new skills and knowledge by producing them.

The Korean affiliates in heavy industries in China may be serving as an export platform for their parent companies. Even though in that case the affiliates' exports from China are displacing exports from Korea, the international fragmentation of production processes has a positive effect on bilateral trade if parts and components are shipped from parent to affiliate firms.

3.2   Trade Patterns of Korean Affiliates in China

As discussed in the preceding section, we are able to make some informed guesses about the effect on bilateral trade of Korea's ODI in China from the knowledge of its motives. In this section we try to find additional information on the ODI–trade nexus by looking into the procurement and sales patterns of affiliates as reported in the KIET and KEXIM surveys. This examination will only provide us, however, with a first approximation of the ODI–trade nexus since it does not take into account the indirect linkage effect of ODI that may take place in other sectors in the economy.

3.2.1   Procurement and Import Patterns

Table 11.5 reports the sources of procurement made by Korean offshore affiliates, as reported in the two surveys. According to the KIET survey (the top panel of the table), 60.5 percent of the total procurement of intermediate goods and materials by Korean affiliates in China came from Korea, 31.3 percent from local suppliers, and 8.2 percent from third countries. It is interesting to note that Korean affiliates outside of Asia (including China) imported a larger share of their intermediate goods and materials from Korea and procured less from local suppliers (with the exception of the affiliates in North America) in comparison with their counterparts in Asia.

According to the KEXIM survey (the bottom panel of Table 11.5), the procurement pattern of large-firm affiliates differs from that of all affiliates: the former imported 44.7 percent of intermediate goods and materials from Korea (78 percent of this share came directly from their parent companies or related affiliates). Local suppliers in China accounted for 39.2 percent of total procurement while third countries accounted for 16.1 percent. In other words, Korea's large-firm affiliates in China imported less from Korea, procured more locally and from third countries, implying that Korea's SME-affiliates in China relied more heavily than their large-firm counterparts on imports from Korea and less from local and third-country sources. This difference may be due to the networks of SMEs being more localized in Korea than

Table 11.5   Sources of procurement by offshore affiliates of Korean firms by region (% of total procurement)

KIET survey (as of 1996)

	Local procurement	Import		Total
		Korea	Third countries	
Asia	37.4	52.3	10.3	100
China	31.3	60.5	8.2	100
North America	34.6	64.8	0.5	100
Europe	19.6	80.1	0.3	100
Latin America	12.6	85.9	1.5	100

KEXIM survey (as of 2000)

	Local procurement	Import		Total
		Korea	Third countries	
Asia	45.4 (3.8)	33.4 (30.2)	21.3 (9.3)	100
China	39.2 (3.1)	44.7 (34.8)	16.1 (8.1)	100
North America	20.1 (8.4)	58.7 (56.9)	21.2 (14.7)	100
Europe	23.0 (7.9)	48.9 (45.4)	28.1 (14.4)	100
Latin America	31.0 (14.8)	51.6 (46.4)	17.5 (8.6)	100

Note: Figures in parentheses of KEXIM survey are the share of the related affiliates out of total procurement.

Sources: Ha and Hong (1998), KEXIM.

those of large firms, which we expect to be more global in reach. Another reason might be that, relative to SMEs, large firms are concentrated in capital-intensive industries, which are internationally more fragmented in production processes than labor-intensive industries in which ODI from SMEs is concentrated.

The results of the KEXIM survey are consistent with the information obtained from the KIET survey. That is, Korean affiliates in China imported a large share of their intermediate goods and materials from Korea, albeit not as much as that by those outside of Asia (including China). They generally procured more from local suppliers, creating substantial backward linkages within China. These results lead to the conclusion that as far as procurement by affiliates is concerned, Korea's ODI in China has had a positive effect on bilateral trade and has created extensive backward linkages, thus contributing to the economic integration of the two countries.

Table 11.6 shows the procurement pattern of offshore affiliates by manufacturing industry, as reported in the KIET survey. For affiliates in food and beverages – natural-resource-based industries in which the motive for ODI is to obtain natural resources in the host country – the share of imports from Korea was, as to be expected, small, 7.2 and 0.9 percent, respectively. Their share of local procurement was quite large, 91.4 and 98.9 percent, respectively, indicating a strong backward linkage effect of ODI.

In a number of labor-intensive industries and in some heavy industries the share of imports from Korea was very large. In the former group are the textile

Table 11.6   KIET survey on sources of procurement by offshore affiliates of Korean firms in manufacturing by industry (as of 1996; % of total procurement)

	Local procurement	Import		Total
		Korea	Third countries	
Manufacturing	47.3	46.0	6.7	100
Food and beverages	91.4	7.2	1.3	100
Textiles	21.8	74.8	3.4	100
Apparel	49.1	49.1	1.8	100
Footwear and leather	7.0	90.8	2.2	100
Wood	32.8	51.5	15.7	100
Paper and printing	62.0	32.6	5.4	100
Petroleum and chemicals	30.9	33.0	36.1	100
Non-metallic metals	48.8	39.5	11.6	100
Basic metals	98.9	0.9	0.2	100
Fabricated metals	0.9	96.0	3.1	100
Machinery and equipment	68.1	27.4	4.5	100
Electrical machinery	25.0	74.5	0.4	100
Electronics and telecomm equipment	16.7	64.7	18.6	100
Motors and freight	31.1	68.9	0.0	100

Source: Ha and Hong (1998), pp. 66–7.

and the footwear and leather industries, where the shares of inputs imported from Korea were 74.8 percent and 90.8 percent, respectively. In the latter group are the fabricated metals, electrical machinery, motors and freight, and electronics and telecommunication equipment industries, where the shares were 96.0, 74.5, 68.9 and 64.7 percent, respectively. For affiliates in those industries local procurement accounted for a small share of intermediate goods and materials, indicating that they are basically assemblers of imported parts utilizing low-cost labor in the host country.

Table 11.7 reports the procurement pattern of Korea's large-firm affiliates in China. In footwear and leather, basic metals, and machinery and equipment at least one half of intermediate goods and materials were imported from Korea. In food and beverages, apparel, non-metallic minerals, and motors and freight a significant portion of inputs was supplied locally, a sign of strong backward linkages of ODI in China by large-firm affiliates. In textiles and basic metals at least a third of inputs was imported from third countries.

Table 11.7   KEXIM survey on sources of procurement by Korea's large-firm affiliates in China in manufacturing by industry (as of 2000; % of total procurement)

		China	
		Import	
	Local procurement	Korea	Third countries
Manufacturing	38.5 (3.1)	45.2 (35.1)	16.2 (8.1)
Food and beverages	80.0 (0.0)	20.0 (0.0)	0.0 (0.0)
Textiles	29.5 (0.0)	32.2 (32.2)	38.3 (22.0)
Apparel	72.1 (0.0)	24.8 (24.8)	3.1 (0.0)
Footwear and leather	29.9 (0.0)	68.5 (68.5)	1.5 (0.0)
Petroleum and chemicals	44.2 (0.0)	27.9 (13.3)	27.8 (0.0)
Non-metallic minerals	100.0 (0.0)	0.0 (0.0)	0.0 (0.0)
Basic metals	17.0 (0.3)	49.8 (21.5)	33.1 (26.4)
Machinery and equipment	10.0 (0.0)	67.4 (67.4)	22.6 (0.0)
Electronics and telecomm. equipment	41.8 (4.8)	45.1 (37.7)	13.1 (6.8)
Motors and freight	55.6 (0.0)	44.4 (44.4)	0.0 (0.0)

Note: Figures in parentheses are the share of related affiliates out of total procurement.

Source: KEXIM.

For manufacturing as a whole the share of inputs imported from Korea was 45.2 percent while the share of local procurement was 38.5 percent. These high figures suggest that ODI in China by Korea's large-firm affiliates has had a positive effect on economic integration of the two countries.[8]

3.2.2 Sales and export patterns

Table 11.8 reports the sales and exports of Korean affiliates as reported in the two surveys. Korean affiliates in China exported 69.9 percent of their output to the rest of the world: 27.9 percent to Korea and 42.0 percent to third countries (the top panel of the table). In comparison, its large-firm affiliates exported 53.3 percent of their output to the rest of the world – 24.5 percent to

Table 11.8   Sales destination of offshore affiliates of Korean firms by region (% of total sales)

KIET survey (as of 1996)

	Local sales	Export		Total
		Korea	Third countries	
Asia	64.5	14.2	21.3	100
China	30.2	27.9	42.0	100
North America	93.9	3.6	2.5	100
Europe	69.9	1.4	28.7	100
Latin America	58.0	10.9	31.1	100

KEXIM survey (as of 2000)

	Local sales	Export		Total
		Korea	Third countries	
Asia	49.1 (2.5)	30.0 (25.5)	20.9 (9.4)	100
China	46.7 (7.1)	24.5 (23.8)	28.8 (13.9)	100
North America	83.5 (2.2)	5.5 (3.6)	11.0 (4.2)	100
Europe	50.1 (6.2)	7.2 (4.4)	42.7 (9.8)	100
Latin America	68.5 (13.2)	20.1 (20.1)	11.4 (4.2)	100

Note: Figures in parentheses of KEXIM survey are the share of the related affiliates out of total sales.

Sources: Ha and Hong (1998), KEXIM.

Korea and 28.8 percent to third countries (the bottom panel of the table), indicating that Korea's SME affiliates in China exported a much larger share of
their output. The share of local sales by the affiliates outside of China was
much larger than that by the affiliates operating in China, suggesting that the
latter performed largely as an export platform for Korean companies, especially for its SMEs.

Table 11.9 shows that the Korean manufacturing affiliates as a whole sold
66.1 percent of their output in the host countries and exported 9.4 percent to
Korea and 24.5 percent to third countries. It also shows a wide industry variation in the shares of local sales and exports. In food and beverages, petroleum and chemicals, non-metallic minerals, basic metals, fabricated metals,
machinery and equipment, and motors and freight, more than half of the affiliate output was sold locally. In contrast, in textiles, apparel, footwear and
leather, wood, paper and printing, electrical machinery, and electronics and

*Table 11.9   KIET survey on sales destination of offshore affiliates of Korean
firms in manufacturing by industry (as of 1996; % of total
sales)*

	Local sales	Export		Total
		Korea	Third countries	
Manufacturing	66.1	9.4	24.5	100
Food and beverages	77.2	10.2	12.6	100
Textiles	31.7	21.0	47.3	100
Apparel	24.5	19.8	55.7	100
Footwear and leather	26.7	21.6	51.7	100
Wood	41.8	41.9	16.3	100
Paper and printing	2.9	23.4	73.7	100
Petroleum and chemicals	64.3	13.5	22.1	100
Non-metallic metals	67.3	20.5	12.2	100
Basic metals	95.4	2.3	2.3	100
Fabricated metals	56.8	3.8	39.5	100
Machinery and equipment	97.5	2.4	0.1	100
Electrical machinery	19.4	44.4	36.1	100
Electronics and telecomm. equipment	27.4	7.6	65.1	100
Motors and freight	86.7	0.9	12.3	100

Source: Ha and Hong (1998), pp. 56–7.

telecommunication equipment, more than half of the output was exported. Reverse imports – exports back to Korea – accounted for 9.4 percent of the entire manufacturing sector output and were especially large in wood (41.9 percent) and electrical machinery (44.4 percent).

The large reverse imports in wood reflect a strategy of Korean firms to develop and import resource-based products, which are in short supply in Korea. In contrast, the large share of reverse imports of electrical machinery in total sales reflects Korea's changing comparative advantage and the displacement of home production with imports in some of the consumer durable goods markets in Korea.

Table 11.10 reports the sales and exports of large-firm affiliates in China, as reported in the KEXIM survey. For the entire manufacturing sector, local sales in China accounted for 45.8 percent of total sales, reverse imports 24.9 percent, and exports to third countries 29.3 percent. Reverse imports were especially large in non-metallic minerals (89.1 percent) followed by apparel (41.1 percent), textiles (38.3 percent), and electronics and telecommunication equipment (32.4 percent). As noted earlier (see Table 11.7), offshore affiliates

Table 11.10   KEXIM survey on sales destination of Korea's large-firm affiliates in China in manufacturing by industry (as of 2000; % of total procurement)

| | | China | |
| | | | Export |
	Local sales	Korea	Third countries
Manufacturing	45.8 (7.2)	24.9 (24.2)	29.3 (14.1)
Food and beverages	76.2 (0.0)	0.0 (0.0)	23.8 (0.0)
Textiles	36.0 (6.1)	38.3 (38.3)	25.7 (0.0)
Apparel	17.0 (0.0)	41.1 (41.1)	41.8 (0.0)
Footwear and leather	0.2 (0.0)	20.3 (20.3)	79.5 (0.0)
Petroleum and chemicals	75.1 (12.9)	11.4 (11.4)	13.6 (11.5)
Non-metallic minerals	10.9 (0.0)	89.1 (89.1)	0.0 (0.0)
Basic metals	97.8 (18.9)	0.0 (0.0)	2.2 (0.2)
Machinery and equipment	100.0 (12.2)	0.0 (0.0)	0.0 (0.0)
Electronics and telecomm. equipment	33.0 (5.1)	32.4 31.2)	34.7 (21.2)
Motors and freight	79.6 (0.0)	20.4 (20.4)	0.0 (0.0)

Note: Figures in parentheses are the share of related affiliates of total sales.

Source: KEXIM.

in most of those industries procured much of their intermediate products from their parent companies; that is, apparel 24.8 percent, textiles 32.2 percent, electronics and telecommunication equipment 45.1 percent. This pattern of procurement, combined with heavy reliance on reverse imports, suggests the importance of intra-firm trade for large-firm affiliates in those industries.

For large-firm affiliates in China in the footwear and leather industry, third-country markets accounted for 79.5 percent of their total sales; for those in apparel 41.8 percent; and for those in electronics and telecommunication equipment 34.7 percent.

Reverse imports resulting from ODI clearly add to bilateral trade between home and host countries and reflect a changing comparative advantage between the two countries.

What motivated Korean firms to invest in China was the rapidly increasing labor cost at home and an abundant supply of low-cost labor in China. An increasing gap in the labor cost between the two countries would have caused a contraction in labor-intensive industries in Korea and an expansion in the same in China even without the transplantation of those industries to China through ODI and would have led to Korea's importing labor-intensive products from China. What ODI has done is to bring about a more rapid response of the international division of labor to changing comparative advantage and a greater expansion of bilateral trade between Korea and China than would have been otherwise (Ogawa and Lee, 1996).

4.   SECTORAL AND GEOGRAPHICAL DISTRIBUTION OF KOREA'S ODI IN CHINA AND ITS DETERMINANTS

FDI in China is not evenly distributed throughout the country, being highly concentrated in the coastal areas (Broadman and Sun, 1997; OECD, 2000). Such geographical concentration implies that the effect of FDI on economic growth and integration into the world economy is not evenly distributed throughout China. If Korea's ODI follows the same pattern, its effect on bilateral economic integration will also be unevenly distributed, some areas in China being more integrated with Korea than others. In this section we investigate the geographical distribution of Korea's ODI in China to find out the spatial distribution of its integrative effect in China.

As is clear from Table 11.11, Korea's ODI in China is, like FDI in China in general, concentrated in the coastal areas, which received 88.9 percent ($2896 million) of total FDI from Korea in 1993–97. The inland areas and the autonomous regions received only 9.3 percent and 1.8 percent, respectively, during the same period.

Table 11.11   *Geographical distribution of FDI in China by region*
(cumulative, US$ million, %)

	From Korea (1993–97)			From the world (1994–97)
	Total	Large firm	SMEs	
Coastal areas	2 896.3	1 777.0	1 119.3	135 609.7
	(88.9)	(90.7)	(86.2)	(85.4)
Shandong	927.2	434.4	492.8	10 650.5
	(28.5)	(22.2)	(38.0)	(6.7)
Jiangsu	369.1	293.7	75.4	19 599.2
	(11.3)	(15.0)	(5.8)	(12.3)
Liaoning	377.0	188.1	188.9	6 968.9
	(11.6)	(9.6)	(14.6)	(4.4)
Tianjin	348.1	209.1	139.0	7 200.0
	(10.7)	(10.7)	(10.7)	(4.5)
Shanghai	367.4	304.7	62.7	13 532.0
	(11.3)	(15.6)	(4.8)	(8.5)
Beijing	248.7	181.0	67.7	5 597.3
	(7.6)	(9.2)	(5.2)	(3.5)
Guangdong	106.0	71.9	34.1	44 112.6
	(3.3)	(3.7)	(2.6)	(27.8)
Hebei	51.9	26.2	25.8	3 003.4
	(1.6)	(1.3)	(2.0)	(1.9)
Zhejiang	72.1	55.8	16.3	5 432.3
	(2.2)	(2.8)	(1.3)	(3.4)
Fujian	19.7	5.6	14.1	16 038.7
	(0.6)	(0.3)	(1.1)	(10.1)
Hainan	9.1	6.5	2.6	3 474.8
	(0.3)	(0.3)	(0.2)	(2.2)
Inland areas	301.8	128.3	173.5	19 611.4
	(9.3)	(6.5)	13.4	12.4
Jilin	125.8	51.0	74.8	1 503.8
	(3.9)	(2.6)	(5.8)	(0.9)
Heilongjiang	108.6	24.7	83.9	2 166.2
	(3.3)	(1.3)	(6.5)	(1.4)
Hunan	29.8	28.6	1.2	2 501.2
	(0.9)	(1.5)	(0.1)	(1.6)
Hubei	14.0	12.3	1.7	2 756.4
	(0.4)	(0.6)	(0.1)	(1.7)
Anhui	4.4	2.0	2.4	1 793.6
	(0.1)	(0.1)	(0.2)	(1.1)

Table 11.11   continued

| | From Korea (1993–97) | | | From the world |
	Total	Large firm	SMEs	(1994–97)
Henan	3.0	0.0	3.0	2 080.9
	(0.1)	(0.0)	(0.2)	(1.3)
Shanxi	2.4	0.3	2.2	502.5
	(0.1)	(0.02)	(0.2)	(0.3)
Sichuan	7.4	6.4	1.1	2 570.7
	(0.2)	(0.3)	(0.1)	(1.6)
Shaanxi	3.9	2.6	1.3	1 517.1
	(0.1)	(0.1)	(0.1)	(1.0)
Jiangxi	0.9	0.0	0.9	1 332.9
	(0.03)	(0.0)	(0.1)	(0.8)
Guizhou	0.4	0.4	0.0	201.8
	(0.01)	(0.02)	(0.0)	(0.1)
Yunnan	1.1	0.0	1.1	393.7
	(0.03)	(0.0)	(0.1)	(0.2)
Gansu	0.0	0.0	0.0	283.1
	(0.0)	(0.0)	(0.0)	(0.2)
Qinghai	0.0	0.0	0.0	7.5
	(0.0)	(0.0)	(0.0)	(0.004)
Autonomous regions	59.3	54.0	5.3	3 516.1
	(1.8)	(2.8)	(0.4)	(2.2)
Total	3 257.4	1 959.3	1 298.1	158 737.2
	(100)	(100)	(100)	(100)

Source: KEXIM, www.koreaexim.go.kr/oeis/index.hml, National Bureau of Statistics of China, www.stats.gov.cn

Among the coastal areas the Shandong province is the most favored destination for Korean investment (28.5 percent of Korea's ODI in China), followed by the Liaoning province (11.6 percent), the Jiangsu province (11.3 percent), the city of Shanghai (11.3 percent), the city of Tianjin (10.7 percent) and the city of Beijing (7.6 percent). It is noteworthy to point out that Korea's ODI is concentrated, relative to FDI from the world, in Shandong, Liaoning, Shanghai, Tianjin and Beijing – areas that are along the Yellow Sea and nearest to Korea.

Another noteworthy point is that three provinces in China's northeastern region (Liaoning, Jilin and Heilongjiang) have received significant amounts of

FDI from Korea, particularly from its SMEs, whereas the same provinces have received relatively negligible amounts from other countries. We explain this difference as due to the fact that those three provinces have the highest concentration of ethnic Koreans in China:[9] the common language and some commonality in culture would have the effect of reducing the transactions cost in investing overseas, such cost reduction being more important for SMEs than for large-firm affiliates.

Table 11.12 reports the distribution of Korea's ODI in China by province and by sector. In 1993–97 Korea's ODI in manufacturing in China amounted to $2649 million, about 81 percent of Korea's total ODI in China. Within the manufacturing sector, electronics and telecommunication equipment registered the largest share (18.8 percent), followed by textiles and apparel (17.2 percent), machinery and equipment (10.4 percent), and petroleum and chemicals (9.4 percent). Investment by SMEs was concentrated in light industries such as textiles and apparel, footwear and leather, and wood and furniture, whereas investment by large firms was concentrated in heavy and chemical industries such as electronics and telecommunication equipment, motors and freight, non-metallic minerals, and basic metals.

The city of Tianjin was the largest recipient of Korean investment in electronics and telecommunication equipment whereas the provinces of Shandong, Liaoning and Jiangsu were the largest recipients of investment in textiles and apparel, machinery and equipment, and basic metals, respectively.

In order to find out the factors that determine the geographical distribution of Korea's ODI in China, we carry out a regression analysis of the following location choice model of FDI that includes variables representing the level of economic development and foreign investment policies of different regions. The model is applied to two different sets of FDI data, one for large firms and the other for SMEs.

$$ODI_i = \beta_1 + \beta_2 Y_i + \beta_3 W_i + \beta_4 E_i + \beta_5 I_i + \beta_6 DP_i + \beta_7 DK_i + \varepsilon_i,$$

where:

ODI_i = log of Korea's net cumulative direct investment in a manufacturing industry in region i in 1993–97,

Y_i = log of nominal GDP of region i in 1995,

W_i = log of nominal annual average wage for staff and workers in region i in 1995,

E_i = ratio of the number of students enrolled in higher education to population in region i in 1995,

I_i = total length of road in region i per square kilometer of land in 1995,

Table 11.12 Korea's net outward manufacturing investment in China (cumulative, 1993–97), by sector and region, US$ thousands, %)

	(1) FB	(2) TA	(3) FL	(4) WF	(5) PP	(6) PC	(7) NM	(8) BM	(9) FM	(10) ME	(11) ET	(12) MF	(13) OT	Total
Shandong	43 296	219 325	80 888	9 242	9 568	48 536	123 016	8 187	20 511	58 437	85 949	119 975	66 699	893 629 [33.7]
Jiangsu	11 798	65 824	6 824	1 556	580	72 128	8 710	87 067	1 196	25 816	70 377	1 680	4 949	358 505 [13.5]
Liaoning	9 281	39 926	27 692	14 290	11 076	16 089	28 907	17 818	9 143	73 104	26 710	19 478	11 391	304 905 [11.5]
Tianjin	4 423	38 997	9 860	1 016	1 214	33 818	3 210	6 102	14 154	11 975	146 740	3 722	59 462	334 693 [12.6]
Shanghai	8 366	17 846	1 214	2 151	21 678	1 608	6 487	300	5 795	8 171	42 506	14 610	8 695	139 427 [5.3]
Beijing	22 709	7 259	2 204	309	680	14 116	18 059	1 190	5 013	18 443	39 092	4 743	5 273	139 090 [5.3]
Guangdong	3 500	3 094	1 760	3 508	308	9 298	150	12 387	2 984	7 657	47 541	8 500	3 986	104 673 [4.0]
Hebei	17 321	8 389	1 204	1 108	86	1 119	2 014	2 824	1 469	8 440	100	141	2 767	46 982 [1.8]
Zhejiang	3 498	8 675	825	797	1 361	28 120	730	521	84	591	220	150	2 169	47 741 [1.8]
Fujian	0	1 256	0	0	0	3 780	280	2 191	52	1 220	888	7 131	2 811	19 609 [0.7]
Hainan	0	0	0	20	0	200	1 800	6 456	0	0	0	0	0	8 476 [0.3]
Jilin	11 906	34 158	643	8 320	2 571	10 663	4 713	3 302	2 890	4 387	6 200	1 894	1 912	93 559 [3.5]
Heilongjiang	6 257	4 725	951	3 090	1 773	2 880	1 167	2 031	898	54 873	1 840	1 048	-2 073	79 460 [3.0]
Hunan		100									28 618		1 100	29 818 [1.1]
Hubei	391	5 480		70		300						6 900	50	13 191 [0.5]
Anhui	1 000					1 254					2 000	25	70	4 349 [0.2]
Henan	906					902	64			526	80		50	2 528 [0.1]
Shanxi							1 120							1 120 [0.04]
Sichuan		781									156			937 [0.04]
Shaanxi	315					12					200		211	738 [0.03]
Jiangxi		146			22					139				307 [0.01]
Guizhou												414		414 [0.02]
Yunnan	0	0	0	0	0	0	0	0	0	0	0	0	0	0 [0.0]
Gansu	0	0	0	0	0	0	0	0	0	0	0	0	0	0 [0.0]
Qinghai	0	0	0	0	0	0	0	0	0	0	0	0	0	0 [0.0]
Total	145 636	456 191	134 065	45 477	50 942	249 050	201 837	150 376	64 189	276 076	499 217	205 926	169 544	2 648 526 [100]
	(5.5)	(17.2)	(5.1)	(1.7)	(1.9)	(9.4)	(7.6)	(5.7)	(2.4)	(10.4)	(18.8)	(7.8)	(6.4)	(100)
Large	80 282	185 955	29 850	7 973	22 893	131 212	149 353	125 341	14 393	136 074	376 661	149 078	57 510	1 466 575
	(55.1)	(40.8)	(22.3)	(17.5)	(44.9)	(52.7)	(74.0)	(83.4)	(22.4)	(49.3)	(75.5)	(72.4)	(33.9)	(55.4)
SMEs	65 354	270 236	104 215	37 504	28 049	117 838	52 484	25 035	49 796	140 002	122 556	56 848	112 034	1 181 951
	(44.9)	(59.2)	(77.7)	(82.5)	(55.1)	(47.3)	(26.0)	(16.6)	(77.6)	(50.3)	(24.5)	(27.6)	(66.1)	(44.6)

Notes: (1) Food and beverages (FB), (2) Textiles and apparel (TA), (3) Footwear and leather (FL), (4) Wood and furniture (WF), (5) Paper and printing (PP), (6) Petroleum and chemicals (PC), (7) Non-metallic minerals (NM), (8) Basic metals (BM), (9) Fabricated metals (FM), (10) Machinery and equipment (ME), (11) Electronics and telecommunication equipment (ET), (12) Motors and freight (MF), (13) Others (OT).

Source: KEXIM, www.koreaexim.go.kr/oeis/index.hml

DP_i = dummy variable for special economic zones and open coastal cities,

DK_i = dummy variable for provinces where ethnic Koreans constitute a major minority group,

ε = stochastic disturbance term.

Y, GDP, represents the market size of a region and is expected to have a positive coefficient, and the variable W, with an expected negative coefficient, is to capture low-cost labor as a motive for Korea's ODI in China. The variable E is to capture the importance of the availability of skilled labor as a motive for ODI and is expected to have a positive coefficient. It is well recognized in the literature that the availability of infrastructure is an important factor in the decision on where to locate FDI and various indicators have been used as a measure of infrastructure availability. In our regression we use the total length of roads within a region (I), normalized by its geographical size, as a measure of infrastructure availability.

The regression model also includes a dummy variable for preferential policies for FDI inflows. As is well known, China has a number of open economic zones such as special economic zones (SEZs) and open coastal cities (OCCs), which offer special tax incentives and maintain a liberal trade and investment regime but are separated from China's internal markets. The policy dummy variable (DP) is assigned value 1 for Guangdong, Fujian, Hainan, Liaoning, Hebei, Tianjin, Shandong, Jiangsu, Zhejiang, areas designated as either SEZ or OCC, and value 0 for other areas. The expected sign for DP is positive. Another dummy variable (DK) is included in the model to find out whether common culture/language mattered in Korean investors' location decisions. It is assigned value 1 for the three provinces of Jilin, Heilongjiang, and Liaoning, where ethnic Koreans constitute a major minority group, and value 0 for other provinces.

The dependent variable employed in the model is the net cumulative manufacturing investment for 1993–97. For estimation we apply the canonical censored regression model, given that the dependent variable is left censored at zero. All the data for the independent variables are for 1995, a midpoint in the 1993–97 period.[10]

We have shown in the preceding sections that there is a significant difference in the motives for ODI as well as in the sales and procurement patterns between large firms and SMEs. Those differences imply that the large-firm affiliates would be much more sensitive to the size of local market and less sensitive to labor cost and would produce more of their output for local markets than SMEs. They also imply a larger regression coefficient of the local market size (Y) for large-firm affiliates than for SMEs and a smaller absolute value of the negative coefficient of labor cost (W) for large-firm affiliates than for SMEs.

Table 11.13   Locational determinants of Korean firms' manufacturing investment in China (1993–97)

	Model I		Model II	
	Large firms	SMEs	Large firms	SMEs
GDP	1.94 *	1.88 ***	2.13 **	2.08 ***
	(1.9)	(4.5)	(2.0)	(3.8)
Wage	-4.83	–7.03***	–2.12	–5.01*
	(–0.8)	(–2.73)	(–0.4)	(–1.9)
Labour quality	6.45	4.02**	9.4***	6.89***
	(1.6)	(2.0)	(2.9)	(4.1)
Infrastructure	11.62	11.02**	–	–
	(1.1)	(2.5)		
Dummy: govern-	5.70***	3.15***	6.6***	3.87***
ment policy	(3.0)	(3.6)	(3.6)	(4.2)
Dummy: Korean				
people	3.92	3.96***	3.02	2.67**
	(1.5)	(3.3)	(1.2)	(2.2)
Constant	30.20	52.76**	8.1	36.5*
	(0.6)	(2.5)	(0.2)	(1.7)
Adjusted R^2	0.55	0.77	0.56	0.73

Notes: *t*-values are in parentheses. ***, ** and * indicate that the coefficient is significantly different from zero at 1, 5 and 10% levels respectively.

Two sets of regression results are reported on Table 11.13. The first set (Model I), which includes all the independent variables discussed above, shows that in the case of SMEs all the explanatory variables are statistically significant and have the correct signs whereas in the case of the large-firm affiliates only the market size (Y) and the policy dummy variable (DP) are significant and have the correct signs. Model I, however, suffers from multi-collinearity as the infrastructure variable (I) is highly correlated with wage (W) and education (E).[11]

The second set of regression results (Model II), which excludes infrastructure as an independent variable, shows that the estimate of the market size (Y) is positive and statistically significant for both large-firm affiliates and SMEs and is larger for the former than the latter, a result consistent with the survey results discussed in a preceding section.

The estimate of the wage-rate coefficient is negative for both large firms and SMEs, as expected, but is statistically significant only in the case of SMEs. This result is consistent with the survey result that low-cost labor is the most important motive for SMEs but not for large-firm affiliates. There is also a notable difference between large-firm affiliates and SMEs with respect to the effect of labor quality (E) on Korea's ODI in China. The coefficient of this variable is much larger for large-firm affiliates than for SMEs.

These results are consistent with the observation made earlier that investments in China by SMEs are concentrated in low-skilled labor-intensive industries such as textiles and apparel, footwear and leather, and wood and furniture, whereas investments by large firms are concentrated in capital- and technology-intensive industries such as electronics and telecommunication equipment, and motors and freight, which require more skilled labor. For the first group of investments, low-cost labor is a more important factor in determining where to locate than the quality of labor and conversely for the second.

The dummy variable for preferential policies has a positive and statistically significant coefficient for both large-firm affiliates and SMEs with the effect being stronger on investments from large firms than those from SMEs. Finally, the estimate of the coefficient of the dummy variable for common culture/language is positive and statistically significant for SMEs but not significant for large-firm affiliates, as expected.

5. CONCLUDING REMARKS

No single motive drives a country's ODI and Korea's case is no exception: some firms have invested in China to take advantage of its cheap labor and others have invested in China for market access or to secure its natural resources. In spite of such diverse motives the data presented in this chapter suggest that Korea's ODI in China as a whole has had a positive effect on the two countries' bilateral trade. We have also found out that Korea's ODI in China is not evenly distributed throughout China, being limited mostly to the coastal areas and the areas with a high concentration of ethnic Koreans.

If by economic integration we mean that capital, labor, and goods and services can move between countries more freely than otherwise, Korea's ODI in China certainly has had and will continue to have a positive effect on the economic integration of the two countries. It will further the integrative process by promoting information and personnel exchange between the two countries and by inducing them to abide by contracts and accept property rights and the rule of law and to realize the importance of cross-border harmonization of rules and regulations on trade and investment. These are the effects of ODI that are rarely quantified and seldom discussed in the literature but perhaps are more important for regional integration in the long run.

Recently, at a meeting in Beijing, a group of Korean business leaders proposed that China, Japan and Korea establish a joint policy coordination body with the aim of creating a Northeast Asian free-trade area (*Digital Korea Herald*, Friday, 7 June 2002).[12] Creating such an area would be a difficult task in the short run because there are a number of economic, historical and political factors unique to the region that many argue hinder its immediate establishment (Lee, 2003; Schott and Goodrich, 2001; Seliger, 2002). Those factors should not, however, be a barrier to the establishment of a joint policy coordination body, which can carry out the task of promoting trade and investment among them and contributing to the creation of a strong regional identity. Thus it will pave the way toward building formal regional machinery in Northeast Asia.

NOTES

* An earlier version of the chapter was presented at the KIEP/NEAFF conference on Enhancing Investment Cooperation in Northeast Asia, Honolulu, Hawaii, 8–9 August 2002, at the 8th International Conference of the East Asian Economic Association, Kuala Lumpur, 4–5 November 2002, and at the Conference on International Trade Essays in honor of Mordechai Kreinin, Johns Hopkins University, 5–6 January 2003. The authors wish to thank the participant in those conferences, especially Chang-Soo Lee, Kazutomo Abe, Mike Plummer, Woonki Sung, Masaru Umemoto and Ronald Jones for their helpful comments on earlier versions.

1. There are disputes regarding the effect of membership in economic union on the member countries' long-term economic growth, but a recent empirical study points out that membership in the European Union has had a positive effect on the long-term growth of the member countries (Crespo-Cuaresma et al., 2002).

2. Economic integration is usually defined as 'a state of affairs or a process involving attempts to combine separate national economies into larger economic regions' and takes place through the establishment of formal regional machinery such as a free-trade area, a customs union, a common market, or a complete economic union (Bende-Nabende, 2002, p.11). In this chapter we take it also to mean increasing economic connectedness between national economies through trade, investment, and labor movement. Thus economic integration can be brought about either through deliberate attempts to create formal regional machinery, or by policy changes toward freer trade and investment, or technological changes that facilitate trade/investment expansion between national economies.

3. If ODI is tariff-hopping and goes into an import-substitute sector it may have a negative effect on economic growth and thus a negative indirect effect on bilateral trade.

4. This difference in motives between ODI in China and that in North America and Europe may, to a certain extent, be due to the fact that China has SEZs and other countries do not. Some of the Korean ODI in China is likely to be in SEZs but with no access to China's internal markets. Due to lack of data we are unable to verify this possibility.

5. According to Tseng and Zebregs (2002), the market size is more important as a determinant of European and US FDI in China than for FDI from Hong Kong and Taiwan. That is, the motive for investing in China by European and US investors is similar to that of large Korean investors whereas the motive of Hong Kong and Taiwanese investors is similar to that of Korea's SME investors. See also Graham and Wada (2003).

6. These survey results are consistent with those of an econometric study that shows that investments from Hong Kong and Taiwan tend to use China to manufacture goods for export to industrialized countries and also tend to be concentrated in labor-intensive industries that only require low-skill labor (Fung, Iizaka and Parker, 2002).

7. Jones (2001) defines international fragmentation in the production process as a phenomenon that allows previously integrated production processes at one location to be separated into various component parts, some of them being 'outsourced' to other countries. He adds that international fragmentation does not necessarily occur within a multinational corporation and can take place as arm's-length transactions whereby the market is utilized between firms.

8. Doner (1997) argues that foreign affiliates in developing countries initially tend to rely heavily on their parent companies for intermediate goods but subsequently reduce their reliance on them as they develop supplier networks within the host country.

9. According to the 1990 China Census Data, ethnic Koreans in China numbered 1.92 million, with 97 percent (1.86 million) residing in the three provinces in the northeastern region (1.18 million in Jilin, 0.45 million in Heilongjiang, and 0.23 million in Liaoning).

10. Data for the variables used in the regression analysis are from the following sources: ODI from KEXIM (www.koreaexim.go.kr/oeis/index.hml), variables Y, W, E and I from National Bureau of Statistics of China (NBS) (www.stats.gov.cn).

11. The table below is a correlation matrix for the explanatory variables.

	Y	W	E	I	DP	DK
Y	1.00					
W	0.14	1.00				
E	0.04	0.63	1.00			
I	0.34	0.73	0.70	1.00		
DP	0.35	0.33	-0.08	0.35	1.00	
DK	0.05	-0.30	0.06	-0.23	-0.02	1.00

12. A similar proposal for establishing a regional economic cooperation body, the Council for Northeast Asian Economic Cooperation, was made by Lee (2001) in August. His rationale for the proposal is that although establishing a free-trade area of China, Japan and Korea in the near future is unlikely, a cooperation body can perform some useful functions such as strengthening the voice of the three countries in the international arena and paving the way to future formal economic integration in the region.

REFERENCES

Bende-Nabende, Anthony (2002), *Globalisation, FDI, Regional Integration and Sustainable Development: Theory, Evidence and Policy*, Aldershot, UK: Ashgate Publishing.

Broadman, Harry G. and Xiaolun Sun (1997), 'The Distribution of Foreign Direct Investment in China,' Policy Research Working Paper 1720, World Bank, Washington, DC, February.

China Statistical Press, *China Statistical Yearbook 1999* (Tables 17–15).

Crespo-Cuaresma, Jesús et al. (2002), 'Growth, Convergence and EU Membership,' Working Paper 62, Austrian Nationalbank, Vienna.

Doner, Richard (1997), 'Japan in East Asia: Institutions and Regional Leadership' in P. Katzenstein and T. Shiraishi (eds), *Network Power: Japan and Asia*, Ithaca, NY: Cornell University Press, pp. 197–233.

Fung, K.C., Hitomi Iizaka and Stephen Parker (2002), 'Determinants of U.S. and Japanese Direct Investment in China,' mimeo, University of California, Santa Cruz, March.

Graham, Edward M. and Erika Wada (2003), 'Foreign Direct Investment in China:

Effects on Growth and Economic Performance,' Oxford: Institute for International Economics, an electronic document posted on February 15, 2003.

Ha, Byung-Ki and Seock-Il Hong (1998), *An Analysis of the Actual Management Conditions of Korean Investors Overseas* (in Korean), Korea Institute for Industrial Economics and Trade, Seoul.

Henley, John, Colin Kirkpatrick and Georgina Wilde 'Foreign Direct Investment (FDI) in China: Recent Trends and Current Policy Issues,' University of Manchester Institute for Development Policy and Management Working Paper No. 7/1998, http://idpm.man.ac.uk

ICSEAD (2002), *East Asian Economic Perspectives: Recent Trends and Prospects for Major Asian Economies*, Vol. 13, Kitakyushu, Japan, February.

Jones, Ronald W. (2001), 'Globalization and the Fragmentation of Production,' *Seoul Journal of Economics*, **14**, (1), 1–13.

Kojima, Kiyoshi (1996), 'A Macroeconomic Approach to Foreign Direct Investment,' in K. Kojima, *Trade, Investment and Pacific Economic Integration*, Tokyo: Bunshindo.

Korea Export–Import Bank (KEXIM) (2000), *Analysis of Business Activities of Korea's Overseas Affiliates* (in Korean), KEXIM, Seoul, March.

Lee, Chang-Jae (2001), 'Rationale for Institutionalizing Northeast Asian Economic Cooperation and Some Possible Options,' paper presented at the 2001 KIEP/NEAEF conference on 'Strengthening Economic Cooperation in Northeast Asia,' Honolulu, Hawaii, 16–17 August.

Lee, Chung H. (1994), 'Korea's Direct Foreign Investment in Southeast Asia,' *ASEAN Economic Bulletin*, **10**, (3), March.

——— (2003), 'Toward Economic Cooperation in East Asia,' in Lee-Jay Cho, Yoon Hyung Kim and Chung H. Lee (eds), *A Vision for Economic Cooperation in East Asia*, Korea Development Institute, Seoul, Korea (distributed by University of Hawaii Press, Honolulu).

Ogawa, Kazuo and Chung H. Lee (1996), 'Changing Comparative Advantage and Direct Foreign Investment: The Case of Six Japanese Industries,' in Richard Hooley, Anwar Nasution, Mari Pangestu and Jan Dutta (eds), *Asia-Pacific Economic Cooperation: Theory and Practice*, vol. 7, part B, Greenwich, CT: JAI Press, pp. 279–96.

Organization for Economic Co-operation and Development (OECD) (2000), 'Main Determinants and Impacts of Foreign Direct Investment on China's Economy,' Working Paper on International Investment, No 2000/4, Paris, December.

Schott, Jeffrey J. and Ben Goodrich (2001), 'Reflections on Economic Integration in Northeast Asia,' paper presented at the 2001 KIEP/NEAEF conference on 'Strengthening Economic Cooperation in Northeast Asia,' Honolulu, Hawaii, 16–17 August.

Seliger, Bernhard (2002), 'Korea's Role in East Asian Regional Cooperation and Integration,' *Korea's Economy 2002*, vol. 18, Korea Economic Institute, Washington, DC, pp. 59–67.

Tseng, Wanda and Harm Zebregs (2002), 'Foreign Direct Investment in China: Some Lessons for Other Countries,' IMF Policy Discussion Paper (PDP/02/3), International Monetary Fund, Washington, DC, February.

APPENDIX

Table 11A.1   Summary statistics for explanatory variables (1995)

	GDP (billion) yuan)	Average wage (yuan)	Education[a] (%)	Infra-structure[b]	SEZs/ OCCs
Beijing	139	8144	1.46	0.69	–
Tianjin	92	6501	0.72	0.38	OCC
Hebei	285	4839	0.20	0.27	OCC
Shanxi	109	4721	0.22	0.22	–
Liaoning	279	4911	0.44	0.30	OCC
Jilin	113	4430	0.39	0.17	–
Heilongjiang	201	4145	0.31	0.11	–
Shanghai	246	9279	1.02	0.60	–
Jiangsu	516	5943	0.30	0.25	OCC
Zhejiang	352	6619	0.21	0.33	OCC
Anhui	200	4609	0.14	0.25	–
Fujian	216	5857	0.22	0.38	SEZ, OCC
Jiangxi	121	4211	0.20	0.21	–
Shandong	500	5145	0.18	0.35	OCC
Henan	300	4344	0.13	0.30	–
Hubei	239	4685	0.32	0.26	–
Hunan	220	4797	0.20	0.28	–
Guangdong	538	8250	0.22	0.48	SEZ, OCC
Hainan	36	5340	0.17	0.44	SEZ
Sichuan	353	4645	0.18	0.18	–
Guizhou	63	4475	0.10	0.18	–
Yunnan	121	5149	0.13	0.17	–
Shaanxi	100	4396	0.37	0.19	–
Gansu	55	5493	0.19	0.08	–
Qinghai	17	5753	0.15	0.02	–
Average	217	5467	0.33	0.28	NA

Notes:
[a]. Education: ratio of the number of students enrolled in higher education to population in 1995.
[b]. Infrastructure: total length of road in 1995 per square kilometer of land.

Source: National Bureau of Statistics of China, www.stats.gov.cn

12. NAFTA and the broader impacts of trade agreements on industrial development: when 'second-order effects' dominate

Robert K. McCleery and Fernando De Paolis

1. INTRODUCTION

The genesis of this chapter is two-fold. On the theory side, we have read with interest the theoretical work of Arndt, Deardorff, Jones, Kierzkowski and others on the international segmentation of production processes.[1] What follows formalizes some of the ideas first (to our knowledge) laid out by Clark Reynolds, on what he termed 'production sharing.'[2] This chapter is meant to be a first step towards looking at some of the empirical implications of that theory.[3] We hope this line of research will ultimately contribute to both this largely theoretical discussion and the empirical debate regarding trade, foreign investment, wages and jobs.[4]

Second, we have been working on and reading NAFTA retrospectives for several years. Many reviews seem to paint an exceedingly bright picture of both NAFTA's impact on the member economies and the forecasting success of NAFTA modelers.[5] We feel that these assessments largely overstate the success of the predictions, particularly in a microeconomic sense of predicting 'winners and losers' at the sectoral level, and hence overstate the discipline's understanding of the impacts of PTAs (preferential trade agreements) in general and NAFTA in particular. Modelers can only be deified if we compare those modeling forecasts to straw men such as predictions made by Choate and Perot. To make an analogy, this is like crediting modern weather people for making better forecasts than people with signs predicting the apocalypse, even though their sophisticated methods performed somewhat *worse* than the prediction that tomorrow's weather would be much like today's. Our own work uncovers a more nuanced picture of NAFTA's impacts, particularly on the Mexican economy.[6]

NAFTA was really an affirmation and continuation of policies put in place in Mexico over the previous decade. And NAFTA did *not* work the way our predictive models suggest, or the way we tell our students in introductory international economics courses. That story of preferential trade agreements goes like this: a reduction in trade barriers to partner countries creates a margin of preference, which increases demand for partner exports (through something like Armington elasticities), creating an incentive for increased output in those sectors over time. Hence we would expect to see all the NAFTA economies, but particularly Mexico's, increasingly specializing, based on: (1) traditional measures of comparative advantage, reflecting relative resource and factor endowments, and/or (2) opportunities for exploiting economies of scale in Mexico, through trade.

Our chapter looks in more depth at the pattern of growth in the Mexican economy in the post-NAFTA period, and attempts to explain the observed pattern of sectoral growth using first the traditional regressors, then some non-traditional ones. While our findings are neither conclusive nor exhaustive, we believe they will cause mainstream international economists to question the traditional wisdom regarding the proper ways to model and understand the impact of preferential trade agreements on member countries.

Section 2 below briefly introduces our data sets. In Section 3, we show that the standard explanation of how PTAs impact industrial development in member countries *does not* explain the observed pattern of structural change in Mexico since 1994. Section 4 introduces and tests our hypothesis of what has occurred in Mexico over the past ten years, liberally borrowing concepts from those that have gone before, as referenced in note 1, without introducing a formal, theoretical model. We close with an appeal to broaden the way we, as economists and social scientists, look at PTAs.

2. DATA SOURCES AND SELECTION

2.1 Trade Data

To explore the relationship between changes in trade barriers and export growth, we used a detailed trade data set at the commodity level. The results reported here are similar to those from earlier research done by the NAID Center for the Department of Labor.[7]

The one problem with such detailed data is that sectoral definitions change over time. Attempts, such as ours, to relate changes in the value of US imports from Mexico to changes in effective tariff rates (duties collected divided by dutiable value) face the challenge of matching trade flows in the initial year to those of the terminal year. Additionally, at the commodity level, many new categories have been created to deal with new products. Our regression appears to do a poor job of this matching process, as it covers 56 percent of trade in 1990, and just 11 percent in 2000. But this lack of coverage precisely illustrates our point.

Nearly 50 percent of US imports from Mexico entered duty-free in 1990. NAFTA did not change their respective effective tariff rates, thus these products were not included in the regression. It is perfectly reasonable to exclude products for which effective tariffs did not change; indeed, to include them would bias the case against finding a significant relationship between tariff changes and changes in import values. Are we to conclude that the class of products that seems to have benefited most from NAFTA relates to those that were already duty-free?

There is one argument to support this assertion. Prior to NAFTA, a product's duty-free status was subject to revision, particularly the 23 per cent that were duty-free under the GSP (generalized system of preferences, under which some products from developing countries enter the US duty-free or at reduced tariffs). The United States had a history of 'graduating' Mexican products from GSP status in response to surges in import values. NAFTA locked in duty-free status, encouraging new investments and trade in those products. Table 4.8B in Hinojosa et al. (2000) provides support for this view. Imports from Mexico that were free under GSP and free under NAFTA increased from $12.1 billion in 1994 to $28.1 billion in 1997, an increase of 132 percent, compared to the 102 percent increase in total imports from Mexico. Imports subject to duty prior to NAFTA that became duty-free under NAFTA rose from $13.7 billion to $23.3 billion, just 70 percent, over the same period. Imports that faced a reduced tariff under NAFTA grew even more slowly, from $14.8 billion to $19.9 billion, just 34 percent. The other large category, imports that were free under MFN and remain free under NAFTA, increased from $6.44 billion to $10.74 billion, a 67 percent rise. These four categories account for 91 percent of Mexican imports in 1994 and 96 percent in 1997. Clearly there is more to the evolution of the US–Mexico trade relationship following the NAFTA agreement than traditional trade theory would indicate.

2.2   FDI Data and Trade–Investment–Production Concordance

To relate trade flows to production levels in Mexico, a concordance table with a substantially higher level of aggregation was necessary. Our FDI data by sector are at an even higher level of aggregation. FDI is allowed in 61 sectors in Mexico, of which 52 are tradable. One of those 52 sectors was dropped from the analysis, however. Virtually the entire tobacco industry of Mexico was sold to British-American Tobacco and Phillip Morris in 1997, for $2.1 billion. We drop this sector due to the suspicion that these investments had nothing to do with trade or profitability, but represented an attempt to shield profits and assets from lawsuits and to escape an increasingly tight regulatory environment in the

US.[8] Charges have even been brought that these firms are preparing to facilitate black- or gray-market exports to the US to circumvent additional tax increases.[9] If tobacco were included, it would introduce an outlier into the analysis, worsening the fit, but not compromising the economic or statistical significant of the relationships described below. The regressions and correlations explored below, unless otherwise specified, use this 51-sector aggregation.

To match the FDI data, trade figures were aggregated from 10-digit HS commodity classification to the 2-digit SIC level. Even then, some 2-digit sectors had to be collapsed together to match the investment data. Since 1994, the initial year of our analysis, trade data from the US Department of Commerce (History of US Exports and Imports, published on CD by the Bureau of the Census, International Trade Division) include 'maquiladora' trade, but do not break such trade out of the totals. Hence our analysis includes both the imports and exports of these in-bond plants, with the exception of the 1990–2000 comparison.

3. THE CONVENTIONAL WISDOM: WHAT IS *NOT* TRUE?

Surprisingly, the reductions in US tariff barriers between 1990 and 2000 (before NAFTA, under NAFTA, and as part of the Uruguay Round agreement) appear uncorrelated with increases in imports from Mexico, across 1410 commodities.[10] As shown in Table 12.1, the sign of the coefficient on tariff change (the change in effective tariff, defined as duties collected divided by dutiable value) is positive, contrary to theory, and the adjusted R^2 of the regression is negative. Increases in the value of Mexican exports by sector do not closely match sectors in which tariffs declined. Hence the margins of preference created under NAFTA seem to have little or nothing to do with increased trade flows with the US.[11]

We further explored the possibility that relative price changes happened to offset changes in trade barriers. But changes in trade volumes did not seem to be correlated with changes in relative prices, calculated from value and volume data, either. One possibility is that Mexican exports are driven by the US market over the period in a more complex way, with strong US demand growth spurring exports and price increases in some sectors, while in others, increased imports drove down US prices.

Furthermore, standard Heckscher–Ohlin (HO) theory fails to explain the pattern of trade increases. In a regression of workers per billion dollars of value added in 1994 (a proxy for labor intensity) and a proxy for degree of economies of scale by sector from Sobrazo (1992) on export growth from 1994 to 2000, the adjusted R^2 is negative (see Table 12.2). Thus there seems

Table 12.1   Relationship between US tariff collections and value of imports, by commodity

---

Dependent variable: Change in value of imports from Mexico 1990–2000
Independent variables: Tariff change = Change in effective tariff 1990–2000

Regression statistics

Multiple R	0.0104
R^2	0.0001
Adjusted R^2	–0.0006
Standard error	186.08
Observations	1410

ANOVA

	df	SS	MS	F	Sig. F
Regression	1	5258.14	5258.14	0.15	0.70
Residual	1408	48751349.10	34624.54		
Total	1409	48756607.24			

	Coefficient	Stand. error	t-stat.	P-value
Intercept	17.861	5.286	3.379	0.001
Tariff change	0.655	1.681	0.390	0.697

---

to be no link between factor endowments, economies of scale, and the pattern of Mexican export growth.

The second theoretical link we explored, that between export growth and value-added growth by sector, also fails the empirical test in the case of NAFTA, as shown in Table 12.4. Furthermore, the relationship between output growth and labor intensity by sector in the NAFTA period was insignificant. Thus we see no evidence that NAFTA has encouraged Mexico to export more and/or produce more labor-intensive goods, and thus specialize according to its comparative advantage in trade with the US in a way consistent with our theories and models.

A caveat is perhaps appropriate at this point. Clearly the Mexican economy was already closely tied and in many ways complementary to the US economy, prior to the signing of NAFTA. And, as US policy-makers were fond of saying during the NAFTA debates, US tariffs on Mexican products were, on the whole, quite low prior to NAFTA. Can it be that the conventional theory is right, but the *additional* specialization according to comparative advantage *subsequent* to NAFTA is not discernible, at the high level of significance required by formal hypothesis testing, in the limited data since 1994?

Table 12.2   Relationship between export growth and labor intensity and economies of scale

Dependent variable: export growth 1994–2000
Independent variables: VA/worker94 = value added per worker in 1994
                        Scale = economies of scale coefficient

Regression Statistics

Multiple R	0.07
R^2	0.00
Adjusted R^2	–0.04
Standard error	0.14
Observations	51

ANOVA

	df	SS	MS	F	Sig. F
Regression	2	0.00	0.00	0.10	0.90
Residual	48	1.00	0.02		
Total	50	1.01			
	Coefficients	*Stand. error*	*t-stat.*		*P-value*
Intercept	0.17	0.04	3.86		0.00
VA/worker94	0.00	0.00	0.33		0.74
Scale	0.00	0.00	0.23		0.82

We suspect not, for two reasons. The 'non-findings' above are robust to choice of functional form, and are not even close to explaining any variation in the dependent variable, either individually or collectively. Second, we have an alternative explanation that *is* consistent with the available data.

4.   OUR ALTERNATIVE HYPOTHESIS AND TESTS

What *is* going on? As a few researchers have been trying to explain since 1991, trade agreements, particularly NAFTA, involve much more than trade.[12] Models that ignore factor flows, intra-industry trade (including international intra-firm trade) and other complexities are doomed to fail the 'predictive power' test. The model we introduce here, although limited by data availability, can be considered a step in what we feel is the right direction. While each PTA is different, perhaps lessons can be learned from NAFTA that will enlighten future modeling efforts aimed at anticipating the impact of a Japan–South Korea FTA, China's accession to the WTO, FTAA, EU enlargement and so on.

We feel that NAFTA fundamentally changed not only or even primarily the *trading* relationship, but the *investment* dynamics between the two countries. NAFTA and the forces of globalization are creating a laboratory for experimenting with the segmentation of production processes for global cost minimization. Hence we propose to show that FDI inflows help to explain the pattern of sectoral growth in Mexico after NAFTA. And we maintain that FDI inflows were not motivated by cheap labor, but by increased opportunities for cross-border production sharing as production processes are segmented internationally.

Thus we model a two-step process. First, sectoral FDI in the NAFTA period is explained by the initial level of openness (and *not* by wage levels or even wage/productivity ratios). Second, value-added growth by sector during the NAFTA period is determined by FDI inflows (and *not* export growth rates). The results of this two-step process clearly reveal the limitations of traditional theory in explaining the evolution of the Mexican economy after NAFTA.

The first step is illustrated in Table 12.3. The dependent variable is total

Table 12.3   Relationship between FDI inflows and initial openness and labor costs

Dependent variable: FDI stock = cumulative FDI 1994–2000
Independent variables: X–VAratio94 = export to value added ratio in 1994
                       W–VAratio94 = wage bill to value added ratio in 1994

Regression statistics

Multiple R	0.77
R^2	0.59
Adjusted R^2	0.58
Standard error	1.08
Observations	51

ANOVA

	df	*SS*	*MS*	*F*	*Sig. F*
Regression	2	80.90	40.45	34.88	0.00000
Residual	48	55.67	1.16		
Total	50	136.57			

	Coefficients	*Stand. error*	*t–stat.*	*P-value*
Intercept	0.17	0.44	0.37	0.71
X–VAratio94	1.88	0.23	8.12	0.00
W–VAratio94	(0.05)	1.18	(0.04)	0.97

FDI from 1994 to 2000, in billions of US\$. The independent variables are a proxy for the level of openness of the sector in 1994 (exports/value added) and a proxy for labor intensity (the wage share of value added in 1994). The adjusted R^2 of 0.58 and the F-statistic of 35 clearly show that the model has some explanatory power, and all of that power clearly comes from the initial openness. The coefficient of 1.88 means that each 1 percent of additional openness in 1994 would have led to about \$19 million in additional FDI for that sector over the next seven years, all else being equal. The labor-intensity proxy has the wrong sign and is completely insignificant (and average wage, our proxy for labor cost, fared no better). The more traditional openness measure of exports plus imports divided by value added works nearly as well as the export share of value added, with a coefficient about half as large. The theoretical problem is that sometimes the openness to imports that matters to potential investors is intra-sectoral (auto parts and autos, electrical components and electronic equipment, and so on), but in other cases it is between sectors (fertilizer to agriculture, textiles to garments, and so on).

We experimented with two other functional forms for FDI. First, we tried to scale sectoral FDI to reflect the different sizes of the 51 sectors. In the absence of sectoral capital stocks, we scaled by 1994 value added. The adjusted R^2 (0.47) and F-statistic (23) fall somewhat, but X–VA remains significant at the 1 percent level. Average wage was significant, but with the wrong (+) sign![13] When we used natural log of total FDI as the dependent variable,[14] R^2 and F declined, but the X–VA coefficient remains significant at nearly the 1 percent level, and the coefficient on W–VA remains negative and non-significant.

In stage two, we regressed total FDI and export growth 1994–2000 on value-added growth, 1994–2000. As shown in Table 12.4, adjusted R^2 is 0.42 and the F-statistic is 19. Total FDI is significant at the 1 percent level. The coefficient indicates that a billion dollars of additional FDI over the period would increase a sector's annual growth rate over this seven-year period by 1.8 percentage points. The sign on export growth is correct, but the coefficient is neither economically nor statistically significant.

Unlike the first stage, where we can claim that initial levels of openness cause subsequent differential FDI inflows by sector, causality here is less clear. How can we say that FDI over the 1994–2000 period 'caused' value-added growth over the same period, and not vice versa? Two problems arise with normal causality tests. First, those who have worked with FDI data know they are more 'discrete' than 'continuous,' hence a time series of annual data can be very misleading. Second, our detailed FDI series begins in 1994; hence we cannot lag it. We attempt to infer causality in Table 12.5, where we examine correlation coefficients between all possible three-year moving averages of FDI and value added growth in the 1994–2000 period. If rapid value-added

Table 12.4   Relationship between sectoral growth and FDI inflows and export growth

---

Dependent variable: VA-growth = annual average value added growth rate
Independent variables: FDI stock = cumulative FDI 1994–2000
                                          X-growth = Annual average export growth rate

Regression statistics
Multiple R	0.668
R^2	0.446
Adjusted R^2	0.423
Standard error	0.033
Observations	51

ANOVA

	df	SS	MS	F	Sig. F
Regression	2	0.04	0.02	19.30	0.0000007
Residual	48	0.05	0.00		
Total	50	0.10			

	Coefficients	Stand. error	t-Stat	P-value
Intercept	0.021	0.008	2.546	0.014
FDIstock	0.018	0.003	6.201	0.000
X-growth	0.017	0.033	0.520	0.606

---

growth in a sector was attracting *subsequent* FDI, we would expect to see the highest correlations in the lower left corner cells. Instead, we see the larger and more significant correlations in the upper right, between FDI inflows and subsequent value-added growth.

For example, sectoral FDI flows from 1994 to 1996 were most strongly and positively correlated with value-added growth from 1996 to 1998 and from 1997 to 1999. Note that 61 sectors are used in this analysis, with non-traded sectors open to FDI included here, since compatibility with trade data is not needed for this exercise. While the general pattern holds if just the 51 traded sectors are used, the additional sectors do allow more cells to be significant at the 5 percent level.

Another way to interpret the implied causality involves dividing the 25 correlations above into three categories: the five contemporaneous correlations, the ten cases where FDI leads value-added growth, and ten cases where value-added growth leads FDI. We observe more than the expected (5 percent by chance) correlations in the first two categories (one of five, and five of ten),

Table 12.5   Correlation coefficients between FDI inflows and sectoral growth

	Value-added growth, moving average				
	1994–96	1995–97	1996–98	1997–99	1998–2000
FDI flows, moving average					
1994–96	0.045	0.030	*0.259**	*0.284**	0.186
1995–97	0.041	0.085	*0.302**	*0.295**	0.210
1996–98	0.054	0.155	*0.337***	*0.285**	0.227
1997–99	0.078	-0.023	0.159	0.182	0.060
1998–00	0.122	0.046	0.195	0.166	0.057

Notes:
** Correlation is significant at the 0.01 level (2-tailed).
* Correlation is significant at the 0.05 level (2-tailed).
n = 61 in all cases.

and less than expected (zero of ten) in the third. Thus we have fairly strong evidence that FDI inflows are correlated with subsequent value-added growth, and not vice versa.

5.   CONCLUSION

In conclusion, we feel we have forced a rethinking of the traditional view of how preferential trade agreements influence the pattern of growth in member countries. Our analysis calls into question traditional economic models, which focus on margins of preference as the motive for trade expansion, and specialization according to comparative advantage, driven by expanding trade flows with partner countries, fueling economic expansion and structural change. Our findings help explain why the raft of economic models commissioned prior to NAFTA did, collectively, a rather poor job of predicting the pattern of sectoral expansion and contraction in Mexico following NAFTA.[15]

We are less sure about the truth of our alternative view. Clearly international flows of capital (and possibly labor, which we were not able to examine in this chapter) have intensified in the post-NAFTA period and have helped shape the pattern of industrial development in Mexico. But more research will be required both to better quantify, test and refine this different view of NAFTA, and to explore its relevance to the many other PTAs forming and evolving in the global economy today. It may turn out that NAFTA is such a 'special case' that traditional international economic models are sufficient for the study of other PTAs. But it may be true that the international factor flows ignored by traditional models are significant factors in the pattern of industrial development across a much wider range of cases than NAFTA.

Another hypothesis we intend to pursue is the idea that, in keeping with the literature on the international fragmentation of the production process, Mexico's economic expansion has come primarily in labor-intensive *segments* of capital-intensive *sectors*. These labor-intensive segments may well have higher capital intensities than Mexico's national average.[16] In the absence of detailed capital stock data at the sectoral level, comprehensive industry studies may be the best way to approach this question. Such sectoral or even firm-level studies may also be the best way of investigating the role of intra-firm trade in the post-NAFTA period. Any of these paths may hold the next breakthrough in our understanding of the impacts of NAFTA in particular and PTAs in general, but the core message of this chapter is that traditional methods are not sufficient.

NOTES

1. Arndt (1997, 1999); Deardorff (2001a, 2001b); Jones and Kierzkowski (1990); Sanyal and Jones (1982); Sanyal (1983); and many others.
2. Reynolds (1980).
3. Feenstra and Hanson (1999) and Egger and Egger (2001) begin the empirical study of the segmentation models, but do so in a rather stylized and highly aggregate fashion.
4. Krugman and Lawrence (1993); Leamer (1993, 1994, 1996); Feenstra and Hanson (1996, 1997); and others.
5. Weintraub (1997); USTR (1999); Burfisher, Robinson and Thierfelder (2001); and more journalistic reviews such as Griswold (2002).
6. For a recent review of the NAFTA models, their predictions and their prediction errors, see Hinojosa Ojeda and McCleery (2003).
7. Hinojosa Ojeda et al. (2000).
8. With good reason, as Phillip Morris, hit by a $10 billion damage award that requires a $10.2 billion bond to be posted before the award can be appealed, threatened to declare bankruptcy, to the dismay of the states currently receiving money from earlier settlements (*Financial Times*, 24 March 2003).
9. C. Everett Koop, 'Remarks Concerning the McCain–Hollings Bill,' presented at the request of the Democratic Caucus of the Senate, 20 April 1998.
10. Changes in *non-tariff barriers*, which must, by definition, be closely correlated with increased trade flows, were not studied.
11. Shelburne (1998) confirms the absence of a correlation between sectors in which tariffs were reduced under NAFTA and growth in exports of those sectors: 'the contention of Hinojosa that the liberalized sectors have not increased significantly faster than the non-liberalized sectors appears to be true.' Shelburne disputes the claim that the *degree* of liberalization is also unrelated to increases in trade values, but it is difficult to see what fraction of total trade is covered by his regression, or how his partial correlation between the amount of liberalization and the amount of increased trade would be affected by the inclusion of other relevant variables in his equation; his regression has an R^2 of just 0.08.
12. McCleery (1988, 1992a, 1992b); Hinojosa and McCleery (1992); Thierfelder et al. (1993).
13. We are considering possible explanations for this odd result in our ongoing work. One possibility is that FDI is attracted to sectors in which wages, while high by Mexican standards, are low by US standards for the type of skilled labor required in that sector.

14. We use the seven-year sum of FDI inflows by sector both to smooth the substantial year-to-year fluctuations caused by individual investment projects and to minimize the negative FDI sums, which allows us to use the logarithmic formulation. Only one sector, glass products, had to be dropped due to a negative FDI sum over the seven years.
15. As detailed in Hinojosa and McCleery (2003).
16. If so, the Stolper–Samuelson theorem, which states that freer trade should benefit Mexico's abundant factors of production (presumably unskilled labor, in trade with the rest of North America), may also not hold in the case of NAFTA. This is another focus of our ongoing research.

REFERENCES

Arndt, Sven (1997), 'Globalization and the Open Economy,' *North American Journal of Economics and Finance*, **8**, 71–9.
——— (1999), 'Globalization and the Gains from Trade,' *Contemporary Economic Policy,* **16**, 480–84.
Burfisher, Mary, Sherman Robinson and Karen Thierfelder (2001), 'The Impact of NAFTA on the United States,' *Journal of Economic Perspectives*, **15**, 125–44.
Deardorff, Alan (1979), 'Weak Links in the Chain of Comparative Advantages,' *Journal of International Economics*, **9**, 197–209.
——— (2001a), 'Fragmentation in Simple Trade Models,' *North American Journal of Economics and Finance*, **12**, 121–37.
——— (2001b), 'Fragmentation across Cones,' in Sven Arndt and Henryk Kierzkowski (eds), *Fragmentation: New Production Patterns in the World Economy*, Oxford: Oxford University Press, pp. 35–51.
Egger, Hartmut and Peter Egger (2001), 'Cross-border Sourcing and Outward Processing in EU Manufacturing,' *North American Journal of Economics and Finance*, **12**, 243–56.
Feenstra, Robert and Gordon Hanson (1996), 'Foreign Investment, Outsourcing and Relative Wages,' in Robert Feenstra, Gene Grossman and Douglas Irwin (eds), *The Political Economy of Trade Policy: Papers in Honor of Jagdish Bhagwati*, Cambridge, MA: MIT Press, pp. 89–127.
——— (1997), 'Foreign Direct Investment and Relative Wages: Evidence from Mexico's Maquiladoras,' *Journal of International Economics*, **42**, 371–93.
——— (1999), 'The Impact of Outsourcing and High-technology Capital on Wages: Estimates for the United States,' 1979–1990,' *Quarterly Journal of Economics*, **114**, 907–40.
Griswold, Daniel T. (2002), 'NAFTA at 10: An Economic and Foreign Policy Success,' CATO Institute December 23. (http://www.cato.org/dailys/12–23-02-2.html).
Hinojosa, Ojeda, et al. (2000), 'The US Employment Impacts of North American Integration After NAFTA: A Partial Equilibrium Approach,' NAID Center Research Report 10/00.
Hinojosa Ojeda, Raul and Robert McCleery (1992), 'US–Mexico Interdependence, Social Pacts and Policy Alternatives: A Computable General Equilibrium Approach,' in Jorge Bustamante et al. (eds), *US–Mexico Relations: Labor Market Interdependence*, Stanford, CA: Stanford Press, pp. 114–54.
——— (2003) 'NAFTA as a Metaphor: The Search for Regional and Global Lessons for the United States,' in Edward Chambers and Peter Smith (eds), *NAFTA and the New Millennium*, Edmonton, Canada: University of Alberta Press.

Jones, Ronald and Henryk Kierzkowski (1990), 'The Role of Services in Production and International Trade,' in Ronald Jones and Ann Krueuger (eds), *The Political Economy of International Trade*, Cambridge, MA: Basil Blackwell.

—— (2001), 'A Framework for Segmentation,' in Sven Arndt and Henryk Kierzkowski (eds), *Fragmentation: New Production Patterns in the World Economy*, Oxford: Oxford University Press.

Krugman, Paul and Robert Lawrence (1993), 'Trade, Jobs and Wages,' NBER Working Paper Series, no. W4478.

Leamer, Edward (1993), 'Wage Effects of a US–Mexico Free Trade Agreement,' in Peter Garber (ed.), *The Mexico–US Free Trade Agreement*, Cambridge, MA: MIT Press, pp. 57–128.

—— (1994), 'Trade, Wages and Revolving Door Ideas,' NBER Working Paper Series, no. W4716.

—— (1996), 'In Search of Stolper–Samuelson Effects on US Wages,' NBER Working Paper Series, no. W5427.

McCleery, Robert (1988), *US–Mexican Economic Linkages: A General Equilibrium Model of Migration, Trade, and Capital Flows*, Ph.D. dissertation, Department of Economics, Stanford University.

—— (1992a), 'An Intertemporal, Linked, Macroeconomic CGE Model of the United States and Mexico Focusing on Demographic Changes and Factor Flows,' in *Economy-Wide Modeling of the Economic Implications of a FTA with Mexico and a NAFTA with Canada and Mexico*, Washington, DC: US International Trade Commission (Publication 2508), May, pp. 371–441.

—— (1992b), 'A General Equilibrium Analysis of the Gains from Trade for the Mexican Economy of a North American Free Trade Agreement–Comment,' in *Economy-Wide Modeling of the Economic Implications of a FTA with Mexico and a NAFTA with Canada and Mexico*, Washington, DC: US International Trade Commission (Publication 2508), May, pp. 655–8.

Reynolds, Clark W. (1980), Private conversations and lectures at Stanford University.

Sanyal, Kalyan (1983), 'Vertical Specialization in a Ricardian Model with a Continuum of Stages of Production,' *Economica*, **50**, pp. 71–8.

Sanyal, Kalyan and Ronald Jones (1982), 'The Theory of Trade in Middle Products,' *American Economic Review*, **72**, (1), pp. 16–31.

Shelburne, Robert C. (1998), 'Those Ever Changing and Unexplainable Mexican Exports to the United States,' in Gulser Meric and Susan E.W. Nichols (eds), *The Global Economy at the Turn of the Century*, Papers and Proceedings of the International Trade and Finance Association Conference, 27–30 May.

Sobrazo, Horacio E. (1992), 'A General Equilibrium Analysis of the Gains from Trade for the Mexican Economy of a North American Free Trade Agreement' in *Economy-Wide Modeling of the Economic Implications of a FTA with Mexico and a NAFTA with Mexico and Canada*, Washington, DC: US International Trade Commission (Publication 2508) May, pp. 601–51.

Thierfelder, Karen et al. (1993), 'Agricultural Policies and Migration in a U.S.–Mexico Free Trade Area: A Computable General Equilibrium Analysis,' *Journal of Policy Modeling*, **15**, (5–6), 673–701.

USTR (1999), *NAFTA Works for America: Administrative Update on the North American Free Trade Agreement 1993–1998*, Washington, DC: US Trade Representative.

Weintraub, Sidney (1997), *NAFTA at Three: A Progress Report*, Washington DC: Center for Strategic and International Studies.

13. Selective intervention and growth: the case of Korea

Marcus Noland[*]

1. INTRODUCTION

Few issues in development economics have been as controversial as the importance of industrial policy in the Republic of Korea's (henceforth Korea) development. This is a topic of growing importance as economists attempt to distill the 'lessons' of the Korean experience for other countries (e.g. Noland and Pack, 2003).

For industrial policies to be successful, the market equilibrium must be suboptimal. Governments must be able to identify these opportunities for welfare-enhancing interventions, formulate and implement the appropriate policies, and prevent political market failures from leading the policies astray. In the case of Korea, most conventional static neoclassical analyses have concluded that these conditions were not met, at least in the most interventionist period, that is, the heavy and chemical industry (HCI) drive of 1973–79.

One can think of the evidence brought to bear as falling into two broad categories. The first of these are studies that document the actual interventions undertaken by the Korean government and assess those interventions according to a variety of static welfare criteria. So, for example, Kim (1990) surveys the fiscal, credit, tax and trade policies undertaken during this period and concludes that the policy was unsuccessful: it had the predictable result of generating excess capacity in favored sectors while starving non-favored sectors of resources, as well as contributing to inflation and the accumulation of foreign debt. Moreover, 'the government [was] reckless in its selection of launch enterprises and in its almost haphazard provision of generous incentives . . . [its] direct, unlimited role in industrial promotion placed it in the position of an implicit, de facto risk-partner, thus complicating efforts at market-determined adjustment' (p. 44).

Yoo (1990) covers similar terrain, distinguishing between the less selective efforts at export promotion in the 1960s, and the more aggressive industrial promotion efforts of the 1970s. Yoo also directly confronts the argument that the HCI policy was a success inasmuch as the industries favored by the HCI policy became major exporters in the 1980s. He addresses this argument by posing two counterfactuals: what would the Korean economy have looked like in the absence of the policy, and how would the Korean trade structure have looked in its absence?

Using reasoning similar to Kim's, Yoo concludes that in macroeconomic terms the Korean economy would have been better off without the HCI policy. But what about industrial upgrading? Yoo compares the Korean experience with other, similarly endowed economies (particularly Taiwan) and concludes that on the basis of upgrading or trade performance the HCI policy was not a success. Indeed, given the high rates of return on capital, the opportunity costs of prematurely promoting a sector could have been enormous. In a subsequent paper (Yoo, 1993) he argues that political influences dominate efficiency considerations as an explanation of the actual pattern of selective intervention.

Kwon and Paik (1995) use a computable general equilibrium model calibrated to 1978 to investigate the potential magnitude of these distortions. They conclude that resource misallocation reduced GDP by less than 1 percent if capital is assumed to be immobile, and more than 3 percent if it is mobile. The welfare impact they calculate is higher.

Lee (1996) regresses indicators of policy interventions against sectoral total factor productivity (TFP) growth rates and other measures of productivity. He finds little support for the notion that policy interventions promoted productivity growth in the targeted sectors.

Another set of analyses has focused on inter-industry linkages and the potentially welfare-enhancing coordination role for the government. Pack and Westphal (1986) argue that, in general, Korea's selective intervention policy has been successful in fostering infant industries without significant losses in efficiency. The key has been to capture latent inter-industry pecuniary and non-pecuniary externalities:

> The Korean government can be seen as having achieved integrated decision-making by acting as a central agent mediating among market agents, forcing and facilitating information interchange and insuring the implementation of decisions reached ... weighing costs and benefits from a collective standpoint and often intervening to reward cooperative players and punish uncooperative ones. (p. 99)

Okuno-Fujiwara (1988) provides a formal example of this in the form of a model of the interdependence of the two industries. One industry, which produces an intermediate product, is assumed to be oligopolistic due to underlying scale economies and engages in Cournot competition. The other industry, which produces a final product from the intermediate product, is perfectly competitive. In this situation there may be multiple equilibria with one equilibrium Pareto-superior to the others. Industrial policy has a positive role in the form of pre-play communication to generate a superior coordinated equilibrium.[1]

Murphy, Shleifer and Vishny (1989) formalize these notions in terms of Rodenstein-Rodan's idea of the 'big push'. Once again, there are multiple equilibria due to pecuniary externalities generated by imperfect competition with large fixed costs. They argue that industrial policy which 'encourages industrialization in many sectors simultaneously can substantially boost income and welfare even when investment in any one sector appears impossible' (p. 1024).[2]

Each of these papers claims that the possibility exists for welfare-enhancing industrial policies through government coordination activities to capture inter-industry externalities, thus promoting growth and industrial development without the standard efficiency losses. The key is the existence of inter-industry externalities, which, when captured, expand the production set of the economy.

Table 13.1 presents correlations of changes in real output for 26 Korean manufacturing sectors and the overall index of industrial output for the period 1975:1 to 1989:4. Changes in output are highly correlated across sectors: in most cases the correlation coefficients are above 0.9, and few are below 0.7. This suggests that selective interventions to encourage output, or coordinated output increases, could indeed be transmitted on an economy-wide basis. Alternatively, the high correlations could be interpreted as evidence that variations in output are largely due to common macroeconomic shocks.

The likely scope for growth-enhancing interventions would be increased if the industries targeted for intervention met three criteria. The first is that they have strong inter-industry linkages to the rest of the economy. Second, they should be leading sectors in a causal sense, so that growth stimulus would be transmitted forward through the economy. One might think of an input supplier industry in the Okuno-Fujiwara model as an example. Finally, variations in output should have a strong industry-specific component; otherwise, variations in output are simply due to macroeconomic shocks and there is little scope for industry-specific stimulus. The existence of industry-specific variation in output suggests the possibility for industry-specific technical change and/or scope for industry-specific policy interventions to increase output.

This chapter analyzes Korean data to explore the potential for growth-enhancing policy interventions and their possible occurrence in the Korean case. This is done by taking sectoral data and putting them through a series of filters to see if any of the industries meet plausible criteria for selective promotion. In the next section the density of the input–output table is analyzed to identify sectors with strong backward and forward linkages. Then, industry times-series data are analyzed to identify possible 'leading' sectors. Last, the time-series data are decomposed to identify sectors characterized by a high

Table 13.1   Correlations of production across industries

	Ind.	Food	Bev.	Tobacco	Tex.	Apparel	Leather	Footwear	Wood	Furniture	Paper	Print
Industrial prod.	1.00											
Food processing	0.99	1.00										
Beverages	0.99	0.99	1.00									
Tobacco prods	0.99	0.97	0.97	1.00								
Textiles	0.81	0.77	0.80	0.86	1.00							
Apparel	0.86	0.82	0.84	0.90	0.99	1.00						
Leather prods	0.97	0.95	0.95	0.94	0.72	0.78	1.00					
Footwear	0.90	0.90	0.91	0.93	0.77	0.81	0.89	1.00				
Wood prods	0.92	0.91	0.92	0.95	0.89	0.91	0.86	0.92	1.00			
Furniture	0.78	0.74	0.76	0.83	0.99	0.98	0.67	0.71	0.84	1.00		
Paper	0.99	0.98	0.98	0.98	0.80	0.84	0.96	0.88	0.91	0.77	1.00	
Printing & pub.	0.98	0.96	0.96	0.98	0.87	0.90	0.91	0.88	0.93	0.84	0.98	1.00
Basic chemicals	0.98	0.96	0.96	0.99	0.87	0.90	0.92	0.91	0.96	0.84	0.97	0.97
Other chem. prods	0.99	0.99	0.99	0.98	0.82	0.86	0.95	0.92	0.93	0.78	0.99	0.98
Petro. refining	0.76	0.72	0.74	0.08	0.99	0.98	0.66	0.73	0.86	0.99	0.75	0.83
Petro. & coal	0.98	0.96	0.95	0.97	0.80	0.84	0.94	0.88	0.89	0.77	0.98	0.97
Rubber prods	0.99	0.98	0.97	0.96	0.76	0.81	0.96	0.85	0.87	0.74	0.99	0.96
Plastic prods	0.84	0.81	0.83	0.89	0.99	0.99	0.74	0.81	0.92	0.98	0.83	0.89
Nonmetallic prods	0.98	0.96	0.97	0.98	0.87	0.90	0.92	0.88	0.94	0.85	0.98	0.98
Iron & steel	0.99	0.98	0.98	0.99	0.81	0.86	0.97	0.90	0.92	0.78	0.99	0.97
Non-ferrous metals	0.97	0.96	0.95	0.94	0.73	0.78	0.94	0.81	0.82	0.71	0.98	0.95
Fabricated metal	0.98	0.97	0.97	0.96	0.76	0.81	0.97	0.86	0.87	0.73	0.98	0.95
Indus. machinery	0.97	0.97	0.96	0.93	0.68	0.74	0.95	0.83	0.84	0.66	0.97	0.93
Elec. machinery	0.99	0.98	0.98	0.98	0.79	0.84	0.97	0.89	0.91	0.76	0.99	0.97
Trans. machinery	0.99	0.97	0.97	0.98	0.82	0.87	0.96	0.88	0.91	0.80	0.99	0.98

Table 13.1   continued

	B. chem.	O. chem.	P refin	P & C	Rub	Plastic	N-metal	I & S	N-fer	Fab m	Ind. m	Elec. m	Tra. m	Prof. g	Misc.
Industrial prod.															
Food processing															
Beverages															
Tobacco prods															
Textiles															
Apparel															
Leather prods															
Footwear															
Wood prods															
Furniture															
Paper															
Printing & pub.															
Basic chemicals	1.00														
Other chem. prods	0.97	1.00													
Petro. refining	0.84	0.77	1.00												
Petro. & coal	0.95	0.97	0.75	1.00											
Rubber prods	0.94	0.98	0.71	0.97	1.00										
Plastic prods	0.90	0.85	0.99	0.83	0.79	1.00									
Nonmetallic prods	0.98	0.98	0.83	0.95	0.97	0.89	1.00								
Iron & steel	0.97	0.99	0.76	0.98	0.98	0.84	0.98	1.00							
Non-ferrous metals	0.92	0.96	0.67	0.96	0.99	0.75	0.95	0.97	1.00						
Fabricated metal	0.94	0.98	0.70	0.97	0.98	0.78	0.95	0.98	0.98	1.00					
Indus. machinery	0.92	0.96	0.63	0.94	0.98	0.72	0.94	0.96	0.97	0.97	1.00				
Elec. machinery	0.97	0.99	0.74	0.98	0.99	0.82	0.98	0.99	0.97	0.98	0.97	1.00			
Trans. machinery	0.98	0.98	0.78	0.98	0.98	0.85	0.98	0.99	0.97	0.98	0.96	0.99	1.00		
Profes. goods	0.98	0.98	0.78	0.97	0.97	0.85	0.98	0.99	0.95	0.97	0.95	0.99	0.99	1.00	
Misc. manu.	0.94	0.97	0.70	0.94	0.96	0.78	0.94	0.97	0.93	0.95	0.95	0.97	0.96	0.96	1.00

degree of industry-specific stochastic variation. These statistical analyses do not constitute any kind of test of the previously described theoretical models; rather, they simply indicate whether conditions that would be associated with successful interventions have existed in reality.[3] The possibility that the interventions undertaken in Korea could constitute a case of successful coordinated intervention is then discussed in the concluding section of the chapter.

2.   INTER-INDUSTRY LINKS

A first step in exploring the possibility of welfare-enhancing coordinated interventions is to identify the strength of inter-industry linkages. Jones (1976) clarified the appropriate way of measuring backward and forward linkages using an input–output table. The jth column sum of the input inverse matrix measures the backward links, indicating the increase in total output of the system required to supply inputs for the initial unit increase in industry j. The ith row sum of the output inverse matrix measures the forward links, indicating the increase in total output of the system required to utilize the increased output from an initial input from industry i. For a given industry, the sum of its backward and forward linkages indicates the total or maximum potential causal links stimulated by an increase in its output.

The measures of backward, forward and total linkages have been computed for 26 Korean manufacturing industries using the 1986 65-sector input–output table published by the Bank of Korea. Since we are interested in measuring the potential stimulus to domestic output, they have been calculated using the domestic flow matrices. These results are presented in Table 13.2.

Forward links were strongest for paper, basic chemicals, and iron and steel. These sectors also had the highest total linkages. Hence, if one were to target industries on the basis of inter-industry linkages, these would be prime candidates. Links were weakest for the tobacco and apparel sectors. Presumably, these are sectors a targeting policy would avoid.

Again, this implicitly assumes a closed economy. If the economy is open, then the relevant criterion is not only the degree of forward linkage, but also the efficiency of the input industry relative to imported substitutes. Likewise, the relevant criterion for backward links would be whether expansion of the downstream sector induced sufficient expansion of the upstream sector to achieve minimum efficient scale and displace imports.[4]

3.   IDENTIFICATION OF LEADING SECTORS

If an economy is at less than full employment, then the targeting of leading sectors could induce an overall expansion of economic activity and put the

Table 13.2   Inter-industry linkages

Industry	Backward linkage	Forward linkage	Total linkage
Food processing	2.267269	1.572321	3.839590
Beverage	1.756841	1.958921	3.715763
Tobacco products	1.281045	1.051235	2.332280
Textiles	2.163114	1.771415	3.934529
Apparel	2.145076	1.024679	3.169755
Leather	1.782901	1.747012	3.529913
Footwear	1.782901	1.747012	3.529913
Wood products	1.698044	2.091918	3.789961
Furniture	2.013180	1.823123	3.836303
Paper	2.060614	3.186488	5.247102
Printing	2.163467	2.438758	4.602225
Chemicals	1.932577	3.181606	5.114183
Other chemicals	1.740605	2.383885	4.124490
Petroleum ref.	1.146829	2.859925	4.006754
Petro., coal prods	1.293919	2.750794	4.044713
Rubber	1.924645	1.327635	3.252280
Plastic	2.042086	2.062823	4.104910
Non-metallic prods	1.938187	2.370438	4.308624
Iron & steel	2.464819	2.938392	5.403211
Non-ferrous metals	1.618080	2.509598	4.127677
Fabri. metal prods	2.130569	1.722996	3.853565
Machinery	2.036547	1.744555	3.781102
Electric mach.	1.790613	1.398499	3.189113
Transport mach.	2.047274	1.292247	3.339521
Professional goods	1.843012	1.446915	3.289926
Misc. manuf.	2.076539	1.280840	3.357379

economy on a permanently higher growth path in growth models where scale economies play an important role. (If the economy is already at full employment, then such targeting would just change the composition of output, and one is back to the neoclassical critique of Kim and Yoo.)

A considerable amount of recent econometric research has focused on the specification and analysis of models in which some or all of the variables may be integrated or possess unit roots. Particular interest has centered on the possibility of cointegration explored by Granger and Engle (1987), where some linear combination of variables exhibits reduced orders of integration.

Sims, Stock and Watson (1990) have shown that the asymptotic distributions of causality tests are sensitive to unit roots and time trends in the series. This underscores the importance of examining the time-series properties of the data prior to model specification and estimation.

Frequently used diagnostic tests include the Stock–Watson (SW) and Dickey–Fuller (DF) tests for a unit root, that is, for a unit root in the series, against the alternative that the series is stationary around a linear time trend (Dickey and Fuller, 1979; Stock and Watson, 1989); the modified Stock–Watson test (MSW) for a single unit root when there might be a quadratic time trend; and the augmented, or higher-order, Stock–Watson and Dickey–Fuller tests for a second unit root, that is, for a unit root in the first difference of the series, against the alternative that the series is stationary in first differences around a linear time trend.

These tests were applied to quarterly data on real output of industrial production and 26 manufacturing industries. For most series the sample period was 1960:1–1989:4, with some having shorter sample periods due to missing data, the shortest sample being 1975:1–1989:4. All data were expressed in logs. Examination of autocorrelation and partial autocorrelation functions indicated that all of the series could be represented as AR2 functions, and consequently all of the diagnostic tests were calculated with this correction.

According to the augmented Stock–Watson and Dickey–Fuller tests the existence of higher-order unit roots could be rejected for all series and for the sake of brevity are not reported. The remaining diagnostic tests are reported in Table 13.3. In 14 industries (apparel, leather, footwear, wood products, furniture, basic chemicals, other chemical products, petroleum, plastic, iron and steel, non-ferrous metals, fabricated metals, industrial machinery, and professional goods, plus industrial production) the existence of a single unit root cannot be rejected. In two cases (rubber and electrical machinery) the test results are ambiguous. In the remaining ten cases, the existence of a single unit root can be rejected in favor of the alternative that the series are stationary around either linear (SW, DF) or quadratic (MSW) time trends.

To ascertain the degree of the polynomial, the first differences of each series were regressed against a constant, time, and four of its own lags. The *t*-statistics of these deterministic regressors are reported in the fourth and fifth columns of Table 13.3. In a number of cases (e.g. wood products, furniture), the time-trend coefficient was significant, indicating that the series has a single unit root around a quadratic time trend. In several other cases (e.g. industrial production, apparel, leather), when the time trend is removed from the regression, the constant is significant, indicating that the series could be characterized as having a single unit root with drift.

Having established the univariate characteristics of the data, the next step was to investigate the possibilities of cointegrating relationships between

Table 13.3   Tests for unit roots, co-integration

Series	MSW	SW	DF	time	constant	CO
Industrial production					a	—
Food processing	b	b	a			
Beverages	c	c	a			
Tobacco products	a				a	
Textiles	c				a	
Apparel					a	
Leather					b	
Footwear					b	
Wood products				b		
Furniture				a		
Paper	b	a	c	b	b	
Printing	b			a		
Chemicals					a	c
Other chemicals				c	a	b
Petroleum refining				b	b	
Petroleum, coal prods.	a	a	c	a	b	
Rubber		c		a	c	
Plastic					a	
Non-metallic products	a	a	c	a	b	
Iron & steel					a	b
Non-ferrous metals				b	b	
Fabricated metal products				b		
Machinery				a		
Electrical machinery				c	a	
Transport machinery	b			c	a	
Professional goods				c	a	b
Miscellaneous manufactures	b	b	b	a		

Note: the letter a indicates significance at the 1% level; b at the 5% level; and c at the 10% level.

industrial production and the industry series. This was done using the augmented Stock–Watson test (CO), and these results are reported in the final column of Table 13.3. In four cases (basic chemicals, other chemical products, iron and steel, and professional goods) the hypothesis of no cointegrating relationship could be rejected at the 10 percent or greater level.

The information in Table 13.3 was then used in specifying bivariate Sims causality tests on industrial production and sectoral indices. The hypothesis that one variable (Y_1) causes another (Y_2) is tested by running a regression of

Y_1 on past, current and future values of Y_2; the null hypothesis that Y_1 does not cause Y_2 implies that the coefficients of the future values of Y_2 are jointly equal to zero. The procedure is then reversed to test the hypothesis that Y_2 causes Y_1. These are estimated using the common practice of eight quarter lags, and four quarter leads. As indicated in Sims, Stock and Watson, the OLS (ordinary least squares) estimates of these regressions are consistent, though in certain cases (when both regressors have unit roots and are not cointegreted), the F-statistics on causality may have non-standard limiting distributions.

Three summary statistics are reported in Table 13.4: the adjusted coefficient of determination, the Box–Ljung Q-statistic for serially correlated errors, and the F-statistic on the future values of the right-hand side variable. According to the F-tests, seven industries Granger-cause industrial production (beverages, textiles, leather, wood products, paper, petroleum and coal products, and non-ferrous metals), four industries are characterized by feedback (non-metallic mineral products, fabricated metal products, transportation machinery, and miscellaneous manufactures), and in five industries (apparel, printing and publishing, other chemical products, iron and steel, and professional goods) industrial production Granger-causes industry output. In the remaining cases no causal ordering could be established. In ten cases (apparel, leather, footwear, wood, furniture, petroleum refining, plastic products, non-ferrous metals, machinery, and electric machinery) the results should be treated with caution due to the apparent presence of multiple roots, as should the results for fabricated metals where the hypothesis of white-noise residuals was rejected at the 1 percent level in one of the regressions.

More generally, as Lütkepohl (1982) has demonstrated, spurious inferences may be obtained in bivariate causality tests due to the omission of relevant explanatory variables. This, however, is simply a particular manifestation of the more general problem of omitted variable bias, and concern does not appear to be warranted in the case at hand in the absence of either any particular reason to believe that the causality relations are more complicated than the simple bivariate approach modeled here, or signs of possible omitted variable problems (such as low coefficients of determination and serially correlated errors). With appropriate caveats about the interpretation of the F-statistics, 11 industries exhibit either leading or feedback relationships with industrial production, and hence might be appropriate targets for promotion. Two of these, iron and steel, and basic chemicals, were identified as sectors with particularly strong inter-industry links. In contrast, the apparel sector would be a uniquely poor choice for targeting, as it has weak inter-industry links, and is a causally lagging sector.[5]

Table 13.4 Causality regressions

Industry	Industry LHS variable			Industrial production (IP) LHS variable			Interpretation
	RBAR**2	BLQ	F	RBAR**2	BLQ	F	
Food	0.80	23.1	1.5	0.73	28.5	1.0	
Beverages	0.89	30.9	8.4[a]	0.71	34.2	1.5	Industry causes IP
Tobacco	0.59	37.8	1.9	0.68	28.4	1.6	
Textile	0.38	24.8	2.2[c]	0.71	19.1	0.9	Industry causes IP
Apparel	0.48	21.4	1.2	0.80	19.7	5.2[a]	IP causes industry
Leather	0.22	17.0	3.0[b]	0.66	31.0	0.8	Industry causes IP
Footwear	0.26	18.8	1.8	0.70	10.1	0.7	
Wood	0.66	17.2	3.4[b]	0.78	27.3	0.6	Industry causes IP
Furniture	0.38	24.4	0.6	0.63	17.1	0.9	
Paper	0.93	24.2	3.1[b]	0.79	24.4	1.8	Industry causes IP
Printing	0.55	20.5	0.2	0.66	34.5	2.1[c]	IP causes industry
Chemicals	0.28	23.6	1.9	0.65	31.5	1.3	
Other chemicals	0.36	21.7	0.4	0.70	25.1	3.9[a]	IP causes industry
Petroleum ref.	0.47	16.5	1.3	0.63	22.7	1.8	
Petroleum, coal	0.88	16.4	4.2[a]	0.69	19.5	1.2	Industry causes IP
Rubber	0.38	26.0	0.3	0.69	20.9	1.5	
Plastic	0.15	18.8	1.4	0.65	17.5	1.6	
Non-metallic	0.87	21.7	3.2[b]	0.77	23.1	4.6[a]	Feedback
Iron & steel	0.34	27.9	0.2	0.72	22.3	3.6[a]	IP causes industry
Non-ferrous metal	0.39	33.9	2.2[c]	0.73	34.6	0.7	Industry causes IP
Fabricated metal	0.43	53.8[a]	2.1[c]	0.75	20.1	2.1[c]	Feedback
Machinery	0.58	15.8	0.8	0.75	31.0	1.1	
Electrical mach.	0.47	26.0	1.1	0.74	23.5	2.0	
Transport mach.	0.40	25.7	2.4[c]	0.70	22.3	2.2[c]	Feedback
Professional	0.30	8.8	0.9	0.74	20.7	2.7[b]	IP causes industry
Miscellaneous	0.88	24.0	3.2[b]	0.78	22.2	4.7[a]	Feedback

Note: [a] indicates significance at the 1% level; [b] at the 5% level; and [c] at the 0% level.

238

4.   DECOMPOSITION OF CHANGES IN OUTPUT

A final criterion for candidates for targeting would be that changes in output be characterized by substantial industry-specific micro shocks, as opposed to economy-wide macro shocks. These industry-specific policy interventions could be associated with things such as technological change, or indeed, when analyzing historical data, industry-specific policy interventions. Macro shocks would presumably be due to economy-wide phenomena such as changes in monetary policy, or the exchange rate, though again, in principle, in historical data they could be due to industry-specific policy interventions that were then propagated economy-wide through inter-industry input–output relations. The point is that if changes in industry output are dominated by either economy-wide macro shocks, or policy interventions in other industries, the industry would be a poor candidate for growth-enhancing interventions.

Changes in output have been decomposed into micro and macro components following the method of Yoshikawa and Ohtake (1987). The equations to be estimated are:

$$Q_t^i = M^i(L)\, Y_{t\,+}\, u_t^i, \tag{13.1}$$

where the dependent variable Q is the log of industry real output, and Y is the log of industrial production, each detrended as indicated by the results in Table 13.3; $M^i(L)$ is a polynomial function of the lag operator L defined as

$$L^n x_t = x_{t-n} \qquad (n = 0, 1, 2, \ldots), \tag{13.2}$$

and i and t refer to industry and time, respectively, and Y_t follows an autoregressive process,

$$Y_t = a(L)\, Y_{t-1} + e_t, \tag{13.3}$$

where e_t is a white-noise error. The industry-specific micro shocks, u, are in turn generated by the autoregressive equations

$$u_t^i = a^i(L)\, u_{t-1}^i + v_t^i. \tag{13.4}$$

In this case, v is a white-noise error and $a^i(L)$ is a polynomial function of L.

From equations (13.1) and (13.4), the industry-specific micro shock can be expressed as

$$Q_t^i - M^i(L)Y_t = a^i(L)\,[Q_{t-1}^i - M^i(L)Y_{t-1}] + v_t^i, \tag{13.5}$$

Table 13.5　Macro regressions

Industry	A1	A2	M0	M1	M2	SEE	SDQ	BLQ	Macro
Food	0.6	0.2	0.2	−0.1	0.1	0.06	0.09	27.8	0.34
	(5.3)	(1.9)	(0.5)	(−0.3)	(0.8)				
Beverages	0.9	0.2	−0.1	−0.5	1.1	0.07	0.12	32.9	0.03
	(7.1)	(0.2)	(−0.4)	(−1.3)	(0.2)				
Tobacco	0.3	−0.1	−0.1	−0.4	−0.4	0.06	0.06	28.2	0.00
	(2.9)	(−1.2)	(−0.3)	(−0.5)	(−0.2)				
Textiles	0.2	0.1	0.0	−0.1	−0.1	0.03	0.03	16.1	0.79
	(1.3)	(0.9)	(0.1)	(−0.4)	(−0.4)				
Apparel	−0.0	0.6	0.0	1.1	−0.2	0.07	0.07	11.4	0.46
	(−0.1)	(0.5)	(0.1)	(0.1)	(−0.2)				
Leather	0.1	0.2	0.0	0.6	−0.1	0.14	0.14	12.6	0.08
	(0.9)	(1.3)	(0.0)	(0.1)	(0.5)				
Footwear	−0.2	0.0	0.1	−0.1	1.6	0.07	0.07	11.4	0.05
	(−1.4)	(0.2)	(1.1)	(−0.5)	(0.2)				
Wood	0.2	0.2	0.1	0.4	0.6	0.07	0.08	18.2	0.12
	(2.0)	(1.8)	(2.7)	(1.7)	(1.9)				
Furniture	−0.2	−0.1	−0.1	0.2	0.8	0.13	0.13	12.2	0.07
	(−1.5)	(−1.7)	(−0.8)	(0.3)	(0.5)				
Paper	0.8	0.6	−0.1	−0.1	0.4	0.05	0.08	9.9	0.07
	(6.5)	(0.6)	(−0.3)	(−0.5)	(0.1)				
Printing	−0.4	−0.1	0.1	0.2	0.1	0.07	0.07	24.7	0.01
	(−3.4)	(−0.9)	(0.2)	(0.2)	(0.0)				
Chemicals	−0.3	−0.3	0.1	0.4	−0.9	0.07	0.08	25.8	0.02
	(−3.0)	(−2.6)	(0.4)	(0.3)	(−0.1)				
Other chems	−0.1	0.1	0.1	0.1	−0.0	0.05	0.05	22.9	0.02
	(−0.6)	(1.2)	(0.3)	(0.2)	(−0.2)				
Petro. ref,	−0.2	−0.1	−0.0	0.0	0.1	0.05	0.05	17.1	0.47
	(−1.5)	(−0.7)	(−0.0)	(0.0)	(0.3)				
Petro., coal	0.3	−0.1	−0.0	−0.1	0.1	0.11	0.11	33.5[c]	0.00
	(2.2)	(−1.1)	(−0.1)	(−0.0)	(0.0)				
Rubber	0.3	−0.2	0.0	0.0	−0.0	0.07	0.07	31.1	0.07
	(2.6)	(−1.6)	(0.9)	(0.3)	(−0.2)				
Plastic	0.1	0.3	0.1	−0.2	−0.4	0.08	0.08	11.9	0.02
	(0.7)	(2.4)	(0.3)	(−0.0)	(−0.2)				
Non-metal	0.7	−0.1	0.1	−0.1	−1.4	0.06	0.09	15.1	0.00
	(6.1)	(−0.1)	(0.3)	(−0.2)	(−0.1)				
Iron, steel	0.3	−0.1	0.2	−0.6	−0.1	0.07	0.07	27.6	0.26
	(2.9)	(−0.5)	(0.4)	(−0.4)	(−0.2)				
Non-ferrous	−0.2	−0.1	−0.0	0.2	0.1	0.09	0.09	17.8	0.31
	(−1.4)	(−1.0)	(−0.9)	(0.4)	(0.2)				
Fabricated	0.5	−0.3	−0.1	0.2	−0.3	0.09	0.09	15.0	0.53
	(0.4)	(−0.3)	(0.2)	(0.2)	(−0.2)				
Machinery	−0.5	−0.1	0.2	−0.2	−0.1	0.12	0.12	40.9[b]	0.30
	(−0.4)	(1.2)	(0.2)	(−0.1)	(−0.3)				
Electrical	0.4	0.4	0.1	−0.1	0.1	0.09	0.09	21.8	0.05
	(3.0)	(0.4)	(0.3)	(−0.5)	(0.1)				
Transport	−0.1	−0.0	0.0	0.1	−0.7	0.16	0.16	23.4	0.00
	(−0.5)	(−0.2)	(0.2)	(0.1)	(−0.1)				
Profession.	−0.3	0.1	0.6	0.3	0.3	0.15	0.15	16.6	0.06
	(−3.7)	(0.5)	(2.1)	(0.4)	(0.1)				
Misc. manf.	−0.2	−0.1	0.0	0.1	−0.1	0.08	0.18	18.5	0.05
	(−1.6)	(−1.2)	(0.3)	(0.1)	(−0.2)				

Note:　Numbers in parentheses are *t*-values. Superscripts in the Box–Ljung Q column indicate level of statistical significance: [a] indicates significance at the 1% level; [b] at the 5% level; and [c] at the 10% level.

and has been estimated by non-linear least squares for a second-order autoregressive model. The percentage changes in Q due to macro shocks can be calculated as

$$\frac{(M_0^2 + M_1^2 + M_2^2)\sigma_y^2 + 2(M_0M_1 + M_1M_2)\sigma_{yy-1} + 2\,M_0\,M_2\,\sigma_{yy-2}}{\sigma_Q^2}, \quad (13.6)$$

under the assumptions that industrial production is exogenous, and that the macro shocks (e) and the micro shocks (v) are orthogonal. The problem is that the results in Table 13.4 indicated that industrial production is not exogenous in a number of cases, violating the assumption underlying this decomposition. A broader measure, real GNP, was tried, but it too was found not to be exogenous in several cases.

Fortunately, Noland (1993) demonstrated that the real exchange rate, real US GNP, and the real US fiscal deficit are all causally prior to real Korean GNP. It is inconceivable that these variables are not exogenous to variations in output of individual Korean industries. Consequently, an instrument for Korean GNP was formed by taking the fitted values of a regression of the real exchange rate, real US GNP, and the real US budget deficit on Korean real GNP. Equation (13.5) was then estimated using this instrument, and the coefficient estimates, their t-statistics, the standard error of the regression (SEE), the standard deviation of the dependent variable (SDQ), the Box–Ljung Q-statistic, and the macro-shock share (MACRO), are reported in Table 13.5.

The macro shares reported in Table 13.5 range from nil (tobacco products, petroleum and coal products, non-metallic mineral products, and transport equipment) to a high of 0.79 (textiles) with a mean value of 0.16, and a median value of 0.07. In only one case, machinery, where the Box–Ljung Q-statistic indicates that v is not white noise, do the assumptions underlying equation (13.6) appear to be violated. These results imply that sectors with relatively high macro shares such as textiles, apparel, petroleum refining, and fabricated metals products would be inappropriate candidates for targeting. Such statements are subject to Lucas critiques, however: sectors with historically high macro ratios might exhibit low macro ratios under a different policy regime and vice versa.

5.   CONCLUSION

This chapter has attempted to employ data-instigated methods to determine if conditions amenable to successful selective interventions to capture cross-industry externalities such as those posited by Pack and Westphal, Okuno-Fujiwara, and Murphy, Shleifer and Vishny exist in practice. This has been done by examining historical data for Korea, a country whose experience is often invoked in these discussions. Three criteria are proposed in selecting good candidates for industrial promotion: (1) that they have strong inter-industry links; (2) that they lead the rest of the economy in a causal sense; and (3) that they be characterized by a high share of industry-specific innovations in output growth.

Taken at face value, the results are summarized in Table 13.6, which indicates whether an industry was found to Granger-cause industrial production (in the case of feedback this is indicated with a question mark); whether it had a macro share of less than half; whether its index of inter-industry linkage was above the sample mean; whether it was promoted during the HCI drive; and finally, the intersection of the first three sets: the candidates for successful intervention. As can be seen from Table 13.6, four of the 26 sectors fulfill the first three criteria, demonstrating that conditions supportive of successful intervention are present in the data. Unfortunately, with regard to the specific historical experience of Korea, with the exception of non-ferrous metals, these were not the sectors promoted during the HCI drive.

Indeed, with one exception, none of the sectors promoted by the HCI policy fulfill all three of the criteria. Basic chemicals, petroleum refining, iron and steel, and machinery all have low macro ratios and strong inter-industry links, but were not causally leading sectors. However, if Korea was assumed to be at full employment, then macro causality is not an important issue, and these sectors could be considered possible cases of successful targeting. Transportation equipment has a low macro ratio and feeds back to national income, but its inter-industry links are lower than average.[6]

The calculations made in this chapter are admittedly quite crude, and they should not be considered a test of the theoretical arguments in favor of selective intervention. Indeed, even accepting the argument put forward here, one could quarrel with the specific statistical results for the reasons cited above. But beyond these questions of econometric technique, it is certainly correct to argue that the level of industry aggregation (imposed by data availability constraints) is far too high, and that both the underlying externalities and the forms of intervention may be far more subtle than the relations modeled in this exercise. Nonetheless, this approach may provide a useful starting point for identifying potential candidates for industrial promotion.

Table 13.6 Summary

Industry	Macro ratio <0.5	'Leading' sector	Strong links	HCI sector	Candidate sector
Food processing	x		x		
Beverages	x	x			
Tobacco products	x				
Textiles		x	x		
Apparel	x				
Leather	x	x			
Footwear	x				
Wood Products	x	x	x		x
Furniture	x		x		
Paper	x	x	x		x
Printing	x		x		
Chemicals	x		x	x	
Other chemicals	x		x		
Petroleum refining	x		x	x	
Petroleum, coal products	x	x	x		x
Rubber	x				
Plastic	x		x		
Non-metallic products	x	?	x		?
Iron & steel	x		x	x	
Non-ferrous metals	x	x	x	x	x
Fabricated metal products		?	x		
Machinery	x		x	x	
Electrical machinery	x			x	
Transport machinery	x	?		x	
Professional goods	x				
Miscellaneous manufactures	x	?			

NOTES

* This chapter was begun while I was a visitor at the Korea Development Institute, and I would like to thank KDI for its more than generous support during my stay. Jeff Nugent, Morty Shapiro and Chris Udry provided helpful comments on an earlier draft, and Chongshan Liu provided diligent research assistance.

1. In both this model and that of Pack and Westphal, the same outcome could presumably be attained through organizational integration. Pack and Westphal argue that in the case of Korea this is not feasible: 'the externalities may flow in complex and inseparable patterns among

(actual and potential) agents covering most if not all of the industrial sector' (p. 99), necessitating government intervention. However, the existence of the giant *chaebol*, spanning the industrial sector, would appear to undermine this argument. If the *chaebol* cannot internalize these externalities, then it is hard to imagine what institution could. Indeed, it is unclear why the government would be any better able to coordinate decisions than the *chaebol*.

The Japanese case does, however, suggest a constructive role for government. In Japan vertical integration is less complete: the *keiretsu*, networks of affiliated firms, strike a balance between the coordination advantage of full integration, and the maintenance of competition among suppliers. In this more loosely organized system the government's coordinating role could be larger.

It should also be noted that the Okuno-Fujiwara model is a closed-economy model. For the intervention to convey some purely *national* welfare enhancement, there has to be some non-traded aspect of the externality. Otherwise, foreigners have access to the same low-cost inputs, and the pattern of production in the downstream industry is indeterminate without additional assumptions.

2. Indeed, Auty (1991) provides detailed descriptions of indivisibilities and other entry barriers in the HCI industries. Even after assessing possible pecuniary and non-pecuniary externalities, however, he concludes that from an economy-wide perspective, resources were misallocated.

3. Of course it would be desirable to test these models directly, but the necessary firm data do not exist, hence the crude but feasible analysis reported here.

4. See Pack (2000) for a further elaboration of this argument.

5. One could object that the horizon for observing causal effects (four quarters) is too short, that the output effects might manifest themselves with only longer leads. The problems with testing this objection are two-fold: as the time horizon lengthens, presumably the power of the *F*-tests declines. Moreover, as the time horizon lengthens, degrees of freedom decline.

6. Dollar and Sokoloff (1990), working from a completely different perspective, concluded that the transport machinery industry was the single 'unqualified success' of the HCI program. They did not consider, however, the issue of inter-industry linkages. If this criterion is ignored, transport machinery is one possible successful HCI candidate identified in the study at hand.

REFERENCES

Auty, Richard M. (1991), 'Creating Comparative Advantage: South Korean Steel and Petrochemicals,' *Tijdschrift voor Economie en Social Geografie*, **82** (1), 15–29.

Dickey, D.A. and W.A. Fuller (1979), 'Distribution of Estimators for Autoregressive Time Series With a Unit Root,' *Journal of the American Statistical Society*, **74** (366), 727–43.

Dollar, David and Kenneth Sokoloff (1990), 'Changing Comparative Advantage and Productivity Growth in Manufacturing Industries,' in Jene K. Kwon (ed.), *Korean Economic Development*, New York: Greenwood Press, pp. 129–42.

Granger, C.W.J. and Robert F. Engle (1987). 'Co-Integration and Error Correction: Representation, Estimation, and Testing,' *Econometrica*, **55** (2) 251–76.

Jones, Leroy P. (1976), 'The Measurement of Hirschmanian Linkages,' *Quarterly Journal of Economics*, **90**, 323–33.

Kim, Ji Hong (1990), 'Korean Industrial Policy in the 1970s: The Heavy and Chemical Industry Drive,' KDI Working Paper No. 9015, Korea Development Institute, Seoul.

Kwon Jene K. and Hoon Paik (1995), 'Factor Price Distortions, Resource Allocation, and Growth: A Computable General Equilibrium Analysis,' *Review of Economics and Statistics*, **77** (4), 664–76.

Lee, Jong-wha (1996), 'Government Interventions and Productivity Growth in Korean Manufacturing Industries,' *Journal of Economic Growth*, **1** (3), 391–414.

Lütkepohl, Helmut (1982), 'Non-Causality Due to Omitted Variables,' *Journal of Econometrics*, **19**, 367–78.

Murphy, Kevin M., Andrei Shleifer and Robert W. Vishny (1989), 'Industrialization and the Big Push,' *Journal of Political Economy*, **97** (5), 1003–26.

Noland, Marcus (1993), 'The Origins of U.S.–Korea Trade Frictions,' in Jongryn Mo Ramon H. Myers (eds), *Shaping a New Economic Relationship: Republic of Korea and United States Economic Relations*, Palo Alto, CA: Hoover Institution Press, pp. 13–39.

Noland, Marcus and Howard Pack (2003), *Industrial Policy in an Era of Globalization: Lessons from Asia*, Washington: Institute for International Economics.

Okuno-Fujiwara, Masahiro (1988), 'Interdependence of Industries, Coordination Failure, and Strategic Promotion of an Industry,' *Journal of International Economics*, **25**, 25–43.

Pack, Howard (2000), 'Industrial Policy: Growth Elixir or Poison?' *World Bank Research Observer*, **15** (1), 47–68.

Pack, Howard and Larry E. Westphal (1986), 'Industrial Strategy and Technological Change,' *Journal of Development Economics*, **22**, 87–128.

Sims, Christopher A., James H. Stock and Mark W. Watson (1990), 'Inference in Linear Time Series Models with Some Unit Roots,' *Econometrica*, **58** (1), 161–82.

Stock, James H. and Mark W. Watson (1989), 'Interpreting the Evidence on Money-Income Causality,' *Journal of Econometrics*, **40** (1), 161–82.

Yoo, Jung-ho (1990), 'The Industrial Policy of the 1970s and the Evolution of the Manufacturing Sector,' KDI Working Paper No. 9017, Korea Development Institute, Seoul.

——— (1993), 'The Political Economy of Protection in Korea,' in Anne O. Krueger and Takatoshi Ito (eds), *Trade and Protectionism*, Chicago: University of Chicago Press.

Yoshikawa, Hiroshi and Fumio Ohtake (1987). 'Postwar Business Cycles in Japan: A Quest for the Right Explanation,' *Journal of the Japanese and International Economies*, **1** (2), 373–407.

Index